NONVIOLENCE

AIN'T WHAT IT USED TO BE

UNARMED INSURRECTION AND THE
RHETORIC OF RESISTANCE

NONVIOLENCE
AIN'T WHAT IT USED TO BE

UNARMED INSURRECTION AND THE
RHETORIC OF RESISTANCE

By Shon Meckfessel

PRAISE FOR:
NONVIOLENCE AIN'T WHAT IT USED TO BE

"From Occupy encampments to urban rebellions against police violence, *Nonviolence Ain't What It Used to Be* provides a wide-ranging analysis of how social movements choose their tactics and to what ends. Rejecting the simplistic divide between violence and nonviolence, Shon Meckfessel strives for a more holistic accounting of radical action. Where else will you find Martin Luther King and Emma Goldman debating the French Revolution with Hannah Arendt and Angela Davis?"—**Dan Berger**, author of *Captive Nation: Black Prison Organizing in the Civil Rights Era*

"Shon Meckfessel considers riot as rhetoric, articulating its discursive strategy and discerning its implicit meaning. His efforts pay off, bringing a fresh perspective to the stubborn debates about violence and nonviolence and suggesting a way to move beyond the left's tactical impasse. *Nonviolence Ain't What It Used To Be* won't settle the old argument, but it may start a new one." —**Kristian Williams**, *Our Enemies in Blue: Police and Power in America*

"Shon Meckfessel's *Nonviolence Ain't What It Used to Be* brilliantly defends physical challenges to capitalist democracy…. Heir to Orwell's sneer that 'Gandhi was very useful to the British government' and King's statement that 'riot is the language of the unheard,' Meckfessel echoes most powerfully Fanon's insistence that all de-colonization is violent. We need a re-constituted public that riots, damaging 'sacred' private property and confronting the police. Justice eschews abstract reflection on the ethics of nonviolence, Meckfessel urges, for a historical revolt with a radical logic: activists must seek and transgress the limits of neoliberal normalcy." —**Rudy Sayres**, independent scholar

"Shon Meckfessel's book *Nonviolence Ain't What It Used To Be* explores how contemporary movements have moved beyond respectability politics and other flawed political frameworks, while also examining what has worked historically and how past movements have evolved. His work here—which, in fact is more tool than text—pulls from experiences in the streets, experiences readers rarely have a window into. This book is particularly helpful for political organizers who serve as bridges across social divides. In short, it clarifies the reasoning behind, and the importance of, social and political defiance and disruption." —**Mara Willaford**, Black Lives Matter organizer

"At a time when profound crises are mounting and, for many, personal comforts are expanding, Shon Meckfessel drops a text that simultaneously challenges both the power structures fomenting calamities and the complacency that leaves them largely unchallenged. By focusing its analysis on moments when people do in fact collectively issue such challenges, this work brings forth a much-needed call to action that defies familiar rhetorical binaries, synthesizes divergent struggles, and offers a constructive pathway forward for scholars and activists alike. Read this book, and your perceptions of effective social change won't be what they used to be." —**Randall Amster**, author of *Peace Ecology*

"With growing resistance movements throughout the world, it is no surprise that interest has also grown about how social change can be made most effective. The strategic, tactical, and philosophical nexus points between the broad concepts of 'revolution,' 'nonviolence,' and/or 'armed resistance' are appropriately undergoing rigorous discussion— with occasional overt attempts at the formation of new theory and practice, but more often in confused and dichotomized debate. In this context, *Nonviolence Ain't What It Used to Be* makes a vital and extremely valuable contribution. Taking us beyond the ahistorical, magical thinking so common in contemporary discourse, Meckfessel constructs a dialogue that looks clearly at the nature of twenty-first century power dynamics, and the role of riots, property destruction, police clashes, and more. Without sectarian bias, he reviews the quasi-religious fervor with which too many approach nonviolence, and suggests powerful alternatives for upcoming movements. For scholars and organizers alike, *Nonviolence Ain't What It Used to Be* is essential reading, a soon-to-be classic that we'd do well to take seriously." — **Matt Meyer**, International Peace Research Association

Nonviolence Ain't What It Used to Be:
Unarmed Insurrection and the Rhetoric of Resistance

© 2016 Shon Meckfessel

This edition © 2016 AK Press (Chico, Oakland, Edinburgh, Baltimore)

ISBN: 978-1-84935-229-1
E-ISBN: 978-1-84935-230-7
Library of Congress Control Number: 2015942535

AK Press
370 Ryan Ave. #100
Chico, CA 95973
USA
www.akpress.org
akpress@akpress.org

AK Press
33 Tower St.
Edinburgh EH6 7BN
Scotland
www.akuk.com
ak@akedin.demon.co.uk

The above addresses would be delighted to provide you with the latest AK Press distribution catalog, which features books, pamphlets, zines, and stylish apparel published and/or distributed by AK Press. Alternatively, visit our websites for the complete catalog, latest news, and secure ordering.

Cover design by John Yates | stealworks.com
Interior design by Margaret Killjoy | birdsbeforethestorm.net

Printed in the USA on acid-free, recycled paper.

CONTENTS

ACKNOWLEDGMENTS

The irony of a work like this is that those who I want and need to thank most have to remain anonymous. You know who you are, and I thank you here more than anonymous thanks could ever express. Keep loving, keep fighting, and don't forget to fuck shit up.

As far as those I can actually name, I first want to thank Dr. Sandra Silberstein, my friend, dissertation advisor, nonviolence insider, and mentor in agonistic strategy. Sandy, you'll never know how right you were that time you said you'd "laundered" me into the world of professionalism. I also want to thank Dr. Anis Bawarshi and Dr. Candice Rai for their challenges and encouragement over the long process of research. Caitlin Palo, Mara Willaford, Kristian Williams, Evan Tucker, and Michael Esveld were all immensely helpful in their critical readings of my drafts and discussions of my analysis, as well as keeping me mostly alive through the process. Carley Phelan, too, for being a rare voice of sanity and generosity in chilly Seattle. Also, my cat Cora, particularly for her critical (if sometimes harsh) feedback. Stephen Zunes and Nathan Schneider were both very helpful interlocutors, despite/because of our differences on these subjects; thank you both for holding me to a high standard of proof, and I look forward to future difficult discussions on these topics. Lastly, I want to thank the various branches of my nontraditional family, in its various senses: my grandmother Irene who always supported me in all of my endeavors even when they must have seemed totally mad, and who died during the time I was writing this; Oskar and Cleo, my twin brothers; Peter, Betty, Pedro Luis, Karla, and Pedro, who I have been very lucky to suddenly be related to; and Shane, Sarah, Josh, Nora, and Cindy, whose alt-familial love I will treasure for my entire life. Finally, thank you to Charles, Suzanne, Zach, Lorna, and Bill for putting up with me yet again.

INTRODUCTION

IN ITS 2016 REPORT, *GLOBAL RIOT CONTROL SYSTEM MARKET, 2016–2020*, the market research firm Infiniti Research Ltd. has some great news for investors who are thinking about putting their money in riot-control technologies: by 2020, the overall riot control market in the United States "is expected to exceed USD 2 billion," with the markets in Europe, the Middle East, and Africa growing at an even higher rate.[1] "Protests, riots, and demonstrations are major issues faced by the law enforcement agencies across the world," and current conditions are unambiguously predicted to further "generate demand for riot control systems." "Growing economic transformations" in the Asia–Pacific region are predicted to produce changes that will "boost demand for riot control systems" there as well. Another recent report

---

1   *Global Riot Control System Market, 2016–2020*, quoted in Nafeez Ahmed, "Defence industry poised for billion dollar profits from global riot 'contagion'," *Medium.com*, May 6, 2016. Accessed June 20, 2016, https://medium.com /insurge-intelligence/defence-industry-poised-for-billion-dollar-profits-from-global-riot-contagion-8fa38829348c#.c3qc3z5ol. All remaining quotes in this paragraph are also from Ahmed's overview.

by the esteemed Lloyd's of London similarly predicts that "instances of political violence contagion are becoming more frequent and the contagion effect ever more rapid and powerful." The Lloyd's report presents three "pandemic" categories, what they term "super-strain pandemic types: "a) anti-imperialist, independence movements, removing occupying force; b) mass pro-reform protests against national government, and c) armed insurrection, insurgency, secessionist, may involve ideology (e.g. Marxism, Islamism)." The report presents the distinctions among these categories as hazy, as unrest of one sort is liable to bleed into that of another. Clearly, the differences matter less than the similar threat various forms of unrest pose and responses they demand.

Ours is a time of riots, without a doubt. Still, not so long ago, protests in much of the world, and particularly in the US and Europe, were generally thought of as "nonviolent" affairs. After the intensity of 1968 and the subsequent repression of armed revolutionary groups in the US, Europe, and Latin America, nonviolence seemed to have become a cornerstone of social movement common sense. Curious exceptions—the Zapatistas with their generally silent guns, Black Blocs of the antiglobalization movement, and the occasional urban riots in Miami, LA, and Cincinnati—seemed to be exceptions that confirmed the rule. Yet, the time when nonviolence could be taken for granted has clearly come to an end. What happened? What is it that people say through rioting that went unsaid for so long?

One of the first things that struck me as I set out to answer these questions was that advocates both of nonviolence and of riot often speak of their preferred approach as if it works by magic. Insurrectionist and nonviolence advocates alike speak in mystical terms about the ineffable power of their activities, often without giving a hint about what actual effects, in what specific conditions, these approaches might have. Rather than being able to lay out the effective mechanisms of these approaches—what purposes such actions serve, what audiences they appeal to, and how exactly they go about making their claims and appeals—most bristle at having their faith so questioned. Indeed, in looking at how people discuss these issues, I often wondered if I was speaking to religious adherents rather than people seeking to bring about social change through worldly action. It is no secret that the Left (including the "post-Left") has suffered dearly from a traumatic break in generational knowledge, for which we should likely thank the

FBI as much as any of our own dysfunctions. In tracing the influence of these generational breaks to discussions of non/violence, I became increasingly interested in this traumatic history, which I see as the root of the dehistoricized, magical thinking evident in these discourses. This book seeks to redress that amnesia and to explore how it is we've gotten to a point where various core approaches in the repertoire of social movements have come to seem opposed, even complete opposites— while in a longer historical perspective, they seem more like points on a spectrum, or tools in a box. If neither "nonviolence" nor "violent" riots work by magic, how, then, do they work?

In answering these questions, I have drawn heavily on post-structuralist theories of discourse, rhetoric, and affect. Far from head-in-the-clouds academic jargon, I see these fields as concrete tools for understanding how meanings are negotiated and contested, and how such struggles are always at the same time a matter of contesting power. Indeed, for those who think of Foucault and his ilk as steering radical critique too heavily toward a fussy preoccupation with language, I hope this work can provide an example of how that doesn't have to be the case. Many assume that "nonviolence" has a monopoly on the reasoned appeal to its audiences, and that political violence—not only the violence of riots, but even less sympathetic forms of political violence of massacre or torture, for example—relies only on coercion and force, rather than possessing a persuasive eloquence in its own right. I think this distinction is fundamentally wrong and not at all helpful. Consequently, throughout this work, I keep coming back to the tension between, on the one hand, the "rhetorical" or "discursive"—that place where meanings happen, within culture and, generally but not always, language—and, on the other, "materiality," that world of necessity, coercion, objects, and force. Like many rhetoricians, I am interested in the way that material reality can work to create meaning, and how certain meanings can only be made through material realities—that is, not only in words. However, "action not words" doesn't really describe the process, because meanings that happen materially don't "stick" un-less we remember and represent those meanings—unless these material changes get us to talk to each other and ourselves in a different way. Reality is not merely "material" (as some vulgar Marxists would have it) or entirely "discursive" (as some vulgar post-structuralists might say), but happens in the friction between the two. More than a minor aside, the study of how social movements change meaning—which is to say, change the world, since meanings are the way we decide how to act—is a way to better understand this friction. Scrappy protests, especially in their most intense forms as riots, are a perfect site to study this, precisely because they have been so long assumed to be "the voice of the voiceless," a mute symptom of lack of political power, rather than an articulate way of constituting it.

When I look at political violence in this book, I primarily focus on violence in public protest, those public acts that seek to contest and cast doubts on the way that power works under current arrangements, and especially on those aspects of it directed at calling capitalist property relations into question. I do not look at the striking increase in right-wing violence, or at the proud tradition of "armed self-defense," or specifically at anticolonial violence, except to briefly discuss its differences from the subject at hand. Although capitalism and modern settler colonialism have been historically co-constituted and interdependent, they present somewhat different challenges to those trying to contest them. I hope understanding these relatively discrete systems of rule can help us better respond in those complex realities (like the contemporary US) where, in practice, aspects of both nearly always appear tangled together. I do look briefly at those times in the history of social movements when guns have come out into the open, in order to try to figure out why they aren't doing so now.

Much of this book began as my PhD dissertation, researched and written in 2012–2013. During this time, I interviewed approximately thirty participants from Occupy Oakland and Occupy Seattle in order to help me work through these ideas. I was very active in these movements as well, as what academics euphemistically term a "participant observer." While I was conducting my research, the FBI was also conducting its own investigation into these same movements and into some of the same episodes I was interested in—such as the 2012 May Day riot in Seattle, which did some $200,000 of damage to the downtown business core. Because of this, I was obliged to carefully avoid asking any specific questions about people's involvement and also to make all my interviewees completely anonymous. Although some narrative coherence might be lost as a result, I hope the wider personal dramas, struggles, and victories come through the words of the people I spoke with. These things are never experienced individually anyway; therefore, somehow this jumbling strikes me as more faithful to the experience. Given the limited pool of participants in these movements, I was also reluctant to give away much demographic data, regardless of how obviously important intersectionalities of race, gender, sexuality, region, etc. are. I have refrained from mentioning very many identity markers, and only when it seems absolutely necessary to the meaning of the comments. In general, I can attest that those I interviewed were diverse in terms of race, gender, and sexuality, although perhaps less so in terms of class (I am thinking in particular of the large contingent of street kids who were difficult to track down once the Occupy camps were dispersed).

While turning my original research into a book, I was also a very active participant in a number of other movements, such as the Block the Boat actions against Israeli shipping companies and the Black Lives Matter movement in Seattle. Even though I was not conducting "research" as a participant in these movements, I could see that the tendencies I was writing about had only become more pronounced. Examples and extrapolations from these more contemporary struggles found their way into my manuscript in what I think are productive ways, despite the less formal nature of the research.

My goal in this book is not to advocate violence or to prescribe nonviolence; it is, in fact, to move beyond the politically obstructive dichotomy of such prescriptions. If I am successful, we will learn to hesitate when we use these words, to pause until we actually have some idea what we're talking about—or perhaps until we've managed to come up with more helpful terminology. If, as Randall Amster says, "the sum total of people killed or physically injured by anarchists throughout all of recorded history amounts to little more than a good weekend for the empire," then why are arguments about violence and nonviolence within our movements so acute?[2] Why do the stakes seem so high? More often than not, we are not even sure what we're talking about when we debate nonviolence and rioting. This book, in its small way, hopes to add a bit more clarity to the discussion by helping us understand, when our rioting bodies enter the streets, what they are saying and how successful they are at articulating it.

---

2   Randall Amster, *Anarchism Today* (Santa Barbara: Praeger, 2012), 44.

CHAPTER 1

WHY DID IT TAKE SO LONG FOR PEOPLE TO RIOT?

It's about power, because capitalism is about a struggle over agency. To live a life of capitalism, for absolutely anyone, is to be perpetually unstable in your own agency...cause there's this outside structure of money that governs it beyond you. That sort of power play is at the core of the capitalist psyche. Playing with that power is so key...taking it for yourself is so key, because that is in the end the fundamentally anticapitalist thing, is to do something that expands your own agency.... That's why [these protests] are a threat, because they're people being like, oh yeah, there's way more of us than there are of you. And we can do whatever the fuck we want.

—Occupy San Francisco participant[1]

---

1   Personal interview (A).

SOMETIME IN THE LAST DECADE, THE FEAR BROKE. PERHAPS IT WAS IN the strip malls of little Ferguson, Missouri, or Hong Kong's intersections, or Istanbul's Gezi Park, or Brazil's buses. Perhaps it was in a Tunisian fruit market, or on the rooftops of Tehran, or in Athens's dusty little Exarchia park. The year 2011 alone witnessed the most disruptive wave of contention to occur on a global scale since at least and perhaps before 1968, with uprisings in Tunisia, Egypt, Libya, Bahrain, Syria, Yemen, Israel/Palestine, Greece, Italy, Spain, Chile, the UK, Canada, and nearly every major city in the United States, to name only some. *None* of these places had experienced such unrest in decades, at least. Not only the number, but also the very character of these uprisings was something new. Lancing the rancid bitterness of generations stricken by suffocating passivity, isolation, and social depression, the relief and rage finally embodied in these global explosions was notable for a vehemence that could sometimes justifiably be called violent. These protests consistently demonstrated an undeniable intensity and confrontational scrappiness, rising up from the love of strangers drawn together in intimate risk and hope. At the same time, with the eventual exceptions of Syria and Libya, the intensity of these revolts was also almost universally nonlethal, on the demonstrators' side at least. Little love was felt by the insurgents for police and ruling elites, and though their uprisings often went well beyond what has come to be called "nonviolence," the millions in the streets were still reluctant to take out their rage on the bodies of their opponents. Why? Why were they so consistently violent, at least in some senses, and yet so consistently nonlethal? And why is it that we lack words for this kind of violence, if that's what it is?

9

This eruption came seemingly out of nowhere. But this scrappy intensity was long in the making and can be directly ascribed to decades of increased inequality under the policies of neoliberalism.[2] The neoliberal era has overseen the greatest unequal redistribution of wealth in human history, and this inequality has been, and remains, an all-pervasive form of violence. As Harvard psychiatrist James Gilligan argues, relative poverty—that is, poverty in the face of wealth, measured by the gap between rich and poor—is not only itself an endemic form of massive structural violence but also the direct cause of more visible forms of violence. Summarizing his findings from three decades studying violence in American prisons, Gilligan states that "structural violence is not only the main form of violence, in the sense that poverty kills far more people (almost all of them very poor) than all the behavioral [individual] violence put together, it is also the main cause of violent behavior. Eliminating structural violence means eliminating relative poverty."[3] So, rather than wondering why recent protests have been so intensely conflictual, one might initially ask why those most affected by neoliberalism's inequalities remained quiet for so long instead of responding with a violence analogous to that of previous eras. Where was what E. P. Thompson describes as the "moral economy" of riots, as in the eighteenth-century, when citizens smashed up and expropriated flour stores and bakeries as a means of community control of pricing?[4] Where was the response?

---

2   Although neoliberal policies have driven social shifts and movement responses in powerfully similar ways across the globe—even in states purportedly outside the global-capitalist sphere like Syria and Iran—this study will focus, with some exceptions, on examples in the recent US context.

3   James Gilligan, *Preventing Violence* (London: Thames & Hudson, 2001), 102.
    This definition of violence alone is adequate to refute the thesis of Steven Pinker's awful *The Better Angels of Our Nature* (New York: Viking, 2011), based as it is on a laughably narrow view of violence, massively downplaying, for example, civilian war casualties in modernity. Nassir Taleb's criticism of Pinker's statistical abuses, or Stephen Corry's bearing out of the dishonest cherry-picking justification of the "brutal savage" trope, among many others, should already have been adequate.

4   E. P. Thompson, "The Moral Economy of the English Crowd in the Eighteenth Century," *Past & Present* 50 (1971): 76–136.

The absence of a violent response to intensified relative (as well as absolute) poverty is particularly puzzling when compared to the proliferation of massive urban riots in the US during the late 1960s and early 1970s. As the Kerner Commission appointed in 1967 by President Johnson recognized, these riots were not mute explosions of brute force.[5] If anything, they were the most articulate expression of grievance that large swaths of the country had available to them, as Black populations, who had only recently arrived to northern cities in what is called "the Great Migration," faced massive exploitation and wretched conditions. Historian Michael Katz compares conditions of marginalized populations under neoliberalism to those faced at that earlier time and finds that, "with the notable exception of the Vietnam War, most of the conditions identified in the [Kerner Commission] report as precipitating civil violence did not disappear" but actually worsened to a severe degree.[6] Asking in his aptly titled 2008 essay "Why Don't American Cities Burn Very Often?" Katz observes,

> Poverty, inequality, chronic joblessness, segregation, police violence, ethnic transition, a frayed safety net: surely, these composed a combustible ensemble of elements, which a reasonable observer might have expected to ignite. In 1985, two sociologists who studied crime and violence observed: "the ghetto poor were virtually untouched by the progress that has been made in reducing racial and ethnic discrimination.... We thus face a puzzle of continued, even increasing, grievance and declining attempts to redress grievance through collective protest and violence." Writing in 1988, Tom Wicker pointed to the same puzzle. The "urban ghetto is, if anything, more populous, confining, and poverty-ridden than in 1968." Yet, the "urban riots that generated so much alarmed attention twenty years ago have long since vanished—rather as if a wave

---

5   National Advisory Commission on Civil Disorders, *Report of the National Advisory Commission on Civil Disorders* (Washington, D.C.: U.S. Government Printing Office, 1968).

6   Michael Katz, "Why Don't American Cities Burn Very Often?" *Journal of Urban History* 34, no. 2 (2008): 188.

had risen momentarily on the sea of events and then subsided." Why did no one light the match?[7]

Katz answers his own question with the idea of *incapacitation*—the means of making dissent powerless—which includes a set of developments in the country since the last wave of popular insurrection. He proposes a set of six "mechanisms" for "the management of marginalization": selective incorporation, mimetic reform, indirect rule, consumption, repression, and surveillance.[8] "Together," Katz notes, "they set in motion a process of de-politicization that undercuts the *capacity* for collective action."[9] Because each of these mechanisms assails the capacity, rather than the righteousness, of dissenters, I argue that movements are pressed to respond in kind by publicly performing *power* in the face of incapacitation attempts instead of arguing the *justice* of their cause. The remaining sections of this chapter will look at how marginalization is managed under neoliberalism and what it might mean for social movements.

Katz observes that the inherent violence of inequality never disappears; instead, it is displaced from public to interpersonal expression. While writing the article, Katz was called up for jury duty in his home city of Philadelphia. The trial involved the murder of an elderly African American man by one of his longtime acquaintances, even a friend, in an argument over a loan of five dollars. The crime took place in North Philly, a neighborhood of apocalyptic poverty (where I also lived for three years) only minutes away from Philadelphia's glitzy Center City. In trying to understand what connection neoliberal developments and the incapacitation of dissent might have to such tragic instances of interpersonal violence, I find it useful to turn to James Gilligan's research on violence in prisons, mentioned above. Gilligan's analysis reminds us that neoliberalism's widespread social incapacitation imposes an essentially *humiliating* powerlessness and that, by making social action unimaginable, this humiliation is likely to express itself through interpersonal situations closer to home. "The German word for attention—Achtung—also means respect. And that makes sense: the way you truly respect someone is to pay attention

---

7   Ibid., 189.
8   Ibid., 193.
9   Ibid., 192. My emphasis.

to them, and if you are not giving them your full attention, you are disrespecting them…we all need attention. When we get it, we know that we are being respected. That also helps to explain the etiology of violence: assaulting people is a foolproof way to get their attention. Since everyone needs respect/attention, if they cannot get it nonviolently, they will get it violently."[10]

Gilligan's analysis of interpersonal violence as stemming from the systematic disrespect of relative inequality helps us reframe Katz's question. Instead of only asking why American cities don't burn very often, we might ask why Americans often shoot each other instead of burning cities. How, in more academic terms, does the endemic violence of neoliberalism's intensification of inequality become systematically displaced from public to interpersonal spheres?

Before trying to answer this question, we should notice how this same shift, from social control by presumed consensus to control by incapacitation of dissent, essentially redefines the work of social movements at every level. As incapacitation of dissent results in a generalized humiliation among the poor and marginalized, movements must turn their focus away from bemoaning the absence of some anticipated justice, which fewer and fewer people expect in the first place—outrage at exceptional injustices may even sound insultingly obvious to those suffering injustices as routine—and instead focus on resisting the imposed sense of powerlessness. Under these conditions, movements arise simply to prove that it's still possible to do something, that incapacitation isn't complete. The focus on the incapacitation of movements, rather than the justice of their cause, can be understood as the most significant shift in social control from the welfare state to the neoliberal era. Consider the foundational 1962 Port Huron Statement that established Students for a Democratic Society. The statement, which in many ways framed New Left concerns, reveals how movement rhetorical strategies of the time were primarily concerned with attacking the *justice* of the status quo: "Many of us began maturing in complacency.… As we grew, however, our comfort was penetrated by events too troubling to dismiss.… Not only did tarnish appear on our image of American virtue, not only did disillusion occur when the hypocrisy of American ideals was discovered, but we began to sense that what

10   Gilligan, *Preventing Violence*, 122.

we had originally seen as the American Golden Age was actually the decline of an era."[11]

Reading these words now, their pained sincerity is no less striking than their absolute distance from our own times. Whatever one's social position or political affiliation, the idea that complacent comfort, virtue, or some sort of Golden Age is in danger of being undermined by a threat of hypocrisy and decline is an idea from some other world. Political radicalization must now happen by other means, since no one—Left or Right—would entertain such naivety in the first place. Even those most likely to bristle at mention of "the hypocrisy of American ideals" would now never argue that the country is in an untroubled, untarnished Golden Age; rhetoric of hypocrisy and the decline of American virtue is now even more typical of the Right than among Left critics—albeit with different alleged causes. Talk of values and righteousness has largely been abandoned by liberals and the Left; such talk persists mostly within the Right, but then only as a thin pretext for the brutal exercise of force by those in a position to do so over those who, until recently, seemed little inclined to fight back. If movements are to do their job and disrupt the daily reproduction of the status quo, they cannot merely point out how unfair things are, which is obvious enough. Instead, they have to figure out, work through, and overcome those social "advances" that have convinced people that they are powerless to do anything about it. In many ways, as later chapters hope to show, they've already started.

DISRUPTION DISRUPTED:
OR, WHY HAVE THE POOR BEEN PUTTING UP WITH GETTING SO SCREWED?

That Katz measures the incapacitation of the poor in the neoliberal era in terms of the vanishing of urban riots—why he asks "why did no one light the match?" instead of asking why they aren't, for example, voting in greater numbers—may need some additional explanation. We'd do well here to turn to Francis Fox Piven and Richard Cloward's classic work on the sociology of social movements, *Poor People's Movements: Why They Succeed, How They Fail*. In the authors' analysis of a series of hard-won gains of the poor against the powerful in American history, "[I]t was not formal organizations but mass

---

11   Students for a Democratic Society, *The Port Huron Statement* (New York: SDS, 1964).

defiance that won what was won in the 1930s and 1960s: industrial workers, for example, forced concessions from industry and government as a result of the disruptive effects of large-scale strikes; defiant blacks forced concessions as a result of the disruptive effects of mass civil disobedience."[12] It is wrong to credit organizations like the AFL-CIO with the gains of labor history, or the Civil Rights Act with the end of Jim Crow. Such institutional measures are in reality more the effect of social change than its cause: "While...symbolic gestures give the appearance of influence to formal organizations composed of lower-class people, elites are not actually responding to the organizations; they are responding to the underlying force of insurgency."[13] The capacity for disruptive intervention is the measure of such "force of insurgency," and hence of the political power of those without other access to institutional deliberation processes:

> It is our judgment that *the most useful way to think about the effectiveness of protest is to examine the disruptive effects on institutions of different forms of mass defiance, and then to examine the political reverberations of those disruptions....* By our definition, disruption is simply the application of a negative sanction, the withdrawal of a crucial contribution on which others depend, and it is therefore a natural resource for exerting power over others.... Indeed, some of the poor are sometimes so isolated from significant institutional participation that the only "contribution" they can withhold is that of quiescence in civil life: they can riot.[14]

For workers at a site of production, the most effectively leveraged disruption—the "withdrawal of a crucial contribution"—might take the form of a slowdown or strike; students might walk out from their school; soldiers might flee into the wilds or attack their superiors. Those with only minimal institutional affiliation—the unemployed or underemployed poor, youth, and indeed the many precarious workers

---

12 Frances Fox Piven and Richard A. Cloward, *Poor People's Movements: Why They Succeed, How They Fail* (New York: Vintage Books, 1979), xv.

13 Ibid., xxi.

14 Ibid., 24–25.

unable to organize in traditional workplace settings—are left with few resources for political intervention besides direct interruption in urban processes of the reproduction of daily life. Such an analysis hardly romanticizes public displays of violence; rather, these are revealed as symptomatic of a final, desperate refusal of powerlessness, an acknowledgment of the severe distance from channels of influence inscribed in the very position of the marginal subject's daily life:

> The poor do not have to be historians of the occasions when protestors have been jailed or shot down to understand this point. The lesson of their vulnerability is engraved in everyday life; it is evident in every police beating, in every eviction, in every lost job, in every relief termination. The very labels used to describe defiance by the lower classes—the pejorative labels of illegality and violence—testify to this vulnerability and serve to justify severe reprisals when they are imposed. By taking such labels for granted, we fail to recognize what these events really represent: a structure of political coercion inherent in the everyday life of the lower classes.[15]

When the force exerted by the "structure of political coercion inherent in everyday life" effectively blocks marginalized subjects from disruptive activity, the basis of their political power is undermined absolutely. Without a means of staking their claim, the poor (and a significant portion of "the middle class" who find themselves sliding into insecurity and poverty in the neoliberal era) have taken loss after loss in the social gains of previous generations, with little means of response. Recent contentious movements, to their tremendous credit, have finally broken through this impasse after nearly half a century of failures to do so but have not always received adequate appreciation for their particular success.

Seraphim Seferiades and Hank Johnston have described what they term a "disruptive deficit" that has resulted in the neoliberal era, as the poor and underprivileged are denied means of enacting disruption, their only real means of exerting influence. This incapacitation

---

15   Ibid., 26.

is made worse by a "reform deficit" occurring within institutions themselves, as neoliberal ideology has favored technocratic consensus—"leave it to the experts"—over the sorts of conflicts that drive reforms even within institutions:

> [A] key element…is the extent to which "conflict" (as non-violence) is premised on claimant *disruptive propensity*, that is, the tendency of contentious actors to act transgressively (though not necessarily resorting to violence) in order to further their goals. Even if states are reform-prone (and, nowadays, many seem viciously counter-reformist, both socioeconomically and politico-institutionally), "conflict" is not possible *unless* protest is sufficiently pungent to disrupt the workings of the system: to exert pressure on opponents, bystanders and authorities…. Prolonged periods of *conflictual irrelevance*, a state of affairs where either claimant actors fail to adequately express grievances, or the state proves perpetually unable (and/or unwilling) to be responsive—what may be construed as a *reform deficit*—leads to "conflict's" eventual collapse (if it had ever emerged). This is where *violence* begins to set in…. [T]his *disruptive deficit* may lead to a great paradox: in seeking conciliation through exclusively conventional protest, institutionalized claimants end up inadvertently fomenting the kind of political violence they most dread and despise. Indeed, this is all the more so, considering that this disruptive deficit coincides with the *reform deficit* characterizing contemporary neoliberal policies.[16]

As much of the rest of this book will attempt to show, performances of *potential* disruption—like peaceful protests, pre-arranged business-union "scheduled strikes," or even petitions and

---

16 Seraphim Seferiades and Hank Johnston, "The Dynamics of Violent Protest: Emotions, Repression, and Disruptive Deficit," in Seferiades and Johnston, eds., *Violent Protest, Contentious Politics, and the Neoliberal State* (Farnham/ Burlington: Ashgate Publishing, 2012), 5–6.

grievances—ultimately derive their power from the threat of actual, material disruption. And once elites have assured themselves that such threats are unlikely to go anywhere in terms of actual disruption, they have little reason to care. Thus, a deficit in disruption makes such petitionary measures—ironically, the very measures held forth as the only way to actually "change the world"—empty and useless. Consequently, the hollowness of these threats, and their inability to win any substantial gains, ends up resulting in a return of actual, unmediated violence. In political theory terms, this emptiness signals the impossibility of containing conflict within any mediating sphere of deliberation—what Chantal Mouffe terms "agonism," the clash of interests and perspectives mediated through a functioning deliberative sphere.[17] Instead, conflict, when it inevitably appears, escalates and is driven outside mediating processes, appearing as unmediated violence, equivalent in Mouffe's terminology to "antagonism," or violence between enemies. By shutting down whatever limited spheres of deliberation that might once have been available for working out conflicts before they exploded, neoliberalism offers the poor and disenfranchised a dismal choice: silence or violence.

MANAGING DISSENT:
ENGINEERING NEOLIBERALISM'S DISRUPTIVE DEFICIT

Political Recuperation and "The Pluralist Prejudice"
Neoliberalism has succeeded spectacularly well, at least until the 2010s, in suppressing dissent; thus, its means of suppression then become the new conditions to which challengers are forced to respond. Clearly, if we are to understand the approaches movements take, we also need to understand *how* the neoliberal age has witnessed such brilliant achievements in the management of dissent. How has power succeeded so well in repressing dissent? What new factors are social movement actors contending with? I will begin by looking at how dissent is managed through four ways potentially disruptive forces are immobilized: co-optation of dissent leaders, indirect rule of potentially unruly subjects, consumerist deferment of antagonism, and "civil society" recuperation of the symbolic resources of disruption. After

---

17   Chantal Mouffe, *The Democratic Paradox* (New York: Verso, 2000).

that, I will turn to the heavy stick of direct force that complements this managerial carrot.

Since the 1970s, many prominent New Left leaders have entered, or at least visited, the halls of power. SDS president Tom Hayden became a state senator in California, and the Black Panthers succeeded in helping Jerry Brown become governor of the same state with their backing. Across the country, minority and radical activists found homes within municipal governments. This growing political heft led many to claim that yesterday's radicals had finally won their voice; they were participating in the serious, grown-up world of change-the-system-from-within politics. However, in the same way that demands for more personal freedom made for a new life for capitalist markets, such political "successes" functioned as a new means of social control, employed to great effect against the very claims from which they originated. While self-identified Marxists largely fled behind the safe walls of ivory-tower academic incomprehensibility, "the Left" in the political sphere came more and more to signify social liberals whose economic policies were hardly distinguishable from their conservative counterparts. Indeed, Democrat Bill Clinton, or the British Labour Party of Tony Blair, pushed through neoliberal reforms often surpassing their more conservative opponents in severity. This bipartisan technocratic ("leave it to the experts") conquest of the political sphere brought together an apolitical consensus, with little room for openly conflictual approaches. Speaking in the European context with its rather more developed institutional Left, Seferiades and Johnston argue that "in contemporary Western democracies, and on a variety of pretexts, official protest organizations, including several [social movement organizations], trade unions, and, above all, the parties of the Left, tend to approach contentious disruption as a relic of the past. Hoping to secure the consensual resolution of pent-up grievances, nominally contentious organizations are increasingly espousing (often in a dogmatic fashion) the modalities of an exclusively conventional protest repertoire."[18]

The range of permissible political expression narrowed as previous movement leaders found themselves accepted into the institutions they'd once criticized and disrupted, and thus less apt to disrupt them. A culture developed within the Left favoring what scholar Doug

---

18   Seferiades and Johnston, "Dynamics of Violent Protest," 6.

McAdam calls a "pluralist prejudice," which delegitimized and deprived the marginalized of their most, and perhaps their only, means of expressing their political interest:

> [N]on-institutional protest was for a long time considered to be pathological owing to what may be construed as the *pluralist prejudice*: the axiomatic assumption that political systems (at least in the West) possessed sufficient expressive channels, which protesters, to their detriment, evaded quite simply because they were "irrational": "Why would any group engaged in rational, self-interested political action ignore the advantages of such an open, responsive, gentlemanly political system?... [Because m]ovement participants are simply not engaged in 'rational, self-interested political action.'" Incorporating insights from social theory and novel research findings (both historical and contemporary), political process and contentious politics approaches have problematized and eventually shattered the pluralist assumption: actors engaged in contentious, non-institutional collective action are *not* irrational; instead their departure from the proper channels reflects systematic channel deficiency and is, if anything, eminently rational.[19]

Such systematic institutionalization of dissent also resulted in what Katz terms "mimetic reform," defined as "measures that respond to insurgent demands *without devolving real power* or redistributing significant resources," most notably through a systematization of conflict which "not only absorbed the energies of insurgents, it also transformed their protests and rendered them harmless.... [It] substituted decentralization for community control, elections for protest, and 'modest but sufficiently tantalizing distribution' for redistribution."[20] Institutionalized dissent talks back to insurgent demands without actually answering them, neither serving their constituency's interests nor allotting them power to do so themselves. The accumulated effects

---

19 Ibid., 4.
20 Katz, "Why Don't American Cities Burn?," 193.

of decades of managed dissent have resulted in a crisis of powerlessness for social movement actors—regardless of the justice of their cause. Material power is replaced with a feeling of "empowerment," which comes to mean just another kind of despair.

Indirect Rule

For many, increased minority inclusion in political representation—the election of a Black president, selection of a Black secretary of state and Supreme Court judges, and particularly the Black entry into municipal politics—has been the most palpable victory won by the civil rights movement. Notably, people-of-color representation among business leadership has continued to be considerably more constrained, which in any case hardly "trickles down" to racialized populations at large. In view of the worsening conditions for large numbers of minorities and the poor, such "selective incorporation" of token elites, by "constructing limited ladders of social mobility," may well be viewed as an ultimately counterproductive strategy, working to confuse without essentially improving the reality of material inequalities and unequal access. Michelle Alexander, former Racial Justice director of the ACLU, for example, criticizes affirmative action programs for this reason, pointing out that their effect in creating small, visible elites may work to mask the widespread degradation in conditions, thus actually perpetuating it.[21] In terms of the more public challenges confronted by social movements, the selective incorporation of holders of municipal public office bears particular significance.

This selective incorporation of marginalized populations did not occur in a vacuum. Housing policies first robbed these populations of assets and networks of influence by first driving them into deteriorating city centers during an explosion in suburban land values, which was policed by real estate covenants often with explicitly racist language. Then, gentrification went on to rob them of the considerable assets and networks they'd built up in these neighborhoods. In the midst of these massive schemes of dispossession through displacement, civil rights era struggles did away with some of the mechanisms that kept members of these communities out of office—primarily, however, only at the municipal level. Invoking a term from the colonialism's

---

21 Michelle Alexander, *The New Jim Crow: Mass Incarceration in the Age of Colorblindness* (New York: New Press, 2010).

vocabulary, Katz points out that this limited representation results in a form of "indirect rule," as the faces of political and bureaucratic rule appear much darker than the faces actually setting policies and determining budgets at the state and national levels. "Like colonial British imperialists who kept order through the exercise of authority by indigenous leaders, powerful white Americans retained authority over cities through their influence on minorities elected to political office, appointed to public and social service bureaucracies, and hired in larger numbers by police forces."[22]

State legislatures have retained effective control over finances, schooling, and housing, but more diverse representation at the city level "meant that civil violence or other claims on city government increasingly would be directed toward African American elected officials, African American public bureaucrats, and African American police."[23] This results in a perverse hesitancy for communities of color to manifest antagonism in the places they live, lest they lose the ambiguous gains won through long struggle; political elites, whatever good or bad intentions they may have, are thus able to demobilize dissent, as urban populations identify more closely with the faces, if not the actual forces, of rule. The contradictions in the practice of such management strategies can be seen in the example of Occupy Oakland, when Chinese American (and former neighborhood organizer and self-described communist) Mayor Jean Quan at first attempted to express sympathy with the movement by visiting the camp, only to order the deployment of near-lethal force by hundreds of riot police less than two weeks later. Quan justified her move by claiming that "white anarchists" were marauding through "our Oakland," which, though misrepresenting the diverse composition of Occupy, seemed true if "our" referred to the racial makeup of the city's political elites. The appeal of this claim must have been noticed by other politicians: on November 24, 2014, when Black Lives Matter protests erupted in Seattle and shut down the country's largest interstate for a full hour, white mayor Ed Murray did not blush to claim that the freeway had been shut down by "a bunch of white anarchists," even though, according to several eyewitnesses I spoke with, every one of those who actually made it on the freeway were Black youth (with the ironic

---

22   Katz, "Why Don't American Cities Burn?," 194.
23   Ibid.

exception of local white hip hop celebrity Macklemore). In both instances, a bizarre rhetorical situation was revealed: minoritized communities were apparently shut off from the sort of public disruption that had historically been a central means of influence, so that their "representatives" could actually claim public disruption to be evidence of *privilege.*

After decades of being assured that racial uplift can work by trickle-down, disprivileged communities are hesitant to stand up to and take on political leaders who, though ultimately lacking power, resemble the face of progress. The political quiescence resulting from such accumulated hesitation is central to disruptive deficits and has become a central challenge that movements are forced to confront.

Consumerism and Credit as "Hope"

Much of the recuperation and displacement of potentially disruptive drives in the neoliberal era has occurred outside the sphere of what is usually understood as political, as for example in the composition of the consumer economy. As the Free Association has brilliantly analyzed, the neoliberal era managed to defer the antagonism that might have resulted from declining real wages by substituting easy consumer credit; so long as one didn't actually have to pay off all these little plastic cards, what was the difference between wages and credit anyway?[24] Suspiciously easy home mortgages became so simple to attain that the entire global economy somehow came to rest on them. The availability of consumer and home credit was coupled with a drastic drop in the price of many commodities due to the slave-like working conditions of globalized labor. This increase in purchasing power gave more and more people a means to feel powerful in their consumer choices just as they had less and less power in their political lives. As New Deal welfare-state labor protections were dismembered and factory-line industrial jobs were replaced with service and information work, increasing insecurity was marketed back to workers as an exciting new world of flexibility and mobility. Credit cards and easy mortgages that could be paid off just after dreams come true, cheap goods made by happy distant workers grateful to work for slave

---

24   Free Association, "Antagonism, neoliberalism and movements: Six impossible things before breakfast," *Antipode* 42, no. 4 (2010): 1019–33.

wages, a long procession of short-term jobs that one hopes will end in untold wealth—what all these changes had in common was a deferral of the essential antagonism of capitalism, between labor and capital, into the future. It is precisely this anxious faith that things would work themselves out that Barack Obama mobilized in his reliance on a message of "hope and change" during his successful 2008 campaign. The Free Association points out that the 2008 economic collapse, when investors very literally lost faith in the future as they sold off debt everyone suddenly realized would never be paid off, was the end of this deferral and "hope." Antagonism could no longer be postponed into the distant future, and it returned to the present in full force, as a wave of protests, riots, and uprisings swept across the globe in 2011.

Although easy credit and other consumer enticements may be losing their magic in the face of economic decline, the ideological function of consumerism as the sole respectable means of exercising one's agency remains. Nowhere is this so obvious as when social movements attempt to call it into question in protests and riots. Those who participate in consumer society, the logic goes, have no right to protest or riot against it; those who do are instantly labeled hypocrites. When, for example, rhetorical scholar Ellen Gorsevski makes a passing mention of protest "violence" in her book on nonviolent rhetoric, she quickly and confidently (and without feeling the need to cite a single source) alleges that the true motive of 1999 WTO protesters in Seattle, who broke the windows of Starbucks, was that they were shopping for coffee:

> [T]he newest stereotype that is an equally challenging obstacle to be overcome by the various peace movement diaspora is that of the spoiled suburban teenager, the proverbial purple-haired punk, dressed in all black clothes, who, out of sheer boredom, takes to the street to smash things. A friend of mine who attended the "Battle of Seattle" protests in 1999–2000 observed with ironic dismay, for example, when a small band of black-garbed, face-masked protesters, self-proclaimed "anarchists," used crow bars to smash into a Starbucks coffee chain store, then proceeded to help one another to bags of coffee, saying: "Hey! Pass me some of that

Mocha Java," or "I'll trade you this Kenya for that Morning blend."[25]

One participant in these actions assured me, on hearing this quote, "There was free coffee in the convergence center. No one needed to shop for coffee. We were good for coffee." In Gorsevski's view, rioters could be understood merely as coffee shoppers who were doing it all wrong. Similarly, within hours of the 2012 May Day riot in Seattle, in which hundreds of thousands of dollars of damage were inflicted on downtown banks and corporate business-es, one masked rioter who sported the characteristic Nike swoosh on his shoes while swinging a wooden stick at the windows of Niketown came to summarize the entire event in much media coverage. Twelve years before at the same Niketown building, another masked pro-tester had climbed its awning and was kicking down its metal let-ters, with shoes apparently marked by a similar swoosh. Then, too, this one pair of shoes among thousands somehow was supposed to explain everything. How, we might ask, is this supposed to be an explanation? Why would one rioter's choice of footwear somehow explain away the presence of tens of thousands of protesters? The "hypocrisy" is not simple wrongdoing, but rather the revealed *in-dividual* contradiction between *legitimate* choice (shopping) and *illegitimate* choice (anything besides shopping). It is as if the riot-er wearing Nikes (probably dumpstered or bought used in a thrift store, in any case) stupidly missed his one legitimate chance to voice his disapproval of the company by not buying their shoes, which is why he ended up so confused as to be smashing windows, which in turn explains why everyone else was probably rioting as well. Besides being a rather simple reading of riots, such an explanation seeks to reassert the idea of society as nothing more than the simple aggrega-tion of individual preferences; an ascription that leaves no room for collective political action against an institution, which a riot would rather obviously seems to be. If anything, such bewildered "expla-nations" indicate that riots still possess a great deal of power, exactly because they are so inexplicable within these dominant frameworks and may actually work to call them into question.

---

25 Ellen W. Gorsevski, *Peaceful Persuasion: The Geopolitics of Nonviolent Rhetoric* (Albany: State University of New York Press, 2004), 21.

Civil Society as Institutionalized Dissent

Of the various developments in the incapacitation of dissent that have undercut the power of social movements to challenge the status quo, none are quite as insidious as those developments that claim to represent and speak for the same concerns that movements do or even to speak for the movements themselves. The neoliberal era has witnessed an astronomical growth in the nonprofit sector: from 50,000 organizations designated by the IRS with charity status in 1953 to over one million tax-exempt organizations in 2012.[26] According to one nonprofit advocacy group, "If the nonprofit sector were a country, it would have the seventh largest economy in the world...the nonprofit arts and culture industry generates $166.2 billion in economic activity every year."[27] Structurally, the more "progressive" among these organizations often operate by grafting the revolutionary symbolic branches of the 1960s and 1970s struggles to a consistent trunk of pluralist-prejudice approaches. The words and slogans of the nonprofit sector—not to mention the participants themselves—are often deceptive carryovers of the radical aspirations of past disruptive social movements, but they are ultimately and unavoidably beholden to the organization's funding cycle, and hence to the political agendas of the funders themselves. What recent scholars have termed the "Nonprofit Industrial Complex" (NPIC) has been a central cause of the disruptive deficit, a fact that today's social movements must (and do) consciously confront.

An instant classic on the topic, *The Revolution Will Not Be Funded*, by the INCITE! Women of Color Against Violence collective, has brought together a watershed and widely referenced collection of essays bearing out this analysis.[28] The history of the collective illustrates the same tensions they came to write about. INCITE! began in 2000 in an attempt to bring together efforts to end endemic domestic violence within communities of color and state violence targeting these same communities. Simultaneously taking on both institutionalized feminist groups that collaborate and legitimize racist institutions like

---

26   See Councilofnonprofits.org.

27   Ibid.

28   Incite! Women of Color Against Violence, *The Revolution Will Not Be Funded: Beyond the Non-Profit Industrial Complex* (Cambridge, MA: South End Press, 2007).

the criminal justice system and organizations that claim to fight racism while ignoring endemic violence directed against women of color, the collective has continued to courageously put themselves squarely in the midst of the deepest contradictions of our time. In their first several years, INCITE! put on a series of well-funded national seminars and authored a widely acclaimed book that gathered the experiences of women of color organizing against the intersection of domestic and structural violence. However, when one of their key sponsors, the Ford Foundation, learned of their outspoken support for Palestinian liberation, their endowment was withdrawn, and they were forced to replace their funding through grassroots efforts. This dynamic revealed to the collective's members the stifling effect of foundation dependency and motivated them to publish *The Revolution Will Not Be Funded* anthology. The book is

> not particularly concerned with particular types of non-profits or foundations, but the non-profit industrial complex…as a whole and the way in which capitalist interests and the state use non-profits to [1] monitor and control social justice movements; [2] divert public monies into private hands through foundations; [3] manage and control dissent in order to make the world safe for capitalism; [4] redirect activist energies into career-based modes of organizing instead of mass-based organizing capable of actually transforming society; [5] allow corporations to mask their exploitative and colonial work practices through "philanthropic" work; [and 6] encourage social movements to model themselves after capitalist structures rather than to challenge them.[29]

At their most innocuous, nonprofits frequently interfere with less institutional approaches to mutual aid and social change, which inadvertently threaten to compete for the legitimacy necessary in successful grant applications. Additionally, the demands of institutional survival are often quite different than those of forcing social change, or even of just helping people. Many of the demonstrators I interviewed

---

29   Ibid., 3.

for this book said that disillusion with the ineffectualness of nonprofit work was a central motivation for their conversion to more directly disruptive approaches. One spoke of her brief tenure in one organization as a sort of training in defeatism:

> I was a canvasser for a day and a half for Working Families Party in Connecticut. The second day they dropped me off in a neighborhood, there were three evictions on the street, and so I was like, alright, I'm obviously not going to be canvassing in this neighborhood, instead I am going to help this person move their couch. So I came back to the person who was running the canvas and I was like, yeah, I didn't make any money, I was helping this person move out of their house. And she was like, "What? How...that's not what you're supposed to be doing." And I was like, "So you wanted me to go through this working-class neighborhood and badger people for money [to lobby against evictions] instead of helping this person out who actually legitimately needed my help? I quit. I can't deal with this anymore." It's like, way to take a bunch of energetic radical kids and turn them into zombies.[30]

Worse, by claiming to be the legitimate voice of wider movement concerns and cooperating with state agencies, nonprofits often end up exposing less institutional approaches to direct repression. Scholar Aziz Choudry terms this phenomenon the "co-opt and clampdown" strategy: nonprofits provide a way for state agencies to claim to be helping the cause, often in the same moment that they are cracking the skulls of those fighting for it in the streets.[31] As authorities often rely on "good protester/bad protester" talk to divide movements and isolate their more radical elements for repression, such characterizations can be devastating. Just as nongovernmental organizations paved the way for military intervention in Afghanistan by advocating from afar for Afghani women's rights, domestic nonprofits conveniently

---

30 Personal interview (B).

31 Aziz Choudry and Dip Kapoor, eds., *NGOization: Complicity, Contradictions and Prospects* (London: Zed Books, 2013).

make those who fall beyond the NPIC pale vulnerable to repression. In their book *Paved with Good Intentions*, Nikolas Barry-Shaw and Dru Oja Jay examine how this strategy has played out among Canadian development NGOs, including NGO-funded counterconferences, Oxfam's close collaboration with the World Bank, and how the Canadian "federal government consciously funded the participation of the NGOs in the [alter-globalization] protest movement as an effort to contain its militancy and limit its demands."[32] By their account, among the greatest foes to movements seeking to force social change in the current era are those philanthropic institutions who claim to be working for the same ends.

POLICING AS A REAL PROBLEM

Another shift in the conditions of neoliberalism that has centrally transformed the character of social movements is activists' core antagonism with police, both because of their social role in general and in protest situations in particular. Members of previous generations of movements are often too quick to ascribe such anticop antagonism to the madness of youth and its dangerous predilection for senseless violence. But this antagonism is anything but senseless. If co-optation, indirect rule, consumerism, and "civil society" domestication form the enticing carrot of dissent management, we should not be surprised when we find a big, heavy stick in the other hand of neoliberal social control—surveillance, police, and prisons. Even those types of enforcement inherited from previous eras have undergone an incredible expansion and intensification over the last several decades. While many excellent studies have focused on surveillance and prisons, the role of police in these "advances" in social control have only—finally—come to light through the Ferguson/Black Lives Matter movement. Yet, even with these struggles, the centrality of policing—both in daily life and in the protests challenging the structures of daily life—is still seriously underrecognized, except by those who do not have the option to ignore it. And even those who know how bad it is still have trouble theorizing how we got here.

Policing has always been a problematic and contradictory institution, despised and spiteful, marbled through with both servitude and

---

32 Nikolas Barry-Shaw and Dru Oja Jay, *Paved with Good Intentions: Canada's Development NGOs from Idealism to Imperialism* (Halifax, NS: Fernwood, 2012).

sadism. In the words of former slave Harriet Jacobs, writing in 1861, "Any white man, who could raise money enough to buy a slave, would have considered himself degraded by being a constable; but the office enabled its possessor to exercise authority. If he found any slave out after nine o'clock, he could whip him as much as he liked; and that was a privilege to be coveted."[33] In the neoliberal era, policing is not simply one means among others to maintain control—it is absolutely central to the existence of the state itself. In *Punishing the Poor: The Neoliberal Government of Social Insecurity*, Loïc Wacquant presents a thoroughgoing analysis of the discursive and material constitution of the neoliberal state.[34] The neoliberal state finds itself challenged not only by the material insecurities generated by a drastic increase in income inequality and the abolition of the social safety net but also by a crisis of appearances. As the state in its roles of distributing social goods ("provisional") and regulating business ("regulatory") gradually vanishes under neoliberalism, it risks the appearance of not being a state at all, of disappearing behind private interests, unless it compensates in impressiveness through the mighty "grandeur" of its functions of policing, military intervention, and imprisonment:[35]

> Thus is resolved what could appear to be a doctrinal contradiction, or at least a practical antinomy, of neo-liberalism, between the downsizing of public authority on the economic flank and its upsizing on that of the enforcement of social and moral order. If the same people who champion a minimal state in order to "free" the "creative forces" of the market and submit the dispossessed to the sting of competition do not hesitate to erect a maximal state to ensure everyday "security," it

---

33 Harriet A. Jacobs, *Incidents in the Life of a Slave Girl* (New York: Dover Publications, 2001), 100.

34 Loïc Wacquant, *Punishing the Poor: The Neoliberal Government of Social Insecurity* (Durham: Duke University Press, 2009).

35 The inverse developments of provisional/regulatory vs. penal functions of the state are helpful in understanding what the Right really means when it argues to "stop big government," and how anarchists, for example, might mean something very different when we call to "smash the state," even if the claims are apparently similar.

is because *the poverty of the social state against the back-drop of deregulation elicits and necessitates the grandeur of the penal state.*[36]

Part of the point, then, is to make sure that state violence is seen and makes an impression on potential rebels. The neoliberal state has a day-to-day need to assert omnipotence through widespread surveillance and forceful repression to make up for the disappearance of its friendlier functions, and to incapacitate expressions of dissent even before they appear.

The penal force of the neoliberal state appears in different guises. In trying to understand the management of dissent and the conditions faced by social movements, the most relevant of these are policing and incarceration. The Black Lives Matter movement has finally begun to bring to attention the way that policing and the entire state apparatus around crime and punishment function to produce inequality directly, not coincidentally. Until this movement, policing and prisons were widely misunderstood as a mere effect of social inequality, a "superstructural" result of racism in the "base." Police and prisons are not mere symptoms of the dearth of opportunity and severity of need in communities of color resulting from "deeper" issues of housing discrimination, access to quality education, and redlining and other banking policies. They do not simply arise from personal prejudicial attitudes endemic among whites. Rather, policing and prisons have arguably become central to the production of racialized power inequalities in the US, as Alexander lays out in her now-famous book *The New Jim Crow*. The successes of the civil rights and Black Power movements made legal practices like the Jim Crow laws, which explicitly inscribed inequality by race, discursively unworkable by the late 1960s. Nevertheless, the material investments of white supremacy did not disappear but instead sought a new manner of social inscription: while the civil rights era succeeded in enormously decreasing white vigilante violence which, since Reconstruction, had helped maintain a Black underclass, police and prisons would soon come to assume the same function. Nixon's successful "law and order" campaign of 1968, which in the 1970s and 1980s evolved into an unprecedented assault on

---

36 Wacquant, *Punishing the Poor*, 19. Emphasis in original.

communities of color, became the new home for white supremacy. Rather than explicitly encoding race, these policies proliferated law enforcement powers under the guise of a supposedly race-neutral War on Drugs, empowering a discretionary policing that allowed but never acknowledged highly racialized logics of application. In turn, political leaders and pundits, conservative and liberal alike, deflected criticism of the obviously racialized consequences of these policies with an incessant hammering of "colorblindness"—a discursive trick that claims pointing out these consequences to actually be the central cause of racism itself. While Naomi Murakawa demonstrates in her book *The First Civil Right* that liberal administrations after WWII actually deserve much of the blame for the resulting mass incarceration crisis, Alexander's analysis shows how policing and crime have come to assume their central place in maintaining inequality in our day.[37]

As policing has become central to the production of general social inequality, it has also had to adjust the way it contains attempts to fight back against this inequality. In the 1960s and 1970s, heavy-handed "escalation of force" responses had entailed a serious loss of political legitimacy from Birmingham to Berkeley and played a key role in mobilizing widespread support for anyone on the wrong end of the police baton. Cops urgently sought a new, less politically costly means of containing demonstrator transgression. With most dissident formations relatively cowed by recent repression and therefore backing off of confrontational methods, police and protesters settled on a modus operandi known as *negotiated management*, in which protest organizers would consult with police beforehand, notify them of the general outline of the action (including even likely number, names, and method of arrests), and sometimes themselves take on policing functions, acting as "peace marshals." As the next chapter will discuss, contemporary "nonviolent" approaches often have not come to terms with this shift in policing strategy. Classic nonviolent approaches brilliantly played up and played off the contradictions of escalation-of-force policing, but using those same approaches within a negotiated management model risks having the opposite effect: aiding, rather than contradicting, the mechanisms police use to contain public disruption and dissent.

---

37 Naomi Murakawa, *The First Civil Right: How Liberals Built Prison America* (New York: Oxford University Press, 2014).

In the Seattle protests of 1999 and within wider waves of alter-globalization contention, the model of negotiated management collapsed—protesters not only refused to notify police beforehand of their plans but also actively (and successfully) strategized to outmaneuver police on the ground. Illegal activity was suddenly no longer limited to predetermined, agreed-upon acts of nonviolent civil disobedience; it included politically embarrassing employments of disruptive tactics—most importantly in Seattle, with the successful blockading of delegates from entering the WTO ministerial and massive disruption of downtown business flow during Christmas shopping season, in addition to Black Bloc property destruction. Employing new electronic communications media, protest organization became utterly decentralized and autonomous, removing the traditional core of coordinators with whom to negotiate or, alternately, target for elimination. Consequently, police had to come up with a new plan. They arrived at a new approach that Patrick Gillham and John Noakes call "strategic incapacitation."[38] By employing fierce but focused violence, scrambling communications, conducting preemptive arrests and detention until protests are over, targeting support networks such as medical and legal assistance, seizing food, interrupting protesters' sleep, and disrupting coordination of actions, police tactics aim primarily to impose limits on the ability of protesters to carry out their plans by miring them in the muck of logistical dilemmas. Publicly, police try to limit sites of political action to "free speech zones" far from the target of the protests, while demeaning protesters through intensified media coordination that limits their larger webs of support. In extreme but increasingly common cases, police encourage right-wing vigilantes to preoccupy demonstrators and organizers with the logistics of their own safety and survival. Attempts to control demonstrators end up mimicking the tactics of the demonstrators themselves, as police, too, become more diffuse and multimodal. In turn, protests tend to be increasingly focused on countering the actions of the police. Responses to strategic incapacitation thus become an unavoidable core "message" in the politics of contemporary protest.

---

38   Patrick F. Gillham and John A. Noakes, "'More Than a March in a Circle': Transgressive Protests and the Limits of Negotiated Management," *Mobilization: An International Quarterly* 12, no. 4 (2007): 341–57.

In this back-and-forth negotiation of power in contemporary protest, the attempt to even define what protest means becomes a key point of struggle. David Graeber presents a compelling analysis in his "On the Phenomenology of Giant Puppets," when he wonders why, during a number of alter-globalization protests, the police often reacted with such outrage to the puppets seized from protesters, gleefully backing their patrol vehicles over or absurdly bludgeoning with batons the heads of these papier-mâché mockups.[39] The antiauthoritarian orientation of many contemporary social movement participants hinges on an assertion of the potency of imagination and a refusal to negotiate the right to define a social situation. This insistence on the realization of a collective imaginary is precisely the confrontational trigger for police, who, far more than worrying about infractions of the law or disorderly social conduct, seek to impose and maintain a "reasonable," agreed-upon definition of the situation. However civil or "nonviolent" the conduct of protesters, this interaction will result in (police) violence the moment protesters refuse to surrender the right to define what, exactly, it is that they're up to. The consequences for protest strategy are significant: while "nonviolent" analyses of protest interactions generally posit protester aggression as the cause of violent police response—a theory inconsistent with most protest experiences in which aggression and violence are most often initiated by police—attention to the right to define the moment shows that conflict arises in the *political* moment when protesters claim their autonomy to understand a situation in their own terms. This issue is completely tangential to their "violent" or "nonviolent" conduct.

The Black Lives Matter movement has been perhaps unique in bringing such widespread concern to policing as a social issue. Such concern, however, is hardly novel. The Boston Knowles Riot of 1747, described by historian Paul Gilje, reveals the centrality of policing to issues to which it might at first seem tangential. The crowd, gathered against new policies of forced naval conscription, threatened to hold several navy officers hostage, but peacefully surrendered them before the home of the governor. Yet "[t]hey did take an under sheriff, physically abused him, and, in a nice bit of role reversal, locked him in

---

39 David Graeber, "On the Phenomenology of Giant Puppets," in *Possibilities: Essays on Hierarchy, Rebellion, and Desire* (Oakland: AK Press, 2007).

the town stocks."[40] As an embodiment of the legal violence forcing them into conscription, which Gilje describes as "practical imprisonment, horrid conditions, and an earlier death," the crowd found the undersheriff—as the functionary finally tasked with driving them into a deplorable situation—a more apt target than the navy officers or governor who might be more obviously held responsible for the policy. While conventional wisdom might hold this decision to be ill considered, the crowd certainly seemed to weigh their decision. Is it so clear that they were wrong?

The refusal to acknowledge policing as a persistent concern in its own right is especially noticeable in the public amnesia around Martin Luther King Jr.'s address to the March on Washington. While the final, "I have a dream" portion of the speech may well be the most frequently cited act of public oratory of the twentieth century, the speech in its entirety is seldom cited, particularly the middle portion, where King extols "[t]he marvelous new militancy which has engulfed the Negro community."[41] Rather than mentioning policing in passing as a local impediment to his campaigns, King presents it as core to the movement's goals, as a sort of summary of actually existing racism in the United States. "There are those who are asking the devotees of civil rights, 'When will you be satisfied?' We can never be satisfied as long as the Negro is the victim of the unspeakable horrors of police brutality."[42] Addressing those who have traveled to the nation's capital from the struggles in the South, King again presents the violence of policing as the epitome of racist hatred faced by movement participants: "Some of you have come from areas where your quest for freedom left you battered by the storms of persecution and staggered by the winds of police brutality."[43] Bizarre metaphors aside, police brutality is of such pervasive importance to King that he evokes it repeatedly, throughout multiple sections of the speech, unlike the incessantly quoted dream of the day when "little black boys and black girls will be able to join hands with little white boys and white girls as sisters

---

40 Paul A. Gilje, *Rioting in America* (Bloomington: Indiana University Press, 1996), 31.

41 Clayborne Carson, ed. *The Autobiography of Martin Luther King, Jr.* (New York: Warner Books, 1998), 225.

42 Ibid.

43 Ibid.

and brothers,"[44] which appears only in the closing passage, when "all of God's children…will be able to join hands."[45] While the horrors of police brutality warranted more space in King's speech (already heavily edited by state censors) than the dream of children of different races joining hands, the latter image came to stand in for the entire message of his speech, and indeed his entire life; his critique of endemic, racist police violence, however, has been utterly erased from public memory.

The prevalence of antipolice slogans under neoliberalism is reason enough to suspect that policing has been an issue of central concern to movements long before Black Lives Matter brought it to wide attention. In the mid-1980s, the once mighty British Left struggled in vain to hold off Margaret Thatcher's brutal neoliberal reforms. The conflict came to a head during the protracted coal miners' strike, which brought the battle to the public eye as starkly as Reagan's firing of 11,000 air-traffic controllers did in the US. Though Thatcher was hardly beloved among miner ranks, it was the helmeted face of police which, for many, served as the face of the violent conflict. Images of police waving generous overtime checks in the face of literally starving miners on picket lines were not soon forgotten. Consequently, in the narrative of some participants, the long-standing motto "ACAB" or "All Coppers Are Bastards," a watchword within British prisons since at least the 1920s, became a favorite slogan in the miners' struggles. The slogan has since entered widespread global usage, helped along by its ubiquitous presence in the youth uprising of 2008 across Greece, and has been widely manifest in contentious protests since.

Similarly, the phrase "Fuck the Police," often abbreviated "FTP," has more recently come to hold a central place in struggles against racism and economic inequality. The words gained popularity through 1990s hip-hop, which was itself largely inspired by the street rhetoric of the 1992 Rodney King riots, for which the phrase served as the most recognizable slogan. For all of their force and magnitude, the 1992 riots are still only occasionally remembered in the annals of Black liberation or social justice history, and they are generally dismissed as somehow more of a race riot than anything political. Only if critique of policing (and the racialized practices of policing) is somehow construed as a personal or collective psychological abnormality,

44 Ibid., 226.
45 Ibid.

divorced from history, can such a claim make sense. The Rodney King riots came at the end of nearly a decade of policing and incarceration policies that had resulted in an exponential growth in incarcerated youth of color and a level of surveillance unrivaled in human history.[46] While falling outside the pale of "Black Power" or other recognized political movements, that uprising dwarfed *all* previous riots in American history by an order of magnitude: it greatly exceeded each of the famous riots of 1965 in Watts and 1967–68 in Newark, Detroit, and Washington, DC, in terms of arrests, injuries, deaths, and fires set. The monetary damage of the 1992 riots totaled three times the combined damage of the previous three.[47] The Rodney King riots were not, however, unusual in their cause. Other than the riots after Martin Luther King Jr.'s assassination, every major riot in the United States since WWII has been set off by police brutality or murder of a youth of color: in Miami and Tampa alone, police violence triggered large-scale riots in 1980, 1982, 1987, and 1989. Dismissing these as "race riots" elides the importance of their obvious concern with policing but also belies their evidently multiracial constituency. In the Rodney King riots in Los Angeles, 52 percent of arrests were Latinos, 10 percent whites, and only 38 percent African Americans.[48] Similarly, although the Tunisian revolution was triggered by Mohamed Bouazizi's self-immolation in response to humiliation by police, and Egypt's Tahrir revolution by Khaled Said's death by torture in police custody, the issue of policing as constitutive of Arab Spring revolutions is generally ignored. Michael Brown's murder had been certainly not the first, but merely the latest, of a long and even global history of police murder of the marginalized; it was precisely this lineage that was invisible to so many confused white Americans, who struggled to understand what could have been so special about the youth. His murder was not special but absolutely mundane, which is precisely what drove the residents of Ferguson, and soon every major American city, to strike out with such brilliant rage.

---

46 In some communities in South Central Los Angeles at the time, *every* young Black male had been entered into a gang database.

47 Oliver et al., "Anatomy of a Rebellion: A Political-Economic Analysis," in Robert Gooding-Williams, *Reading Rodney King/Reading Urban Uprising* (New York: Routledge, 1993), 119.

48 Ibid.

	DISCRIMINATION	EXCLUSION	GOVERNMENT	SARKOZY	IMMIGRATION	DELINQUENCY	POLICE	OTHERS	% OF TOTAL STATEMENTS
GOVERNMENT (N = 62)	24	0	10	5	19	29	0	13	27
OPPOSITION (N = 44)	20	5	20	30	20	0	0	5	19
PRESIDENT (N = 25)	33	56	0	11	0	0	0	0	11
EXPERTS (N = 41)	25	38	13	8	4	4	8	0	18
ASSOCIATIONS (N = 30)	27	27	18	9	0	0	18	1	13
INHABITANTS (N = 14)	33	0	0	33	0	0	0	34	6
YOUTH (N = 14)	0	0	0	0	0	0	40	60	6
% OF TOTAL STATEMENTS	23	17	11	13	10	9	6	11	100
TOTAL STATEMENTS (N = 230)	54	40	25	29	23	20	14	25	—

Figure 1

Source: Donatella della Porta and Bernard Gbikpi, "The Riots: A Dynamic View," in Seferiades and Johnston, eds, *Violent Protest, Contentious Politics, and the Neoliberal State* (Farnham/Burlington: Ashgate Publishing, 2012), 95.

Even within communities of color, the recognition of policing as a central social movement concern has often been starkly generational. Research concerning perceived causes of the massive 2005 riots in the Paris *banlieues* is borne out by analysis summarized in Figure 1, looking at 366 statements culled from *Le Monde*.[49] Older neighborhood residents, spokespeople for the government and opposition parties, and Sarkozy himself favored explanations blaming either personal discriminatory attitudes, structural exclusion from access, Sarkozy and the parties in power, or, predictably, excessive immigration and youth delinquency. Of the seventeen statements by neighborhood youth, not one of them mentioned any of these as a related issue; fully 100 percent of their statements attributed the riots either to police (40 percent) or to other causes (60 percent) not understood as "political." Not one of the 145 statements by older inhabitants or political figures mentioned police. Experts and volunteer associations, presumably comprising and having contact with both of these constituencies, offered even more mixed statements. Older inhabitants' responses more closely resembled those of political parties than their own youth; this would indicate more of a generational divide rather than solely an ethnic, class, or geographical one.

So why haven't police been understood as a core concern by older and more establishment respondents? This is a question for future research, but for the purpose of understanding the particular situation faced by contemporary social movements, one brief hypothesis will suffice: the centrality of policing, particularly in the neoliberal era of hypertrophied penality, is not taken up as a legitimate social concern because of its very centrality. Seeped in the ideology of the age, even policing's strongest critics find it next to impossible to imagine life without policing—although the Ferguson and Black Lives Matter movements have begun to change this.[50] The purpose of the vast networked apparatus of dissent management might well be understood as an elaborate means of talking around this difficulty. While I will return in the next chapter to the slippage of "nonviolence" from a means of conflict with power to an excuse to avoid it, the propensity

---

49 Ibid.

50 For a great suggested reading list, see "Thinking Through the End of Police," Prison Culture website, accessed May 23, 2016, http://www.usprisonculture .com/blog/2014/12/29/thinking-through-the-end-of-police.

of such "talking around" the issue at the center of contemporary conditions of repression suggests a tragic, self-defeating hope for risk-free social change—one often expressed in our time through appeals to nonviolence.

FROM MASSES TO PUBLICS

Why Elizabeth Is Alive but Erin Is Dead

On the morning of September 4, 1957, taking the recent *Brown vs. Board of Education* at its word, Elizabeth Eckford and eight other black students attempted to attend classes at Little Rock Central High School, Arkansas, but were prevented from doing so by the National Guard, in coordination with a virulent mob of whites. After three-quarters of a century of the rule of white terrorism that undid the gains of Reconstruction, themselves won by force of armed freed slaves,[51] Eckford and her colleagues' dignity and courage could very well have been met with immediate and lethal response. Only two years before, fourteen-year-old Emmett Till had been murdered and horrifically mutilated in Money, Mississippi, for allegedly flirting with a white woman. After Till's gruesome murder, Till's mother had courageously insisted on circulating a photograph of his disfigured face to recently established Black newspapers and magazines around the country, and the image played a key role in galvanizing national support for the civil rights movement. Just as that photograph worked to bring the systemic violence of southern white-supremacist rule into the national arena, so the mass media coverage of the Little Rock Nine helped ensure Eckford's survival in the midst of a venomous white mob and the quick success of the immediate aims of the integration campaign:

> The drama…was played out before a national, even a world, audience. The affair at Little Rock was not an isolated event in a provincial backwater. News cameras and reporters captured every move of both Elizabeth and the segregationists. In the contest for this larger

---

51   William E. B. Du Bois, *Black Reconstruction in America 1860–1880* (New York: Simon and Schuster, 1999).

audience, although greatly outnumbered, Elizabeth won.... When Elizabeth, joined by eight other black students, reenrolled at Central later that month the reporters were again there. This time the crowd beat four reporters—a sign that racist whites understood the implications of the presence of the media—and officials withdrew the students for their own safety. Again, however, isolation was not possible. On the next day President Eisenhower federalized the National Guard and sent paratroopers to guarantee that the nine African-American youths could proceed with their education.[52]

Strategists of the civil rights movement were well aware of their dependency on mass media; their articulation of nonviolent tactics was an explicit response to the novel occasions presented by television and the still novel technologies of newsreel, radio, and print. Such tools opened unprecedented opportunities for a heavily disenfranchised minority population to turn the local balance of power. This dynamic corrects a frequent misconception among the critics of nonviolence (and many of its less-informed proponents as well): classic nonviolence never, in truth, sought to convert its opponents; rather, it played to the cameras of mass media by embarrassing its opponents before a wider audience—and very effectively so. As one civil rights movement participant said, "We were not simply addressing our immediate opponents. What we were doing was addressing the larger audience, the nation, the world, *because the strategy in nonviolence is that you educate a large number of constituents and win them on your side.* In fact, even though we as African Americans were the minority, no change could happen unless you have the sympathy of the majority, if not the active participation."[53]

Classic nonviolence, in the hands of figures such as Gandhi and King, was anything but a naive faith in the innate goodness of the

---

52   Gilje, *Rioting in America*, 151.

53   Bernard Lafayette Jr., videotaped interview by Steve York for the documentary television series *A Force More Powerful: A Century of Nonviolent Conflict* (Princeton, NJ: Films for the Humanities and Sciences, 2002), DVD, Part 1, 20:22. My emphasis.

imperial British officers with their bludgeons or the Bull Connors with their dogs. However, just as past means of successful dissent have been skillfully preempted in the neoliberal age through indirect rule, consumerism, nonprofit recuperation, and policing patterns replacing explicitly racial laws, so the mass publics that classic nonviolence relied on have been reconstituted by shifts in the nature of mass media. Once again, hegemonic forces have done quite well in foreclosing the opportunities successfully exploited by previous generations. Modern images analogous to those of My Lai are scant when journalists must choose between "embedded" reporting and being shot. The only exceptions are occasional internal leaks carried out with great courage in the certainty of terrible reprisal: Chelsea Manning, rather than receiving the Gandhi Peace Prize, as Daniel Ellsberg did for his leak of the Pentagon Papers, instead gets solitary confinement, pain-compliance holds, and a thirty-five-year prison sentence; Edward Snowden, as of this writing, waits in uneasy exile, likely facing worse than Manning if he is extradited. These are precisely the acts which, a generation ago, won accolades for Ellsberg and for the courageous exercise of free press powers by the *Washington Post* and the *New York Times*. Coverage of domestic dissent has followed suit; nearly all media outlets are owned by the same few parent companies that set their editorial policy, with disastrous consequences for breadth of permissible dialogue on domestic issues. Mass media in the neoliberal era works to hide rather than publicize the present-day Little Rocks and other forms of state and racist violence. The highest rate of incarceration in world history, with a total of seven million citizens under correctional supervision; daily killings of African Americans by police (one African American death at the hands of police and vigilantes every 28 hours);[54] daily deaths by enforced exposure along the United States–Mexico border—all have been rendered invisible to the public eye by near-absolute exclusion from mass media coverage, at least until the limited successes of Black Lives Matter and more local movements.

In a tragic synecdoche of this shift, Elizabeth Eckford's only child, her son Erin, a student at University of Little Rock, was gunned down by police on New Year's morning in 2003, after reportedly firing an assault rifle into the air. Police did not allege that Erin was directly

---

54 "We Charge Genocide Again!," Malcolm X Grassroots Project website, accessed May 23, 2016, https://mxgm.org/we-charge-genocide-again-new-curriculum-on-every-28-hours-report.

threatening anyone, merely that he fired it into the air, just as many thousands of others do across the country on New Year's morning. The killing barely merited a paragraph of local coverage for Erin's relation to his mother's past role in Black freedom struggles, but nothing was said of Erin's own freedom struggles in his time; his voice silenced by six bullets before he could give his own account to a mass media unlikely to listen in the first place. A grand jury declined to indict the officers who gunned him down, and media outlets showed no interest in following through with the story. No one seemed to remark that the very tool that had saved his mother's life was actively complicit in Erin's murder.

When older movement participants fail to appreciate these shifts in media, it is not that they naively trust mainstream media or expect it to transparently convey their messages. As one veteran nonviolence trainer who I interviewed suggested, in an attitude she attested as "old guard," mainstream media can be seen as a reliable way to get a message across, even while the representation of this coverage is likely to be unsympathetic. This might be termed the "message-in-a-bottle" approach:

> I would never assume that mainstream media were going to cover things accurately, but I think maybe I'm old guard in thinking that they still influence a lot of people.... I would never do stuff trying to make it look good for the media so that they would put out the right message—because they don't.... I like actions that in themselves embody what we're trying to change, or show without words, without needing words, what we're trying to do. So I think it's definitely worth keeping media in mind, mainstream media in mind, to some extent at least, but not designing everything around it.[55]

In this view, even if media representations of activist events are likely to be unfair, decisions should still be made with the expectation that mass media use a modicum of referential, factual representation in their coverage. Even approaches as radical as ACT UP's ultimately relied on this analysis of the available means of persuasion: corporate

---

55 Personal interview (C).

media cannot be trusted to be sympathetic or accurate, but the media can certainly be trusted to be the media.[56] Sensational actions, like the public scattering of the ashes of AIDS casualties on the White House lawn by their militantly mourning beloveds, will not be ignored, the logic goes, and can reliably be used as a vehicle of counterhegemonic communication, whatever the institutional bias of the vehicle's drivers.

Yet, by the time of the alter-globalization movements, feelings toward mass media hardened among many younger activists, who increasingly suggested that the media might not be worth addressing at all. The skepticism of previous generations hardened into a distinct cynicism. According to the statement released by the Barricada Collective during the 2001 WTO protests in Quebec City: "[W]e have nothing to hope for from the corporate media, we should expect nothing from them, and we should absolutely not change any of our tactics or messages in order to pander to them. We should instead treat them as the servants of capital, and thus our enemies, that they are."[57]

Although perhaps overstated here, media cynicism has only become more endemic in the years since. In an era of embedded journalism, institutional press releases, and image management, social movement participants are also no longer grappling with the question of which federal power can be invoked against a regional injustice. They face issues involving the nature of federal and transnational dominance, and they justifiably wonder if the media are worth attempting to address at all, however difficult it might be to find alternative means of reaching and constituting a public. The predominance of insurrectionary anarchism in some regions is related to this shift: it involves constituting new publics through direct means rather than mobilizing already existing publics. The insurrectionary anarchist movement has fractured into local sectarian schisms over ambiguities of definition, or even whether to constitute a new public at all, or, rather constitute an illegible *antipublic* with no attempt at appeal to outsiders at all. While

---

56 *How to Survive a Plague*, directed by David France (New York: Sundance Selects/ MPI Media Group, 2013), DVD.

57 In David Van Deusen and Xavier Massot, *The Black Bloc Papers: An Anthology of Primary Texts From The North American Anarchist Black Bloc 1999–2001, The Battle of Seattle Through Quebec City* (Shawnee Mission, KS: Breaking Glass Press, 2007), 136. Available online at http://www.infoshop.org/amp/bgp /BlackBlockPapers2.pdf (accessed May 23, 2016).

the latter approaches might be excessive for their absolute hopelessness in *any* appeal to those outside the fold, the concerns expressed through these tendencies are certainly reasonable (however much most insurrectionist anarchists might bristle at being called reasonable).

While the Black Lives Matter movement has been widely covered in mass media (as in both discussed and obscured), excoriated and extolled by commentators of every stripe, the movement itself has consistently prioritized constituting new publics over performing for the cameras. In the words of Seattle's Black Lives Matter organizing group Outside Agitators 206,

> Often, when news reports come out about our movement, our experiences get reduced to feelings, as if there's no factual basis for why we're in the streets. Let's set the record straight. First off, it is a fact that in 2012 there was a Black person executed by law enforcement every 28 hours in the United States, but the mainstream media are completely silent about true injustice committed by law enforcement. Why is that?
>
> We know that the cycle of police terror that we have experienced will never stop until the people who give police their orders are no longer allowed to make a profit from anti-Black racism. Specifically, the owners of 6 media giants who also make money from legalized slavery in the private prison industry. We know that 90 percent of all media are owned by these 6 corporations. We know that these same corporations hire lobbyists that affect the laws that oppress us. Honest depictions of Black experience are seen few and far between because anti-Black racism is profitable for them. We don't expect the mainstream media to tell the truth about our movement. We will win, and we expect that they will lie about it until they can't breathe...
>
> We don't directly speak to corporate media, nor do we need them. We are our own voice.[58]

---

58   "To the Media," Outside Agitators 206 website, accessed May 23, 2016, https://outsideagitators206.org/statements/to-the-media.

Such words show little hope for fairness from mouthpieces deeply embedded in the same systemic racism that the movement fights to expose, but immense hope and determination for other means of constituting a voice. What kind of means could they have in mind?

Constituting Immediate Publics (Despite It All)

Taking the above concerns seriously, movement participants are left with the question: if the mass media are, at least in some circumstances, no longer worth addressing, how should movements go about constituting a public?[59] If we look closely, some of those other means may already be well underway.

On February 11, 2012, the paper edition of the *Oakland Tribune* printed the results of an online poll, to which 10,829 readers had responded; the online edition of that day neglected to post the results. The poll posed a simple question: "Do you support the Occupy Oakland movement?" The paper had spent the previous five months being consistently critical of Occupy Oakland, ranging from an initial bewilderment to later indignation and even outrage. Just two weeks before the poll, it headlined an article with a quote from Mayor Quan addressed to protesters, "Stop Using Oakland as Your Playground!" The paper tended to highlight the voices of local political, business, and nonprofit leaders dismissing Occupy Oakland as beyond the boundaries of legitimate dissent. One might have expected, then, for *Tribune* readers to harbor few warm feelings for the movement. The results of the poll, quietly published in a sidebar, were surprising: 94 percent voted "yes" to supporting the movement, and only 6 percent

---

59   The role of social media has been so exhaustively discussed, to the point of fetishization, without convincing conclusions, that I have chosen to leave it aside in this study. People hear about events because of social media, but dependency on platforms like Facebook make them profoundly vulnerable to authorities in new ways. Tools of communication facilitate new connections, but also introduce new pervasive isolations. This study will focus not on the role of digital platforms but on those using them, and particularly those moments when people come together, physically, and leave their phones in their pockets or at home for the day. For readers interested in social media's role in contemporary movements, I recommend Todd Wolfson, *Digital Rebellion: The Birth of the Cyber Left* (Urbana: University of Illinois Press, 2014).

voted "no."[60] Evidently, the 10,829 respondents bore little relation to the audience constituted through the paper's daily discursive practices—a puzzling outcome indeed.

The passivity or activity of mass-mediated publics has been a heated debate within cultural and media studies since the field's inception. On the one hand, theorists of the Frankfurt School spoke of the "culture industry," a depressing, fatalistic, and seamless model of social control, in which masses are passively molded by capitalist culture. On the other hand, there is John Fiske's "semiotic democracy," in which audiences, with joyful irreverence, freely go about creating their own meanings to sabotage unequal access to the means of representation. Arguably, however, neither of these models can account for the sort of public that appears in the *Tribune*'s poll—materially real, yet somehow invisible in all but this one sidebar. The more this material public begins to appear, the more the "average reader" addressed by the paper is revealed as an *empty public*; ghost-like, disappearing into the realm of the supernatural. How is it possible, one must wonder, that some previously invisible public believes precisely the opposite of the audience that the paper's consistent editorial policy seeks to discursively constitute, and that they believe so to such an extreme degree? An independent survey cited by "Occupy Research" claims equally surprising results from the businesses surrounding the encampment as well:

> Similarly, there was a charge that Occupy Oakland was hurting local businesses, until a survey of local businesses found 80% of 106 shops within two blocks of Oscar Grant Plaza reported a positive or neutral impact from the encampment. In another instance, Police Chief Howard Jordan worried in email to Mayor Quan about how to share the good news of a 19% crime reduction in downtown Oakland during the Occupy encampment. This fact directly contradicted Quan, the City Council, and Oakland Chamber of Commerce's

---

60   "Bay Area News Group Poll Finds 94% Support Occupy Oakland," Occupy Oakland website, accessed May 23, 2016, https://occupyoakland.org/2012/02 /bay-area-news-group-poll-finds-94-support-occupy.

claim that Occupy Oakland was causing an increase in crime.[61]

What these figures show is that Occupy Oakland's claims and rhetorical appeals, which were negatively received (if at all) by mainstream media and leading figures among indirect-rule political institutions and nonprofits, do indeed reach certain immediate publics. Those publics seem to be created by some resonance of actions, invisible to the channels of mass mediation that usually serve as the exclusive measure of contemporary publics. The choices that virtually ensure antipathy from news editors and political representatives may simultaneously work to constitute publics through other channels—a fact that organizers seem well aware of and consider worth the risk.

The approach of constitution publics immediately does not lay claim to any pretensions of a universal audience, without race, class, gender, or any positionality. Responding to the slogan "Black Lives Matter" with "All Lives Matter," or insisting that the movement has to moderate its acts to appeal to "normal people," ignores the fact that the "All Lives" and "normal people" are themselves instances of the status quo. Organizing a collectivity or public—mainstream or marginal—is already and inherently political; it implies and determines the possibilities of consciousness and action available to that public. "All Lives" are not equally murdered by police, but people of various "races" gathered together on the basis of resisting police violence against Black lives might find themselves acting as a powerful body against racism. The same group of people thinks and acts very differently depending on how and under what logic they gather. Marginality isn't incidental—the very means of coming together, of constituting a new public, is an attack on how the center is constituted. All are welcome, but not necessarily as they are: if everyone showed up as they are, then the new group would be indistinguishable from the status quo. Challenger publics must transform participants in the very act of coming together. This transformation is central to what contemporary disruptive social movements work to achieve.

Hannah Arendt and the Direct Demos

The notion that mass publics, brought together by mass media, are resources better left untapped is not entirely new. Emma Goldman,

---

61   Ibid.

who in 1893 was arrested on inciting-to-riot charges for exhorting a large crowd of unemployed workers to take bread if they were not given work, could hardly be called an elitist; yet the hazards "the masses" present to real democracy is an ongoing theme in her work. Near the end of her essay "Minorities Versus Majorities," she addresses this apparent contradiction in her concerns:

> Not because I do not feel with the oppressed, the disinherited of the earth; not because I do not know the shame, the horror, the indignity of the lives the people lead, do I repudiate the majority as a creative force for good. Oh, no, no! But because I know so well that *as a compact mass* it has never stood for justice or equality. It has suppressed the human voice, subdued the human spirit, chained the human body. *As a mass* its aim has always been to make life uniform, gray, and monotonous as the desert.... I therefore believe with Emerson that "the masses are crude, lame, pernicious in their demands and influence, and need not to be flattered, but to be schooled. I wish not to concede anything to them, but to drill, divide, and break them up, and draw individuals out of them. Masses! The calamity are the masses. I do not wish any mass at all, but honest men only, lovely, sweet, accomplished women only."[62]

Scholars of Goldman have often stumbled over her position, finding her affection for Nietzsche and his idealization of the solitary genius of the Übermensch in contradiction with her anticapitalist populism. But as she makes clear, she is not making an elitist assertion against the differentiated Many (what Paolo Virno calls the "Multitude"), but is warning against their unitary constitution—through representative media of politics, information, or sociological instruments—into an undifferentiated whole. Rather than being an embittered, secret aristocrat, Goldman reveals herself to have a very contemporary concern with *how* people are drawn into a

---

62 Emma Goldman, *Anarchism and Other Essays* (New York: Dover Publications, 1969), 84. My emphasis.

collectivity, without assuming that their mode of collective being is given by their demographic. For many years, Goldman herself served as the English spokesperson of the Spanish CNT-FAI, consisting at times of some millions of members—certainly a "mass" of participants in some sense—but which was organized along decentralized, direct-democratic, rather than mass, lines.

No modern political thinker has been so misunderstood for her opposition to mass constitutions of publics as has Hannah Arendt. Arendt is, indeed, consistently terrified by mass entrance into politics, viewing mass politics as characterized by an unavoidable tendency toward totalitarianism. She typifies "the masses" as possessed with the irrationality of inarticulate desire. Appropriate to neither the public nor private spheres, these masses dwell in the cursed realm of "the Social," with the overreaching of this sphere responsible for the disappearance both of public and private in the modern world. At the same time, in apparent contradiction, she embraces the direct democratic model of workers' councils of Hungary in 1956, in which representative governance was replaced by direct collective self-governance. Why are not these the very "masses" Arendt fears will exert undue—or perhaps any—influence? Arendt directly answers such concerns from critics who assume that a critique of "the masses" is evidence of an equal distaste for popular self-governance. "[T]he assumptions [of such criticisms] are not difficult to point out. Theoretically, *the most relevant and the most pernicious among them is the equation of 'people' and masses*, which sounds only too plausible to everyone who lives in a mass society and is constantly exposed to its numerous irritations."[63]

Arendt's thought in her earlier *The Human Condition* focuses on the way that different types of political or personal activity determine the values and meaning of human life; thinking in terms of such meaning-producing activity can clarify the difference between "people" and "masses." What we do determines who we are, not only individually but also collectively; and as any sociologist could attest, collectivities come in many different forms. For Arendt, groups are not even necessarily determined by those in them, as with the "working

---

63   Hannah Arendt, *On Revolution* (New York: Viking Press, 1965), 274. For a recent critical look at some of Arendt's serious shortcomings, see Kathryn T. Gines, *Hannah Arendt and the Negro Question* (Bloomington: Indiana University Press, 2014).

class" of orthodox Marxism wholly determined by its given position in production; Arendt was consistently critical of orthodox Marxism for this very reason. Instead, she argues that the manner of political activity itself constitutes the agent; in this way, the passive "masses"—with all their political party representation, television watching, and mass-produced commodities—are the precise opposite of ancient Athens's direct *demos*. Seen in this way, the public constituted through Gallup polls, Nielsen ratings, and mass representative voting is an extraordinarily *thin* public: existing only in statistical average but with little resemblance to or resonance with the thoughts and passions of those mysterious persons surveyed in its construction. This thinness, at its extreme, is precisely what I'm calling an "empty public." More akin to the democracy of ancient Athens, in Arendt's view, are the sorts of assemblies present in workers' councils and revolutionary streets. She does not oppose the masses to a professional political elite, as she is often unfortunately read, but distinguishes between groups of people as a mass, and any collectivity of the same bodies constituted by political self-activity. For her, the ancient Athenian plenum offers a participatory ideal:

> [T]he two-party system…has by no means enabled the citizen to become a "participator" in public affairs. The most the citizen can hope for is to be "represented," whereby it is obvious that the only thing which can be represented and delegated is interest, or the welfare of the constituents, but neither their actions nor their opinions. In this system the opinions of the people are indeed unascertainable for the simple reason that *they are non-existent*. Opinions are formed in a process of open discussion and public debate, and *where no opportunity for the forming of opinions exists, there may be moods…but no opinion.*[64]

Arendt considers that politics and deliberation are inseparable from and unthinkable outside participation, since "[w]henever knowing and doing have parted company, the space of freedom is lost."[65]

---

64   Ibid., 272. My emphasis.
65   Ibid., 268.

Political deliberation, the working-out of dissensus, which can only emerge from collective activity, is the arena in which meaning is produced; outside of its commotion, only "moods," but not actual "opinions," are possible. That Arendt has been drastically misread by her followers on the right is nowhere as evident as in her passages on councilism, when she openly calls "for a new form of government that would permit every member of the modern egalitarian society to become a 'participator' in public affairs."[66]

Arendt's vision is strikingly mirrored in the "Solidarity Statement from Cairo," written by participants in the Tahrir revolution in Egypt to advise their American counterparts. In the Egyptian revolutionaries' formation, Arendt's egalitarian "participation in public affairs," and the very physical spaces that make such participation possible, are clearly more than a precondition of politics; they become the core political content of the struggle itself:

> In our own occupations of Tahrir, we encountered people entering the Square every day in tears because it was the first time they had walked through those streets and spaces without being harassed by police; it is not just the ideas that are important, these spaces are fundamental to the possibility of a new world. These are public spaces. Spaces for gathering, leisure, meeting, and interacting—these spaces should be the reason we live in cities. Where the state and the interests of owners have made them inaccessible, exclusive or dangerous, it is up to us to make sure that they are safe, inclusive and just. We have and must continue to open them to anyone that wants to build a better world, particularly for the marginalized, excluded and for those groups who have suffered the worst.[67]

As the next chapters will attempt to bear out, the Tahrir statement indicates a profound shift shared by contemporary movements

---

66 Ibid.

67 Comrades from Cairo, "Solidarity Statement from Cairo," Occupy Wall Street website, accessed May 23, 2016, http://occupywallst.org/article/solidarity-statement-cairo.

around the world. After decades of disastrously effective demobilization strategies, contemporary social movement actors have finally found new ways to mobilize, or rather constitute, publics founded on a fundamental revulsion to those very demobilizing strategies. These publics are necessarily immediate, unmediated, by mass media or political representation. The goal of these immediate publics is less communication (of the justice of their cause or anything else) than constitution: they are forming new collective subjects through the intimacies of shared risk and power, persisting in spite of state attempts at repression, and articulating their power through this very persistence.

CHAPTER 2

THE STRANGE MAGIC OF NONVIOLENCE

I've been living my life for twenty years through the word "nonviolence." After hearing how it was used in Occupy, I think I have to find a new word.
—Nonviolence trainer, Seattle[1]

I've lost track of what "nonviolent" actually means at this point. *I* am not violent; as a person, my character is deeply not violent. We certainly didn't do anything that any reasonable person would consider violent inside that bank [lock-down].... In that sense I guess you could say that we were *not* violent. But I don't know if I could say that it was *nonviolent* anymore. At that time I probably would have said it was. We did make a commitment to not actively physically aggress upon either bank employees or customers or the police, and in that sense our tactics were nonviolent ones, but it seems...I don't know if I would even use that language anymore. In so many conversations, in so many debates over the past few months, I've felt this *strange magic* coming from that word that I don't know I want to invoke anymore.
—Arrestee in Nov. 2 Occupy Seattle "Chase 5" event[2]

---

1 Personal interview (C).
2 Personal interview (D).

ON NOVEMBER 18, 2011, MEMBERS OF THE LOCAL OCCUPY MOVEMENT at UC Davis were peacefully sitting with linked arms in the Quad, when, before a number of cameras, Lieutenant John Pike casually strolled past them and dispensed a huge quantity of pepper spray into their faces. The incident went globally viral, as commentators compared Pike to Martin Luther King Jr.'s Birmingham antagonist Bull Connor, and the nonviolent nature of the protesters' conduct was widely cited as a victorious moment for nonviolent protest. Susan Thistlethwaite in the *Washington Post*, for example, characterized the incident as proof of "the power of nonviolent witness."[3] Author Chris Hedges held the incident up as proof of the Occupy movement's nonviolent orientation:

> The first principles, of course, were nonviolence and non-property destruction.... We don't accept violent language. When you're violent you undermine everything. If the protesters in [Manhattan's] Union Square, who were pepper-sprayed, had been throwing something at the police, you would not have had the movement. It was because they were nonviolent and didn't react when they were being pepper-sprayed that the movement grew. At UC Davis, when those cops just walked down the line and sprayed, the nonviolent reaction by those kids was fantastic.[4]

Pike was dismissed from the university, the protesters won a compensation lawsuit of over $1 million, and the Occupy movement was

---

3   Susan Brooks Thistlethwaite, "UC Davis Pepper Spray and the Power of Nonviolent Witness," *Washington Post*, November 22, 2011.

4   Chris Hedges, "Thank You for Standing Up," *Truthdig*, January 23, 2012. Accessed May 24, 2016, http://www.truthdig.com/report/item/thank_you_for _standing_up_20120123.

given widespread sympathetic coverage in an increasingly hostile national media environment. The incident functioned as indisputable testimony to the enduring power of "nonviolence." Or did it?

"Justin," one of the recipients of Lieutenant Pike's generosity, clarified to me the events leading up to the moment recorded in the famous video.[5] Protesters were standing with linked arms around the Occupy tents to protect them against a police raid, and police started grabbing and detaining people from the line. Justin watched helplessly as his fellow protesters were taken one by one, cuffed, and deposited on the Quad before being loaded into a police car bound for jail. Given the protesters' overwhelming numbers and the widespread support he knew they enjoyed, Justin found the passivity frustrating. He realized that, being arrested on Friday, his fellow protesters would be held in jail over the weekend before being booked. At that moment, he remembered seeing "de-arrests" during the 2003 Iraq War protests, when some protesters wrested others who had been detained out of police custody, and the feeling of empowerment and exhilaration in the crowd at those moments. Justin stepped away from the line and sat down between the detained protesters and the police vehicles that were pulling up to take them away. "I was just thinking about that, about having some of these people not go to jail, if we prevented the cops from transporting these people into the cop cars. Once we were sitting down we were just entrenched and the cops couldn't move us." Some sat down and joined him, while others gathered around at a distance, worried about confronting the police. The growing number of seated protesters started chanting, "From Davis, to Greece—Fuck the Police!" After they'd chanted this line about four times, those standing around, whom Justin described as "spectators," started to yell in a near panic, "Remain nonviolent!" Justin reflected, "They shouted us down. It was so strange; it was like saying 'fuck the police' was a violent act." Justin later interpreted their use of the word "nonviolent" to mean their own fear at confronting the police, rather than any perceived physical aggression on the seated protesters' behalf. A few minutes later, Lieutenant Pike sprayed the faces of the seated protesters. In retrospect, the famous event was as contingent on the protesters' contestation of policing practices as it was on their own physical passivity while being sprayed.

---

5   Personal interview (E).

Were the seated protesters being "violent" or "nonviolent"? Passively interfering with police conduct, particularly while seated, is in some senses a classic example of nonviolence. Yet the speech acts of those seated, in labeling their action as specifically antagonistic to policing rather than to some more distant issue, and using profanity in doing so, somehow put them outside the category in the eyes of some spectators present. Despite his stated sympathies with those pepper-sprayed, had he been present, Hedges's own take would likely have put him on the side of those characterizing the antipolice slogan as violence. "I would classify violence as the destruction of property and vandalism, the shouting of insulting messages to the police, physical confrontations with the police. Those are very clear cut-acts of violence."[6] In Justin's account, however, without the confrontation with police—which was motivated for participants by the same affectual commitments as their chanting "Fuck the Police"—the political tensions inherent in the moment would never have been made visible, and Hedges wouldn't have had anything to praise.

Justin's experience, and those of the people whose quotations open this chapter, pose a set of difficult questions. What constitutes the difference and the tension between "violence" and "nonviolence"? Why would longtime proponents of nonviolence reconsider their commitments in recent contexts? How is it that nonviolence has in the past enacted such powerful "magic," and what might have caused this efficacy to decline? I argue that nonviolence is not the opposite of violence in any simple, stable way. Rather, nonviolence is a rhetorical move of disavowal whose meaning relies on calling violence into the audience's mind, just as the speaker is disavowing it. Nonviolence deftly exploits ambiguities in the shifting definition of violence, particularly by equating apparently very dissimilar phenomena together as "violence." Instead of merely "demystifying" some deep affinity between nonviolence and its opposite, understanding nonviolence's traditional and contemporary manifestations helps elucidate the supposedly magical power of its appeal. As will become clear, nonviolence has suffered from a slippage in meaning in the neoliberal era, to the extent that even previously devout advocates of nonviolence have

6   J. A. Myerson, "Interview with Chris Hedges about Black Bloc," *Truthout*, February 9, 2012. Accessed May 24, 2016, http://www.truth-out.org/opinion/item/6587:interview-with-chris-hedges-about-black-bloc.

begun to question its relevance to current conditions. Unlike classic nonviolence, contemporary forms consistently display an aversion to disruption and conflict, which is symptomatic of its inadequacy under today's conditions of social control.

THE NONOPPOSITION OF NON/VIOLENCE

As discussed in Chapter 1, the civil rights, anti-Vietnam War, and Black Power movements of the last century were faced with social conditions quite different than those of the present, but their era's frameworks often persist in the description and evaluation of movements in the present. When discussing political violence, particularly counterhegemonic violence, it helps to begin by taking a look at the social conditions that defined violence in the last era of mass social movements in the US to see how those definitions have outlasted the conditions that created them.

In early 1971, a Swedish film crew visited Angela Davis in prison and asked her if she approved of violence as a means of achieving social change. Davis, a core participant in both the civil rights movement and the Black Power movement that had come to supersede it, responded with a breathtaking exegesis on political violence, timeless and yet marked by the political conditions of her time:

> [Y]ou ask *me*, whether I approve of violence, I mean that just doesn't make any sense at all. Whether I approve of guns.
>
> I grew up in Birmingham, Alabama. Some very, very good friends of mine were killed by bombs, bombs that were planted by racists. I remember, from the time I was very small, I remember the sounds of bombs exploding across the street, our house shaking. I remember my father having to have guns at his disposal at all times because of the fact that at any moment...we might expect to be attacked. The man who was at that time in complete control of the city government, his name was Bull Connor, would often get on the radio and make statements like, "Niggers have moved into a white neighborhood. We'd better expect some bloodshed tonight." And sure enough, there

would be bloodshed. [halting] After the four young girls who, one of them lived next door to me, I was very good friends with the sister of another one, my sister was very good friends with all three of them, my mother taught one of them in her class… In fact, when the bombing occurred, one of the mothers of, one of the young girls, called my mother and said, "Can you take me down to the church, to pick up Carol, we heard about the bombing and I don't have my car." And they went down, and what did they find? They found limbs, and heads, strewn all over the place. And then, after that, in my neighborhood, all the men organized themselves into an armed patrol. They had to take their guns and patrol our community every night because they did not want that to happen again.

I mean that's why, when someone asks me [laughs] about *violence*, [shudders] I just find it *incredible*. Because what it means, is that the person who's asking that question has absolutely no idea what Black people have gone through, what Black people have experienced in this country, since the time the first Black person was kidnapped from the shores of Africa.[7]

Notably, Davis never takes the position of *advocating* violence; she uses a rhetorical strategy that I call *forced comparison*, which I'll discuss more in the next chapter. She gives presence to a series of overwhelming images that expose previously invisible violence, inducing shame in the audience for comparing the relatively minute measure of revolutionary force to the disproportionately horrific violence it seeks to end. Davis corrects herself the one time she begins to speak positively about "violence"—recasting "whether I approve of violence" as "whether I approve of guns" after a moment's reflection. For Davis, a category of "not-violence" presents itself as opposed to both the true violence of oppression and the "nonviolence" of the civil rights movement. Davis posits the *opposite of nonviolence* as "guns," ("whether I approve of violence.... Whether I approve of

---

7   Angela Davis, video interview in *The Black Power Mixtape 1967–1975*, directed by Göran Hugo Olsson (Stockholm: Sveriges Television, 2011), DVD.

guns") leaving aside the question whether counterhegemonic "violence" should even be considered violence as such. Similarly, although less involved in lethal confrontation than their counterparts in Black communities or overseas, white revolutionary groups of the time, such as the Weather Underground, often used images of AK-47s and slogans like "Bring the War Home" and "Give Piece a Chance" to call American exceptionalism into question.[8] By espousing guns in their public visual design, if not generally in act, such groups asserted solidarity by acknowledging the severity of the conflict faced by those in Black communities and overseas, whom they mimicked.

Under the conditions faced by Davis or in the jungles of Vietnam, such armed response is more than understandable; however, contemporary participants in the US generally attest that taking up "guns" in armed conflict is no longer a tenable "opposite of nonviolence." Even those identifying as "militants" grow quickly indignant when their opposition to nonviolence is conflated with armed struggle. In the words of one self-described "radical" I interviewed, "It's important to emphasize that none of the radicals are advocating a position of guerilla warfare or armed revolutionary warfare.... This is a straw man argument that some liberals have raised to discredit us."[9] According to another interviewee, nonviolence proponents tend to read disavowals of nonviolence as commitments to conquer the state by *direct force*, with no concern for claims to social power and legitimacy. In the recent global proliferation of disruptive dissent, even in the vivid and intense examples of riots, material consequences were arguably *not* the primary effect. The hundreds of police cars, political party headquarters, and state offices burned in Cairo during the Tahrir uprising certainly brought material consequences to the state for their corrupt, exploitative, antidemocratic policies, but their importance was in the emotions and values enacted and embodied, argued through practices of material rhetoric—the fearlessness of youth before police terror and

---

8   Dan Berger, *Outlaws of America: The Weather Underground and the Politics of Solidarity* (Oakland, CA: AK Press, 2006) and Jeremy Varon, *Bringing the War Home: The Weather Underground, the Red Army Faction, and Revolutionary Violence in the Sixties and Seventies* (Berkeley: University of California Press, 2004).

9   Personal correspondence (A).

the invisible but very "present absence" of torture, the long-repressed public rage given body in flames and shattered facades.[10] These arguments were only made more articulate by the resulting lack of injury, in stark contrast to the bloodied hands of the Mubarak regime.

In a similar vein, the myriad of banks, political offices, and police stations destroyed by arson in the uprising of youth across Greece in 2008—touched off by the police killing of fifteen-year-old anarchist Alexandros Grigoropoulos—lyrically expressed the tearful, enraged despair of an entire generation. The lack of any injury in a month of massive public property destruction successfully associated the destruction with the side of youth and life, while implicating the order of police and the prison society they represented as one of *batsoi, gourounia, dolofonoi—cops, pigs, murderers*, a historic staple of Greek protests, embodying both the long tradition of antiauthoritarian heritage and a grassroots distrust of police. The importance of the noninjurious nature of these actions to the social formation they constituted became tragically clear on May 1, 2010, when three bank employees perished in a bank that had been lit on fire; the movement of numerous millions effectually demobilized in shame over the deaths, however accidental. These events in Greece, for many around the world, defined a new era in repertoires of social movement rhetoric; their noninjurious character was as integral to their meaning as was their immense violence against material sites of status quo power.

A few factors are worth noting as likely contributing to this shift away from armed struggle. First, contemporary social movement actors are well aware of the general supersaturation of surveillance under neoliberal governance, the widespread infiltration of marginalized communities, and the exponential increase in militarization of police forces.[11] These factors alone suffice to make guerrilla warfare,

---

10 "Solidarity Statement from Cairo."

11 Christian Parenti, *The Soft Cage: Surveillance in America; From Slavery to the War on Terror* (New York: Basic Books, 2003) and Glenn Greenwald, *No Place to Hide: Edward Snowden, the NSA, and the U.S. Surveillance State.* (New York: Metropolitan Books/Henry Holt, 2014). On police militarization, see Christian Parenti, *Lockdown America* (London, New York: Verso, 2008) and Radley Balko, *Rise of the Warrior Cop: The Militarization of America's Police Forces* (New York: PublicAffairs, 2013).

either in the *foco* or deterritorialized variants, unfeasible.[12] Secondly, as will be discussed in my final chapter, *prefiguration* has become a key concept in social movements since Angela Davis's time; consequently, the tendency for social movements relying on murder as a method of political transformation to keep on killing long "after the revolution" has become widely acknowledged to the point of cliché.[13] As I will argue, the grievances of contemporary social movements frequently include the low value given to human (and nonhuman) life in comparison to the value given to commodities; injurious violence would thus starkly conflict with the movements' own values.

Lastly, contemporary social movements since the alter-globalization uprisings have generally preferred dispersed, diffuse, nonhierarchical, and antiauthoritarian deliberative structures, for reasons as tactical as philosophical.[14] Nonviolence theorist George Lakey observed that "[s]ecrecy brings divisiveness into movement life because there must always be those who know and those who do not know. Those who are outside feel resentful; those who are inside develop feelings of superiority. Knowledge is a form of power, and secrecy ensures that there be a power structure with a distinction between the haves and have-nots."[15] Syrian anarchist Leila al-Shami offers a painful example from this process at work within the Syrian revolution; although four hundred areas persist in running by self-organized popular councils and decentralized networks of work and distribution, these areas find themselves suffering under the dual oppression of Bashar al-Assad's massacres and the authoritarianism of armed groups responding to Assad's violence:

---

12   For the *foco* model, see Régis Debray, *Revolution in the Revolution? Armed Struggle and Political Struggle in Latin America* (New York: Monthly Review Press, 1967) and Che Guevara, *Che Guevara on Guerrilla Warfare* (New York: Praeger, 1961). On more deterritorial variants, see Robert Taber, *The War of the Flea: A Study of Guerrilla Warfare Theory and Practice* (New York: L. Stuart, 1965).

13   Andrew Cornell, *Oppose and Propose! Lessons from Movement for a New Society* (Oakland: AK Press & Institute for Anarchist Studies, 2011).

14   Gillham and Noakes, "More Than a March in a Circle."

15   George Lakey, *Strategy for a Living Revolution* (New York: Grossman Publishers, 1973), 97.

These experiments in self-organization are caught in a complex web of challenges. The liberated areas have been the main target of Assadist (and more recently Russian) airstrikes, in an attempt to crush any alternative to the regime.

The relentless assault has contributed to the depopulation of these areas and sent waves of refugees seeking safety abroad. Militarization of the uprising, which was on the rise in the summer/fall of 2011, transformed it from a horizontally organized, inclusive and non-sectarian movement into a struggle amongst numerous competing authoritarian factions attempting to assert their hegemony and deny liberated communities self-determination.

The clearest examples are some of the more extreme Islamist factions which have tried to wrest control away from the local councils and impose their own parallel structures, such as Shura Councils and Sharia courts, despite popular protest in areas where this has occurred.

These groups remain part of the armed anti-Assad struggle (and now, with the military involvement of imperialist powers, part of the struggle against foreign occupation) as well as the fight against Daesh (ISIS). But they've never been part of the Syrian people's struggle for freedom, social justice, and self-determination. They seek to replace one authoritarian state with another.[16]

In the same vein, several acquaintances have spoken to me about the difficulties faced by Zapatista communities in attempting to both maintain territorial presence through force of arms, and to foster bottom-up methods of community control. The severe demands of

---

16 Leila al-Shami, "Challenging the Nation State in Syria," *Fifth Estate* no. 396 (2016). Available online at https://www.fifthestate.org/archive/396-summer -2016/challenging-the-nation-state-in-syria. For an immensely informative and moving look at the Syrian revolution, see Robin Yassin-Kassab and Leila al-Shami, *Burning Country: Syrians in Revolution and War* (London: Pluto Press, 2016).

clandestinity required by their military confrontations have proven increasingly incommensurate with the egalitarian, community-based methods of deliberation they seek to put into practice.

Those voices that recognize a function for *insurrectionary* violence often share the intense aversion to arms usually associated with nonviolence adherents. As one Occupy Oakland participant stated,

> I understand two views of [counterhegemonic] militancy, of violence. One is the Party, the Party is precision, order, precision violence, orders coming down the chain of command to execute some kind of violent action, whether that's small terrorist cells, or an armed movement, or a guerrilla force. And another is the chaotic riot, the spontaneous action, no one is giving orders, it's more like, it's decentralized, it's horizontal, it's spontaneous. Those are two [very different] conceptions of violence. I'm against armed struggle, I'm against hierarchical, Leninist vanguard, militant party, stuff like that.[17]

In an essay explaining the centrality of riots as an aspect of contemporary social movement rhetoric, Piven unhesitatingly agrees with nonviolence scholars Peter Ackerman and Jack DuVall in their description of unarmed, social change mechanisms:

> People power in the twentieth century did not grow out of the barrel of a gun. It removed rulers who believed that violence was power, by acting to dissolve their real source of power: the consent of acquiescence of the people they had tried to subordinate. When unjust laws were no longer obeyed, when commerce stopped because people no longer worked, when public services could no longer function, and when armies were no longer feared, the violence that governments could use no longer mattered—their power to make people comply had disappeared."[18]

---

17 Personal interview (F).

18 Frances Fox Piven, "Protest Movements and Violence," in Seferiades and

Where the rest of Piven's essay departs from Ackerman and DuVall's analysis is not in their shared rejection of armed struggle, but rather in leaving aside the (generally unstated) *assertion of moral equivalence between riot and war*, characteristic of so many nonviolence advocates. Because *violence* is a far less definable term than *arms*, some advocates of "strategic nonviolence" have begun to prefer the term "unarmed insurrection" to "nonviolence," a term that resonates with the language of many in contemporary social movements who reject the term nonviolence.[19] The "nonviolence vs. armed struggle" dichotomy, carried down as a traumatic condensation from the 1970s, is being displaced by a more contemporary opposition between, on the one hand, anti-authoritarian "strategic nonviolence" and riotous approaches, and on the other, authoritarian "principled nonviolence" and armed struggle approaches.[20]

Johnston, eds., *Violent Protest, Contentious Politics, and the Neoliberal State* (Farnham/Burlington: Ashgate Publishing, 2012), 28.

19 Stephen Zunes, "Unarmed Insurrections against Authoritarian Governments in the Third World: A New Kind of Revolution," *Third World Quarterly* 15, no. 3 (1994): 403–26.

20 Longtime anarchist and friend Sylvie Kashdan, who participated in the social movements of the 1960s, reminds me that the "nonviolence vs. armed struggle" dichotomy was indeed *never* actually representative of the spectrum of approaches within the New Left regarding violence. As such, the very title of this book might be rather misleading—perhaps nonviolence never was what it used to be, and neither was armed struggle. This project is dealing more with the memory and amnesia of that time and its effect on our present categories of understanding, which, I would argue, *has* been a dichotomous memory. But I eagerly anticipate scholarship correcting this amnesia—particularly on the distinction between "armed struggle" of the generally Maoist variety (which I argue has left such an imprint on our memory of the opposite of nonviolence) and the much more widely embraced but often neglected history of "armed self-defense," particularly as part of the civil rights and Black Power movements. Recent works such as Akinyele Omowale Umoja's *We Will Shoot Back: Armed Resistance in the Mississippi Freedom Movement* (New York: NYU Press, 2013), Charles E. Cobb Jr's *This Nonviolent Stuff'll Get You Killed: How Guns Made the Civil Rights Movement Possible* (New York: Basic Books, 2014), Lance Hill's *The Deacons for Defense: Armed Resistance and the Civil Rights Movement* (Chapel Hill: University of North Carolina Press, 2004), and Neal Shirley and Saralee

A passing look at the ways contemporary approaches to strategic nonviolence characterize themselves provides strong evidence for this idea. In his 2005 work *Unarmed Insurrections: People Power Movements in Nondemocracies*, which has quickly become a cornerstone among "strategic nonviolent" proponents, Kurt Schock identifies what he sees as an ascendance of nonviolent approaches but makes sense of it in a way quite similar to the Occupy Oakland participant quoted above:

> Whereas totalizing ideologies and permanent vanguard parties seem more suited to the tasks of overthrowing a state through violence and ruling society from above, oppositional consciousness and temporary organizations seem more suited to rolling back authoritarian relations and building more democratic and just relations through nonviolent action from below. Oppositional consciousness is open-ended, nontotalizing, and respectful of diversity, and it facilitates the mobilization of a broad-based opposition. Widespread resistance is significant in that there is a greater distribution of the risks involved in engaging in collective action, it is more difficult for the state to focus its repressive apparatus on a particular group or organization, and campaigns of noncooperation need broad-based support to succeed. Mobilizing through oppositional consciousness has consequences for organizing as well. It rejects permanent, centralized organizations and vanguard parties, opting for united front politics, shifting alliances, and temporary organizations that engage in struggles as situations arise.[21]

Stafford's *Dixie Be Damned: 300 Years of Insurrection in the American South.* (Oakland: AK Press, 2015) have opened up more complex understandings of the role of violence and guns in the civil rights movement and before. I am excited to see what continues to come from this extremely important, and long-neglected, line of inquiry and scholarship.

21 Kurt Schock, *Unarmed Insurrections: People Power Movements in Nondemocracies* (Minneapolis: University of Minnesota Press, 2005), 165.

And again, like the Occupy Oakland activist, Schock describes this approach by referring to the conjuncture of military force and authoritarianism: "Whereas the goals of violent challenges are often to capture state power or gain control over territory, in the late twentieth century the goals of many of the challenging movements in the Third World were not to capture state power or exercise a monopoly of power over a piece of territory, but rather *to roll back the frontiers of the authoritarian state, make the polity more inclusive, and promote sociopolitical empowerment.*"[22]

Not only do Schock's characterizations of strategic nonviolence not hold exclusively true for nonviolent actions, but his descriptions of the rhetorical efficacy of contemporary protest closely resemble the processes of the riots I analyze in later chapters. "For the oppressed to engage in collective action, there must first be cognitive liberation, that is, a diminution of fatalism coupled with a perception that conditions are unjust, yet subject to change through collective action."[23] Schock returns time and again to this central importance of *fostering agency* under neoliberal conditions, precisely the goal espoused by contemporary insurgents looking for methods beyond "nonviolence," including but certainly not limited to riots. The *subjective* processes fostered in public performances of confrontation, Schock says, should not be confused with merely *personal* ones, because such processes also produce social relations: "Protest and persuasion are important in that they may help aggrieved populations overcome quiescence and the fear of repression, and provide them with social visibility while alerting reference publics and third parties to an unjust situation. Moreover, methods of protest and persuasion are often the crucibles in which frames are elaborated and disseminated, solidarity is forged, and members of the aggrieved group are mobilized to participate in other methods of nonviolent action."[24]

Notably, Schock goes on to clarify that "[i]n democracies, protest and persuasion have become more or less institutionalized and therefore by themselves may not necessarily provide a direct and immediate challenge to the power of the state."[25] Schock contrasts this to the still

---

22   Ibid., 23. My emphasis.
23   Ibid., 27.
24   Ibid., 39.
25   Ibid.

powerful potential of protest in nondemocratic states, but nowhere does he attempt to answer how such challenges might be brought about under conditions where conventional protest forms have been institutionalized. When they question "pluralist prejudice" and work outside institutionally recuperated channels, dissidents in democratic countries confront conditions not entirely dissimilar to conditions in nondemocratic states. This, I think, is precisely the reason for a return to more conflictual (and often illegal) means of protest.

Advocates of nonviolent approaches also frequently cite the importance of "democratic availability" of methods of nonviolent protest, in contrast to the methods of "violence." In clarifying the superiority of nonviolence over theories that entrust social change to a vanguard, Schock argues that

> a virtue of these methods is that the means for challenging the regime are at hand. Symbolic actions, noncooperation, and intervention can theoretically be implemented by anyone at any time…no special equipment beyond what is typically available to people is needed to undermine state power and legitimacy through nonviolent action. Moreover, although some particular acts of nonviolent action may require more physical strength and endurance than others, just about anyone in the population can participate in nonviolent action: men as well as women, the old as well as the young, the less physically fit as well as the physically fit. This contrasts sharply with violent action, which requires special weapons—weapons that are likely to be monopolized by the state—and military campaigns, in which participation has historically been limited to young, physically fit, ideologically indoctrinated or mercenary males. It also contrasts sharply with theories of social change that privilege a particular class or "vanguard" as the agents of social change, thus excluding networks of exploited groups from struggles against oppression (Galtung 1980, 396–98). Thus, nonviolent challenges have the potential to allow the maximum degree of active participation in the struggle by the highest proportion

of the population. Whereas the arrest or killing of a dozen or so members of a guerrilla cell can devastate an armed campaign, the death or arrest of hundreds or even thousands of nonviolent activists may fail to weaken challenges incorporating mass nonviolent action due to their much greater size (Zunes 1994, 415; Zunes and Kurtz 1999). The greater scale of participation in such challenges also makes it more difficult for the state to differentiate between movement participants and nonparticipants, making targeted repression, which is more effective in quelling dissent, more difficult to implement and indiscriminate repression [sic], which may undermine the regime and promote more widespread mobilization.[26]

Although this difference in democratic availability of repertoire (perhaps overstated, considering, for example, the frequency of women in both guerrilla groups and armies) is often held to distinguish between violence and nonviolence, riot is again seen to resemble nonviolence more than armed struggle by the standards Schock applies, and thus within reach of a wide variety of participants. As British riot scholar Roger Ball clarified to me, what made the destruction during the 1990 Poll Tax riots so effective (ultimately bringing down Margaret Thatcher) was not the concerted, intensive work of any organized contingent within the protests, but rather a broad, dispersed exercise of small amounts of violence by many members of the giant protest, each getting a kick in to a riot cop here and there, or turning over objects into the streets, or breaking a random window—certainly "technologies" available to demonstrators of all shapes and sizes.[27] Traditionally, riot was seen as the particular domain of the most marginalized; indeed, the same activities that might be thought of as "making oneself heard" for more enfranchised parties would often be called "riot" if enacted by the disprivileged. In Rebecca Hill's analysis, "race became a determining factor in what was defined as violent or insurrectionary activity, as opposed to what was defined as popular justice, and the

---

26 Ibid., 40.

27 Roger Ball, personal interview.

ability to use violence in an orderly way became evidence of whiteness itself."[28] Paradoxically, by the time of the alter-globalization and Occupy movements, riots were often dismissed as a sort of vanguardist tantruming of white adolescent boys. Although the charge seems obviously untenable after Ferguson and Black Lives Matter, it also seems to be too useful a tool for recuperation for some people to abandon, which warrants our brief attention.

This recent unfortunate application of privilege theory relies on an inversion of the traditional racialization of riots, associating them exclusively with white people who "have the privilege" to engage in public disruption. This critique was a favorite of nonprofits in Oakland during Occupy, which, as the anonymous collective of people of color, women, and queer folks who authored the "Who is Oakland" pamphlet point out, complemented police force by delegitimizing militant social movements. "Indeed, the exponential growth of NGOs and nonprofits could be understood as the 21st century public face of counterinsurgency, except this time speaking the language of civil, women's, and gay rights, charged with preempting political conflict, and spiritually committed to promoting one-sided 'dialogue' with armed state bureaucracies."[29]

Although, as Jackie Wang points out, people of color certainly face harsher consequences for participation in disruptive performances, this has not and certainly does not equate to impossibility or inadvisability of enacting public disruption. The relative severity of repression may be taken as an acknowledgement of these populations' greater political capacity, a capacity sorely needed to disrupt internal colonialism's physical and material effects, both at the level of the individual and as a social practice:

> When an analysis of privilege is turned into a political program that asserts that the most vulnerable should not take risks, the only politically correct politics

---

28 Rebecca N. Hill, *Men, Mobs, and Law: Anti-Lynching and Labor Defense in U.S. Radical History* (Durham: Duke University Press, 2008), 10–11.

29 CROATOAN, "Who Is Oakland: Anti-Oppression Activism, the Politics of Safety, and State Co-optation," Escalating Identity website, accessed May 23, 2016, https://escalatingidentity.wordpress.com/2012/04/30/who-is-oakland-anti -oppression-politics-decolonization-and-the-state.

becomes a politics of reformism and retreat, a politics that necessarily capitulates to the status quo while erasing the legacy of Black Power groups like the Black Panthers and the Black Liberation Army. For Fanon, it is precisely the element of risk that makes militant action more urgent—liberation can only be won by risking one's life. Militancy is not just tactically necessary—its dual objective is to transform people and "fundamentally alter" their being by emboldening them, removing their passivity and cleansing them of "the core of despair" crystallized in their bodies. [30]

Moving on to the contested gender of riot, Hedges is again worth quoting at length for his allegation that rioting (which he inaccurately terms "the Black Bloc movement") in Occupy was the purview of males, equating it to *war*:

> The Black Bloc movement is infected with a deeply disturbing hypermasculinity. This hypermasculinity, I expect, is its primary appeal. It taps into the lust that lurks within us to destroy, not only things but human beings. It offers the godlike power that comes with mob violence. Marching as a uniformed mass, all dressed in black to become part of an anonymous bloc, faces covered, temporarily overcomes alienation, feelings of inadequacy, powerlessness and loneliness. It imparts to those in the mob a sense of comradeship. It permits an inchoate rage to be unleashed on any target. Pity, compassion and tenderness are banished for the intoxication of power. It is the same sickness that fuels the swarms of police who pepper-spray and beat peaceful demonstrators. It is the sickness of soldiers in war. It turns human beings into beasts. [31]

---

30 Jackie Wang, "Beyond Innocence," *LIES* 1 (2012), 163.

31 Chris Hedges, "The Cancer in Occupy," *Truthdig*, February 6, 2012. Accessed May 24, 2016, https://escalatingidentity.wordpress.com/2012/04/30/who-is -oakland-anti-oppression-politics-decolonization-and-the-state.

Any reading of the history of rioting in America or elsewhere belies such a complete erasure of feminist, queer, and trans struggles, indicating nearly the opposite of Hedges's claims. The modern LGBTQ movement began, it should be remembered, with the quite violent Stonewall riots of 1969 and the lesser-known Compton's Cafeteria riot of transgender patrons in San Francisco's Tenderloin district three years before.[32] The woman suffrage movement, precisely as a movement contesting the stricture of access to legal decision-making instruments, was at times synonymous with rioting.[33] E. P. Thompson's classic work "The Moral Economy of the English Crowd in the Eighteenth Century" details an exhaustive rationale behind the era's plentiful riots, as crowds quite self-consciously sought to exercise the only means of price-control within reach during the onset of capitalist policies.[34] These riots were, again, gendered disproportionately as female. One picturesque passage from Gilje bears repeating:

> Crowds also rioted over prices. Women, like in bread riots in England and France, dominated many of these disturbances. In July 1777 about one hundred Boston women went to merchant Thomas Boylston's shop demanding coffee at a set price. When he refused, they started to drag him to a wharf for a dunking. Before they could do so, Boylston surrendered the storeroom's keys. The women then left him to get the coffee, which they promised to sell to the poor. Similar disturbances occurred elsewhere. In the state of New York a crowd of twenty-two women and two continental soldiers came to Peter Messier's house in May 1777. Refusing to pay his price for tea, they set a just price and beat him. The same concerns for the good of the local community lay behind some resistance to recruitment during the war. A crowd of approximately one hundred in April 1781 prevented a

32   David Carter, *Stonewall: The Riots That Sparked the Gay Revolution* (New York: St. Martin's Press, 2010), 105.

33   A. K. Thompson, *Black Bloc, White Riot: Anti-globalization and the Genealogy of Dissent* (Oakland: AK Press, 2010) and Gilje, *Rioting in America*.

34   E. P. Thompson, "Moral Economy of the English Crowd," 76–136.

draft of men in Roxbridge County, Virginia, claiming that they had given enough to the war and feared that they would not be able to get their crops in with a further drain on man-power.[35]

The evident lack of any clear-cut opposition between nonviolence and violence goes beyond the fact that their protest repertoires can share qualities of openness, diffuse deliberation, emancipatory processes, and the democratic availability. There is a longer-term rationale of social transformation as well. These claims sound strange in contemporary context, when the presence of what was called "revolutionary nonviolence" has all but vanished—those few I interviewed who identified with such approaches all expressed a bewilderment at not finding a clear place within recent movements.[36] Advocates of revolutionary nonviolence were suspicious of those "militants" who refused to avow "nonviolence," but they found little in common with other "nonviolence" advocates, who were generally averse to conflict and talk of radical social transformation. People often confuse the dichotomy of violence/nonviolence with that of revolution/reform, inexorably linking violence with revolution and nonviolence with reform. However, Gene Sharp, essentially the founder of the "strategic nonviolence" approach, clearly puts forth a nonviolent revolutionary project that sounds very much like the discourse of contemporary "radicals":

> The subjects usually do not realize that they are the source of the ruler's power and that by joint action they could dissolve that power. Failure to realize the role they play may have its roots either in innocent ignorance or in deliberate deception by the ruler. If the subjects look at their ruler's power at a given moment, they are likely to see it as a hard, solid force which at any point may fall upon them in their helplessness; this short-range view leads them to the monolith theory of power. If they were to look at their ruler's power both backward and forward in time, however, and note its origins and growth,

35   Gilje, *Rioting in America*, 50.

36   David T. Dellinger, *Revolutionary Nonviolence* (Indianapolis: Bobbs-Merrill, 1970).

its variations and fragility, they would begin to see their role in the genesis, continuance and development of that power. This realization would reveal that they possess the capacity to destroy that power.[37]

One Occupy Oakland participant described both the 2008 uprising in Greece and what occurred over the course of Occupy Oakland as applications of precisely the same revolutionary process:

> What happened in 2008 never happened before in Greece. It was never like that. Probably right after the junta but, like, in collective memory that never happened before. It kind of came on the tail-end of the neoliberal attack against Greece and it had been building for a year, two years—many, many months at the very least—and culminated in an actual insurrection where the government was like, "Do we call in the soldiers?" And they're like, "Actually, we can't trust the soldiers." That's an insurrection. It would have been the revolution if they had called in the soldiers, because then, you know, who knows, the soldiers would've turned over their weapons.
>
> So, let's say Oakland, then is an example of the zenith of militancy in the context of the US. What's been happening in Oakland is kind of like a low-grade insurrection. It's kind of an insurrection. The insurrection has come. Now, what does the insurrection mean in the context of California, of the United States, of the Bay Area? It doesn't actually mean car bombs and assassinations by protesters against police or government forces. It doesn't mean that. I think nationally that it just doesn't make any sense, it's not within our spectrum of political horizon. It's not within our collective consciousness as something being possible. But what is possible for the first time is like constant and never-ending confrontation with state forces and with

---

37   Gene Sharp, *Power and Struggle: The Politics of Nonviolent Action, Part 1* (Boston: Porter Sargent, 1973), 44.

flashpoints of militant street action. Like flagrant disregard for the law, open hostility, a challenge, a response to each kind of infraction brought against us by the police. All these things constitute an insurrection. It's not just bands of militants, bands of radical people—obviously they exist, but when it's sort of like normal people on the street who will pull over, to help you yell at the cops who are hassling kids.... Or the families who aren't like, white radicals, who are just like, black working-class...or like students of all shapes and colors coming together actively doing the same thing in terms of challenging state authority, it's an insurrection. No one's dying, but no one really died in Greece either.[38]

In rare moments, such similarities between insurrectionary militancy and "strategic nonviolence" are acknowledged by strategic nonviolence theorists. Sharp, for example, sees a greater distance between "action" and "nonaction" than between "violence" and "nonviolence":

> It is widely assumed that all social and political behavior must be clearly either violent or nonviolent. This simple dualism leads only to serious distortions of reality, however, one of the main ones being that some people call "nonviolent" anything they regard as good, and "violent" anything they dislike. A second gross distortion occurs when people totally erroneously equate cringing passivity with nonviolent action because in neither case is there the use of physical violence.... Careful consideration of actual response to social and political conflict requires that all responses to conflict situations be initially divided into those of *action* and those of *inaction*, and not divided according to their violence or lack of violence.[39]

Nevertheless, the patent *nonopposition* between the strategic "nonviolence" purported by Schock, Zunes, Sharp, Lakey, and others, and

---

38 Personal interview (G).

39 Sharp, *Power and Struggle*, 64–65.

the material rhetoric enacted by riots does not in any sense imply their acceptance of or reconciliation with the "violence" of riots and non-injurious counterhegemonic violence, particularly in contemporary contexts. In fact, however much "nonviolence" discourses attempt to move beyond a simple negation of "violence" to claim an inherent, positive, and nonpassive content, "nonviolence" in its traditional, strategic, and principled variants remains inextricably joined to its Other in just the manner that its name attests, as a gesture of dis-avowal of an indefinable "violence." It is precisely through this mor-phological disavowal of "violence" that nonviolence has accomplished vast rhetorical victories in the past and upon which it flounders in contemporary applications.

DISAVOWAL BY NON/DEFINITION

During the video of a training session aimed specifically at increasing the presence of nonviolence in Seattle protest movements, a Kingian nonviolence trainer from the Positive Peace Warrior Network, who came up from Oakland for the occasion, attempts to assert a meaning independent of the ambiguity of "violence." The trainer writes the two words "Non-violence" and "Nonviolence" on a white board and then asks, "Someone tell me the difference between those two words. [long silence] It's not a trick question."[40] One audience member final-ly responds, "I would say, non-violence with a hyphen is not violence, and nonviolence below is a positive concept, *ahimsa*, meaning a cer-tain attitude, a positive one, that you take towards your enemy and towards everyone." The trainer responds, "Exactly. I've certainly seen nonviolence written both ways. When you put the hyphen in there, it changes everything, 'cause all this [non-violence] says is it's not vi-olent, it's an adjective, it's the absence of something. Right?" In the words of another facilitator of the session,

> [This trainer] heard neighbors in a fistfight. When he
> looked around, a bunch of people had gathered on the
> street. They were all technically being "non-violent."

---

40   "Kazu Haga in Seattle on Kingian Nonviolence in the Context of Occupy," Youtube video, accessed May 24, 2016, https://youtu.be/PtPLYUe-occ. The scene described starts at 0:52.

Those bystanders were witnessing injustice but standing there meant they were not being violent at the basic level of its definition. But our interpretation of what being truly "nonviolent" would mean goes beyond doing nothing. So he went and intervened. Being truly nonviolent means exposing and doing something to disrupt and prevent a system and circumstance of injustice without using the tools of injustice themselves in order to create peace. It doesn't mean being inactive or passive and watching as inadvertent but nevertheless involved cohabitants of an unjust world.[41]

Such neighborly intervention is certainly commendable, although one might reserve ultimate judgment without knowing the topic of the disagreement. However, what is not clear is why the intervention qualifies as *nonviolence* (without a hyphen) rather than an intervention not involving violence. Would a different neighbor who did not share his convictions be unwittingly engaging in nonviolence if they were similarly to intervene? How would this action, intentions aside, qualify as anything beyond not-violent neighborly intervention? Even generals and *génocidaires* at times seek to deescalate and resolve conflicts; are they practicing nonviolence? The question remains: can the promised positive meaning of nonviolence, this "certain attitude" attested to by the workshop participant, be defined apart from an act of disavowal of a persistently indefinable violence? What is a difference in attitude if its effects are indistinguishable?

In a debate titled "How Will the Walls Come Tumbling Down? Diversity of Tactics vs Nonviolence in the Occupy Movement," held in Oakland in December 2011, this same trainer again attempted to disavow nonviolence's disavowal. He again began with a promise to go beyond simple negation of an undefined Other. "One of the biggest misconceptions about nonviolence is that we think nonviolence means not being violent," he said. "Nonviolence is a whole lot more than that."[42] However, the positive content he tries to map out is just as ambiguous. "Nonviolence means taking a stand against violence,

---

41 Personal interview (H).
42 Positive Peace Warrior Network, "How Will the Walls Come Tumbling Down?"

and taking a stand against injustice, and taking a stand against this belief that we can use violence, fear, and intimidation to bring about the changes we want to see in our society. That's what the government does, that's what the police, the corporations do, they have this belief that they can just take what they want, and use fear and intimidation to get what they want. Nonviolence means taking a stand against that belief."[43]

The trainer's move from simple *nonbeing*—nonviolence as something that *is not* violence—to defining it as "taking a stand against violence" remains just as dependent on a vaguely loathsome Other. Defining violence as a *belief* "that they can just take what they want, and use fear and intimidation" only increases the ambiguity; the move attempts to lay hold of a power of open definition, with consequences in establishing value-laden equivalencies (to be explored in the next section).

Todd Gitlin doesn't fare much better:

> The movement's great majority rightly understand nonviolence not as a negation, the absence of destructiveness, but as a creative endeavor, a repertory for invention, an opening, an identity. Occupy does not take nonviolence for granted. It holds workshops—though perhaps not rigorously enough—to train demonstration monitors as to how to contain provocateurs and control large crowds. MoveOn.org and other supportive groups added their own training on a large scale. When theoreticians crop up to argue for a laissez-faire attitude toward tactics, critics step up to refute the point.[44]

What begins as a "creative endeavor" and "repertory for invention" for Gitlin quickly descends into "refuting" unnamed "theoreticians" and even forcibly "containing" and "controlling" other protesters. The promised creativity, the "repertoire of invention," remain ill-defined promises. The claim of "identity" possesses little content beyond

---

43 Ibid.

44 Todd Gitlin, *Occupy Nation: The Roots, the Spirit, and the Promise of Occupy Wall Street* (New York: It Books, 2012), 127–28.

disavowal of other movement participants—one rather ominously opposed to "a laissez-faire attitude toward tactics."

Among theoreticians of "strategic nonviolence," the difficulties of asserting a positive definition prove no less troublesome. In his foundational list of 198 methods of nonviolent direct action, Sharp includes a great many that might well be understood as violent, like "fear and intimidation," "nonviolent harassment," land seizures, counterfeiting, dumping, and "disclosing identities of secret agents."[45] While Sharp is glad to disagree with followers of what he terms "principled nonviolence," who are more concerned with their own spiritual or ethical state than with effective social change, many of his examples of "strategic nonviolence" not only disagree with "principled" ideas of nonviolence but also with Sharp's own claims to nonviolence as well. The inevitable presence of violence as a consequence and component of many of his methods suggests a critical inconsistency at the heart of his own philosophy. Sharp acknowledges that the historical practitioners of these methods (as for example, general strikes in the labor movement) never claimed them as "nonviolent"; for Sharp, this presents a sort of curious oversight—why didn't they notice they were being nonviolent? Given the ubiquitous presence of some form of violence in the actual application of these methods, however, participants may have had more obvious reasons for not claiming them as nonviolent: they weren't.

Lakey, a contemporary of Sharp, makes a similar claim in his description of the May 1968 events in France: "There was astonishingly little violence by the students and workers, and also less violence by the agents of repression than one might expect in a situation so threatening to the state. Estimations place the number of dead at five to ten, in a month-long struggle by millions! The three weapons most used in the struggle were strike, occupation, and demonstration—all nonviolent methods."[46]

Regrettably, defining strikes, occupations, and demonstrations as nonviolent does not make them so. Lakey quickly contradicts himself in his account of the events in Paris, which began with around a hundred militants clashing with police. As events escalated, the demonstrations remained generally noninjurious (though not

---

45 Gene Sharp, *The Methods of Nonviolent Action: The Politics of Nonviolent Action, Part Two* (Boston: Porter Sargent Publisher, 1973), xv–xvi.

46 Lakey, *Strategy for a Living Revolution*, 36.

without uninjured, including fatalities) but hardly "nonviolent" by any definition:

> *A major impetus to the movement* occurred the night of May 10, when thousands of students returned to the Latin Quarter from a march and *attempted to encircle the police* who were surrounding the Sorbonne. A few of the students began to build barricades. The action spread quickly. Paving stones were torn up, cars were overturned, and any materials lying around were pressed into service in the dozens of barricades erected that night. The students repeated their demand that the police leave the Sorbonne. Instead, the police began to clear the streets, taking barricade after barricade with the help of concussion grenades, heavy use of tear gas, and truncheons. Indignant residents threw flowerpots at the police and gave water for relief from the tear gas to the students.[47]

Lakey's own analysis ("A major impetus to the movement") makes clear that the very violence of the conflict between students and police was instrumental in its massive escalation into a potential revolution. Even if such events are included within Lakey's category of "astonishingly little violence" and remain within certain limited phases of the conflicts, his analysis acknowledges them as integral to the later, less directly violent phases; police violence defined the initial mobilization, while once millions had mobilized in the later phases, there was little that police force could do to restore order. It is undoubtedly preferable if protesters outnumber police to such a degree that violently repressing them is difficult; but can this "nonviolent" phase be isolated from the violent clashes that brought it about? Both Sharp and Lakey frequently select their examples inconsistently—a practice acknowledged only through the telling ubiquity of qualifiers like "less" and "mostly" in their studies. Including a "little violence" within the category of nonviolence reveals that violence is not actually the factor being studied. If a "little violence" is not necessarily detrimental, shouldn't we be using less dichotomous vocabulary in order to decide what determines these limits?

---

47   Ibid, 31.

And wouldn't this also call into question the slippery slope that contemporary nonviolence advocates such as Hedges warn against, even as they cite these studies? What does it mean when even rude language qualifies for placement within an undifferentiated category of "violence," inviting analogies with murder and catastrophic warfare?

Violence is not only present and instrumental in "nonviolence" of the massive revolutionary sort; indeed, few serious political confrontations have occurred without it in some measure. Regarding labor strikes (held up by Sharp as absolutely central in the history of nonviolent struggle, and a vital proof of its inherent efficacy and overall superiority) the turn-of-the-century anarchist theorist Voltairine De Cleyre writes as a first-person witness that

> [n]ow everybody knows that a strike of any size means violence. No matter what any one's ethical preference for peace may be, he knows it will not be peaceful. If it's a telegraph strike, it means cutting wires and poles, and getting fake scabs in to spoil the instruments. If it is a steel rolling mill strike, it means beating up the scabs, breaking the windows, setting the gauges wrong, and ruining the expensive rollers together with tons and tons of material. If it's a miners' strike, it means destroying tracks and bridges, and blowing up mills. If it is a garment workers' strike, it means having an unaccountable fire, getting a volley of stones through an apparently inaccessible window, or possibly a brickbat on the manufacturer's own head. If it's a street-car strike, it means tracks torn up or barricaded with the contents of ash-carts and slop-carts, with overturned wagons or stolen fences, it means smashed or incinerated cars and turned switches. If it is a system federation strike, it means "dead" engines, wild engines, derailed freights, and stalled trains. If it is a building trades strike, it means dynamited structures. And always, everywhere, all the time, fights between strike-breakers and scabs against strikers and strike-sympathizers, between People and Police.[48]

---

48 Voltairine De Cleyre, "Direct Action," quoted in Piven, "Protest Movements and Violence," 20.

Even those demonstrations widely touted as examples of "the power of nonviolence" are perhaps only nominally so. As one participant in the 1999 WTO protests told me, "Everything was advertised as strictly nonviolent, the power of nonviolence, but what were we doing? Here we are, these delegates are trying to get into the convention center, and we're forcibly preventing them from entering, they're trying to push through our line and we're actually pushing them back, hitting them with our crossed arms, to keep them from doing so. I mean, it's fine, but can you really call that *nonviolence*? I'm really not sure."[49]

In one recent work widely acknowledged as *the* reference work in nonviolence scholarship, offering the first serious quantitative empirical study demonstrating the "power of nonviolence" as positive content, Erica Chenoweth and Maria Stephan take a more nuanced stance than their predecessors.[50] The scholars acknowledge the co-presence of violence and nonviolence in social movement phenomena but deny that this implies that they are interdependent elements constituting larger processes. (I will argue later that, by accepting the same dichotomies in the course of reversing them, some advocates of "violence" commit exactly the same error.) Chenoweth and Stephan confidently assert the possibility of a clear distinction between categories, despite their complementary presence in phenomena through nonviolence scholarship:

> [T]he separation of campaigns into violent and nonviolent for analytical purposes is problematic. Few campaigns, historically, have been purely violent or nonviolent, and many resistance movements, particularly protracted ones, have had violent and nonviolent periods. Armed and unarmed elements often operate simultaneously in the same struggle. Still, it is possible to distinguish between different resistance types based on the actors involved (civilians or armed militants) and the methods used (nonviolent or violent). Scholars have identified the unique characteristics of these

---

49 Personal interview (I).

50 Erica Chenoweth and Maria J. Stephan, *Why Civil Resistance Works: The Strategic Logic of Nonviolent Conflict* (New York: Columbia University Press, 2011).

different forms of struggle, and we feel comfortable characterizing some resistance campaigns as primarily violent and others and primarily nonviolent."[51]

What constitutes these "comfortable" scholarly findings, which finally promise to elucidate the boundary between violence and nonviolence, especially when it comes to ambiguous forms of non-injurious violence like riots? In some cases, the authors rely on circular logic, either their own, as in "Campaigns where a significant amount of violence occurred are not considered nonviolent,"[52] or that of previous scholars, ultimately replaying disavowal of an undefined Other: "Sharp defines nonviolent resistance as 'a technique of socio-political action for applying power in a conflict without the use of violence.'"[53] At times, as in the block quote above, the presence of arms ("armed militants" as opposed to "civilians," "armed" versus "unarmed") defines violence, while at other times their definition seems quite a bit more general, as in, "Violent tactics include bombings, shootings, kidnappings, physical sabotage such as the destruction of infrastructure, and other types of physical harm of people *and property*."[54] Why such a grouping of disparate actions might form a coherent category for the basis of a massive research project is never addressed.

Chenoweth and Stephan's quantitative findings arrive at an unambiguous (if hardly an absolute) implication—looking at many thousands of conflicts, nonviolence has proven more than twice as effective as violence. Their methods are "rigorous": "We have established rigorous standards of inclusion for each campaign. The nonviolent campaigns were initially gathered from an extensive review of the literature on nonviolent conflict and social movements. Then these data were corroborated with multiple sources, including encyclopedias, case studies, and the bibliography by Carter, Clark, and Randle (2006)."[55] In case their own approach may have proven incomplete, they consulted experts to check their results: "Finally, we circulated

---

51 Ibid., 16.
52 Ibid., 13.
53 Ibid., 12.
54 Ibid., 13. My emphasis.
55 Ibid., 15.

the data set among experts in nonviolent conflict."[56] A critical reader might ask if these experts might possibly share professional and ideological predispositions to reproduce an ambiguous definition of violence, but the concern is not acknowledged. It is only by looking at the data set forming the basis of their study that an astounding disparity is revealed between their stated definition and the functional definition of violence at work in their study: "Violent campaign data are derived primarily from Kristian Gleditsch's (2004) updates to the Correlates of War (COW) database on intrastate wars, Jason Lyall and Isaiah Wilson's (2009) database of insurgencies, and Kalev Sepp's (2005) list of major counterinsurgency operations. *The COW data set requires all combatant groups to be armed and to have sustained a thousand battle deaths during the course of the conflict, suggesting that the conflict is necessarily violent.*"[57]

In other words, without any explanation or justification, Chenoweth and Stephan conflate interstate or large-scale civil warfare, in which both sides are armed and suffer massive casualties, with their more general "destruction of infrastructure, and other types of physical harm of people and property." This sleight of hand is stunning, particularly given the vast predominance of riots (taking the US as an example)—which would fit their stated definition but certainly not their functional one—over civil wars and armed uprisings. To some extent, the authors understand such reservations: "Our book demonstrates that scholars can take a reasoned look at the relative effectiveness of nonviolent and violent resistance, even if the measures of such terms are imperfect."[58] Still, the disparity between claim and evidence calls into question even the basic categories through which the study argues its premise. Such a "reasoned look" has gone on to inform substantial public conversation despite being applied to actions utterly irrelevant to the actual categories guiding the study.

Ultimately, these shifting definitions of non/violence are more than the result of simple opportunistic manipulations; they may in fact be impossible to overcome within current hegemonic framings. An examination of foundational texts in liberal ideology, as we'll see in the next chapter, reveals that violence functions to guarantee a very

---

56 Ibid.

57 Ibid., 16. My emphasis.

58 Ibid., 17.

capitalist equivalence between commodities and bodies—as forms of "property." Acknowledging this, of course, would be inherently embarrassing for any ideology making humanistic legitimacy claims, so the equivalence must be mystified even as it is employed. The primacy of property can be neither disowned nor avowed. This constitutive contradiction is but another face of Marx's famous claim that the tension between a universal humanism and the very nonuniversal nature of the articulation of property relations is at the heart of bourgeois ideology—and will ultimately summon its demise. As we will also discuss in the next chapter, it is precisely this embarrassment that radical dissidents are trying to bring into public view with their sacrilegious attacks on nonbodily property. For now, let's examine the other ways nonviolent discourse opportunistically imputes a negative evaluation of its shifting Other.

RIOT AS THE MORAL EQUIVALENT OF WAR

One of the things that the people considered to be, quote unquote, the top of society, what they oftentimes do to all of us, is they criminalize us. They say that you guys are just a bunch of criminals, hippies, dirty anarchists, whatever, protesters. But we sometimes do the same thing back. And we demonize those at the top, and we say, you're just a bunch of imperialists, capitalists, pigs, racists. So there's no effort at dialogue, not an effort made at trying to understand the other person's perspective.

—Nonviolence advocate, Oakland.[59]

When Gandhi disavowed any inclination to bring harm upon the British in India, he may have spoken of an egalitarianism of universal humanity, but his actions were in fact tactical moves within a larger rhetorical strategy of reversal. Anyone, whether the war-weary British or the international audience, watching the news clips of British troops beating in the skulls of *satyagrahis* publicly demonstrating their spiritual strength had no ambiguities about who were the truly civilized and who the obviously brutish. Gandhi's great discursive victory was not, then, one of asserting equality where colonial discourse had devalued the captive population as much as it was one of *reversing* it. This was precisely

---

59   Positive Peace Warrior Network, "How Will the Walls Come Tumbling Down?"

the strategy that King took up from Gandhi: his words of universal love for humanity worked all the more powerfully to contrast with the monstrosity of Birmingham dogs and fire hoses; they sought and performed no shared humanity with Bull Connor and his social order, but an undeniable *superiority* before the courts of northern liberal television and newspapers that King knew was his real audience. Indeed, despite his professed faith in converting one's enemy through an assertion of triumphant humanity, King certainly never claimed that Connor himself might be the target of his egalitarian appeals. According to historian Adam Fairclough, King's approach in fact failed in the 1963 Albany, Georgia, campaign, when Chief of Police Laurie Pritchett himself professed a belief in "nonviolence" and instructed his officers to use a "nonviolent approach" by beating demonstrators only after they had been removed to jail and setting high cash bonds for protester arrests to delay their release until after demonstrations.[60] These prescient practices, so akin to today's "strategic incapacitation" policing, defeated King's tactics and left the SCLC on the verge of "imminent collapse."[61] "Albany," according to Fairclough, "disabused the Civil Rights Movement of its more romantic notions about nonviolence."[62] What, then, would be the use of such strategies today, with no distant audience external to the conflicts at hand, no superior executive force that might be called in against the bigoted locals, and no print and broadcast media that would ever deign to carry the message even if such an audience were found?

As we've seen, nonviolence has continually mobilized the ambiguity in the definition of "violence" to constitute and then disavow its Other; this disavowal would carry little effect, however, if it didn't impute its Other with values repulsive to its audience. Such valuation has consistently relied on the rhetorical move of *equivalization*, in which other social movement participants, who could just as well be construed as fellow travelers, are made out to be as loathsome as their shared enemy.

In what may well have been the very first use of "nonresistance" as a secular concept, adapted from Quaker doctrine, abolitionist William

---

60 Adam Fairclough, *Better Day Coming: Blacks and Equality, 1890–2000* (New York: Viking, 2001). On delaying beatings until jail, ibid., 269. On high cash bonds, ibid., 270.

61 Ibid., 271.

62 Ibid., 270.

Lloyd Garrison declared in an early statement his opposition to the violence of state involvement in wars and slavery. He refused any participation in such institutions, other than that obliged by force, which nonresistants could not ethically resist—a position that precluded his wing of the abolitionist movement from entanglement in the political party vulgarities of his day. While detailing his stance of opposition to state practices of violence, Garrison suddenly moves without transition or explanation to distance himself from Jacobinism, in a powerful reference to the "Terror" that accompanied the French Revolution, which, occurring less than half a century before, was still within living memory:

> We advocate no Jacobinical doctrines. The spirit of Jacobinism is the spirit of retaliation, violence, and murder. It neither fears God nor regards man. We would be filled with the spirit of Christ. If we abide by our fundamental principle of not opposing evil by evil we cannot participate in sedition, treason, or violence. We shall submit to every ordinance and every requirement of government, except such as are contrary to the commands of the Gospel, and in no case resist the operation of law, except by meekly submitting to the penalty of disobedience.[63]

However catastrophic The Terror proved to the development of the Revolution, Garrison's equivalence sits oddly. He suddenly equates "sedition," "treason," and "fear[ing] neither God nor man"—all forms of *disobedience* to ruling authority—with *obedience* to those same authorities in the practices of state violence he had just been condemning. With these charges, Garrison was very likely seeking to implicate other militants within the abolitionist movement with whom he had just broken. His charge that his former allies' behavior was somehow analogous to the catastrophes of interstate warfare were odd enough for their time; that this move has remained so flexible and robust over time is even more puzzling. At the end of the nineteenth century, Tolstoy, a major figure in the discourse of nonviolence whom Gandhi

---

63 Quoted in Leo Tolstoy, *The Kingdom of God Is Within You* (New York: Dover Publications, 2006), 5.

named as his greatest influence, and who himself cited Garrison as a central influence on his thought, asserted in *The Kingdom of God is Within You* that

> the principle of non-resistance to evil by force has been attacked by two opposing camps: the conservatives, because this principle would hinder their activity in resistance to evil as applied to the revolutionists, in persecution and punishment of them; the revolutionists, too, because this principle would hinder their resistance to evil as applied to the conservatives and the overthrowing of them. The conservatives were indignant at the doctrine of non-resistance to evil by force hindering the energetic destruction of the revolutionary elements, which may ruin the national prosperity; the revolutionists were indignant at the doctrine of non-resistance to evil by force hindering the overthrow of the conservatives, who are ruining the national prosperity.[64]

Given Tolstoy's central thesis in the book, that "government is violence" and thus that the Gospels demand a stateless society, this statement comes as a surprise. Tolstoy has just been arguing for many pages, completely agreeing with the revolutionists, that the conservatives *really are* "ruining the national prosperity" and that the conservative claims he cites were *dishonest*; but suddenly, the revolutionaries have gained analogical equivalence to the very systematized violence which they, together with Tolstoy, oppose. Tolstoy, who, given his egalitarian vision of the future, might have been seen as a dangerous brother of the revolutionaries and "their resistance to evil as applied to the conservatives and the overthrowing of them," has suddenly and effectively distanced himself from such suspicion. By distinguishing his own spiritual stance from the material action of the revolutionaries, Tolstoy asserts a foundational disavowal. In clarifying that, whatever his vision, only spiritual means of transformation are permissible, he defines "non-resistance" precisely as never meaning any material action, only a spiritual one. By classing *any* material process that might bring about

---

64 Tolstoy, *Kingdom of God*, 39.

social transformation as "violent" and explicitly defining this as morally equivalent to the czar's police, Tolstoy perfects a foreclosure of his own vision, safely containing it as an edifying dream that works to enhance one's reputation as a (very literal) idealist, with the reassuring guarantee that, by definition, such dreams are constituted precisely out of the impossibility of their material realization.

The consistent disavowal of rioting by generations of nonviolence proponents, particularly when they compare it to warfare, belies the long-standing recognition of the stark differences in origin of the phenomena. "War," as General Smedley D. Butler famously wrote, "is a racket," organized at the behest of elites, whether in its inter- or intrastate forms.[65] Riot, in turn, has always been unambiguously a means of claims-making associated with the otherwise poor and powerless. In Piven's pithy axiom, "the long history of protest movements is in fact mainly the history of mobs and riots."[66] In analyzing more than four thousand riots in American history, Gilje documents events that time and again demonstrate that aggrieved parties with little access to other means of claims-making resort to riot as their means of articulation, not the least in the formative years of the labor movement:

> Even in the opening years of the nineteenth century, just as workers refined their strike tactics, coercion was needed to enforce unity and to persuade owners of the legitimacy of the laborers' demands. That coercion frequently took the form of rioting—whether it was tarring and feathering a recalcitrant shoemaker in Baltimore, or brawling with strikebreakers on New York docks. Force was often garnered to meet force, and riots and violence represent the signposts of American labor history from the 1830s to the twentieth century…much of the history of American labor is written in blood as riots.[67]

---

65 Smedley D. Butler, *War Is a Racket: The Antiwar Classic by America's Most Decorated General, Two Other Anti-interventionist Tracts, and Photographs from the Horror of It* (Los Angeles: Feral House, 2003).

66 Piven, "Protest Movements and Violence," 20.

67 Gilje, *Rioting in America*, 3.

Current memories of rioting are tied up with the urban riots of the 1960s and 1970s, which were of a massive enough scale to destabilize the ruling order with their intensity and reach, as examined in the congressional Kerner Commission Report.[68] Later, after Black communities had silently suffered a decade of the War on Drugs, the 1992 Rodney King riots far surpassed in every measure—as I noted earlier, economic damage, arrests, injuries, and deaths—*any* riot in the history of the country.[69] By contrast, rioting for the majority of US history has been so commonplace as to be rather banal. Gilje writes:

> Rioting never became legitimate...all moments of popular disorder were viewed as potentially dangerous.... Yet having made this qualification, what stands out in examining eighteenth-century popular disorder is not the doubts and threats it posed; instead, it is the general acceptance of the mob as a quasi-legitimate part of the standing social and political order....
>
> Anglo-Americans never forgot the upheaval of the mid seventeenth century. The main ideological legacy of that political disruption was a belief in the need to limit the power of government.... To protect liberty it was necessary to limit the power of government. One means of doing so was through the people in the street. Commonwealth writers recognized that mobs could create problems since "one may at any Time gain an interest in a Mob with a Barrel of Beer" or "by Means of a few odd Sounds, that mean nothing, or something very wicked." But some popular disorder was preferable to granting the monarch too much power, since "all tumults are in their nature, and must be, short in duration" and "must soon subside, or settle into some order," while "Tyranny may last for ages, and go on destroying till at last it has nothing left to destroy." In other words, rioting could be tolerated because it offered an important check on the power of government.[70]

---

68   National Advisory Commission on Civil Disorders, *Report*.

69   Gooding-Williams, *Reading Rodney King*.

70   Gilje, *Rioting in America*, 20–21.

Even in their most powerful manifestations, riots were unambiguously interpreted as public expressions of grievance by the disprivileged.[71] In the hugely violent 1849 Astor Place riot, whose immediate cause, oddly, was an interaction of two actors on stage, one commentator interpreted the events as evidence that "hatred of wealth and privilege is increasing over the world and ready to burst out whenever there is the slightest occasion."[72] It was, as Gilje explains, only by gradually enfranchising sectors of the population that such claims-making became mediated through institutions:

---

71 Clearly, this claim could merit an extended study of its own. Gruesome apparent counterexamples such as the persistent race riots in South Asia, mob violence of whites over people of color in the US (articulated, at times, within labor or antiwar claims), and Kristallnacht all rush to mind. Without here fully analyzing the idiosyncratic nature of hegemonic and non-counterhegemonic riots, two things are to be noted: 1) Paramilitary violence, such as that of the Brownshirts on Kristallnacht or Ku Klux Klan-led attacks and lynchings in which local or regional elites and state actors play a key role, can be analytically distinguished from riots by their involvement with elite command structures. Such actions are better considered crypto-state violence rather than the nonstate violence of riots. 2) Quite clearly, actors may be disprivileged relative to elites by certain measures, yet possess social privileges over other demographics in society, who indeed may form the target of their violence. The above formulation certainly does not claim that the distance from channels of decision-making which drives certain demographics to express their political grievances through riot somehow dictates the targets of their violence or makes this violence immune to manipulation by elites. The history of race in America, particularly in the period between Reconstruction and the civil rights movement, provides an incontrovertible illustration of both potentials. However horrific these examples, the literature reveals them as relatively exceptional. For an analysis claiming sports violence as an example of riot by actors in no sense disprivileged, see Bill Buford, *Among the Thugs* (New York: Vintage, 1993). Without asserting any inherent characteristic of riots other than that they are generally enacted by people without access to less risky means of influence, we should note that, as with any other rhetorical phenomena, the meaning of riots can only be interpreted in dynamic interaction with their context.

72 Gilje, *Rioting in America*, 74–75.

Persistent disorder strengthened popular faith in mobs. Rioting had proven itself a useful tool of resistance against a government that seemed distant, alien, and intent on usurping the liberty of the people. Moreover, the experience with crowds during the 1760s and 1770s had helped to translate long-standing plebeian notions of antiauthoritarianism into an egalitarianism that gave the people preeminence in society and government. Although whig [sic] leaders often had opposed excessive rioting, and the people out of doors were defeated in incidents like those at Fort Wilson, many common folk continued to believe that the tumultuous crowd held a special place as an expression of the people's immediate will. Whig leaders accepted the centrality of the "people" in the novel world order of the 1780s and 1790s. They argued, however, that the new republican forms of government now made politics out of doors unnecessary. With the government theoretically in the hands of the people, the people no longer needed to riot.[73]

In addition to the Jacobin=*ancient regime*, state=challenger, and riot=war equivalences, the personal=institutional equivalence appears persistently throughout the history of nonviolence, particularly in its "principled nonviolence" variant, which seeks to equate conduct at the personal scale with institutional action. In their purest form, personal-ethical standards of conduct do not even claim to influence institutions but simply act out of faith for lack of alternatives. In Tolstoy's classic statement of this position, "'*Fais ce que dois, advienne que pourra*'—'Do what's right, come what may'—is an expression of profound wisdom. We each can know indubitably what we ought to do, but what results will follow from our actions none of us either do or can know. Therefore, besides feeling the call of duty, we are further driven to act as duty bids us by the consideration that we have no other guidance, but are totally ignorant of what will result from our action."[74]

---

73 Ibid., 51.

74 Tolstoy, *Kingdom of God*, 74.

For Tolstoy, self-aware action is dependent solely upon perceived "call of duty" (which, apparently, is exempt from any potential misinterpretation, since "we can know indubitably" its message) and is independent from consequence. This is the basic meaning of what has been termed "principled nonviolence." Total ignorance of consequences forms a sort of subject-that-can-never-know, an individual with only ethical, but not political, agency. Wendy Brown classifies such political resignation in place of public engagement as depoliticizing *personalization* that removes matters properly political from shared deliberation, making them a matter of one's psychological constitution or preference.[75] That personalistic discourses, reframing the political as matters of as psychological health and "well-being," should prove loudest under neoliberal conditions was already predicted in 1973 by Lakey, whose criticism of principled nonviolence relies on the prophetic diagnosis of this particular anomie:

> Many Americans, especially in the middle class and in the counter-culture, are like psychic hypochondriacs: they constantly have an inner ear cocked to their emotional condition, testing to see where the aches and pains are today. In the name of liberation (from "neurosis" or from "the straight world"), they seem anxiously driven on their search for a continued sense of wellbeing. Although this "hypochondria" results basically from the dissolution of Western culture, it is intensified by mobility and individualism, both of which drive the person even more back upon him- or herself.[76]

As contemporary poet and critic Wayne Koestenbaum suggests, considering the renunciation of political agency as a form of *humiliation* clarifies how it might benefit those embarrassed by their own social position:

> Humiliation is bliss if the experience of largeness or magnitude has become overwhelming or unpleasant

---

75 Wendy Brown, *Regulating Aversion: Tolerance in the Age of Identity and Empire* (Princeton: Princeton University Press, 2006).

76 Lakey, *Strategy for a Living Revolution*, 81.

and you need relief. When magnitude hurts, humiliation (or demotion) qualifies as remedy. For Shakespeare's querulous King Lear, humiliation provides the bonus pleasure of being exiled on the heath, after his venomous daughters kick him out of their castles; at last, after kingship's ordeal, he can enjoy the aftermath balm of wandering with fellow madmen in the storm. Bliss, to be disqualified from power! (Bliss, perhaps not. But at least Lear relaxes, and rediscovers language, and redefines the meaning of internal sovereignty).[77]

It is not surprising that such personalistic approaches might prove inappropriate to contemporary social movements, whose primary purpose is to assert the possibility of agency against an ideological regime that works by administering away any sense of alternatives. The bliss of renouncing agency holds considerably less charm for those whose concerns stem more from *lack* of power than for those overwhelmed by their excess of it. For an audience suffering from powerlessness, distancing themselves from agency aggravates, rather than ameliorates, their suffering. (The appeal for so-called white allies of the idea that "it's not my place to fight," as opposed to the obligation to become "accomplices" who take risks and take sides, might be understood in this light as well.)[78]

When "principled nonviolence" does claim to influence institutions, it often does so through the thought of modeling ideal ethical behavior, as if institutions functioned like individuals and were somehow capable of being impressed by and wanting to imitate them. The argument goes that, if we model peaceful behavior on a personal level, social structures and institutions such as the state, capitalism, patriarchy, the Red Army, etc. might be compelled to mimic our morally admirable model. Unfortunately, such formations lack both any site of agency to mimic admirable personal behavior, should they even

---

77 Wayne Koestenbaum, *Humiliation* (New York: Picador, 2011), 14.

78 See Indigenous Action, *Accomplices Not Allies: Abolishing the Ally Industrial Complex* (Indigenous Action Media, 2014) and Cindy Milstein, ed., *Taking Sides: Revolutionary Solidarity and the Poverty of Liberalism* (Oakland: AK Press, 2015).

somehow want to. Even public enactments of such "modeling" behavior have little purchase; they are easily recuperated, so long as they are not disruptive enough to prove *intolerable*, and as Schock pointed out in the previous section, representative democracies often enact strategies specifically designed to neutralize them. In Lakey's words, "Unfortunately, the strategy of change by example has most of its power muted by tolerance. When governments learn to tolerate peculiar sects a kind of accommodation takes place: the government stops interfering in the business of the sect, and vice versa…. The growth of the new way declines because the example is taken for granted."[79]

Marcuse famously termed just this strategy "repressive tolerance." In short, in a sort of "declining rate of profit" law of social movements, recuperation through repressive tolerance makes innovative disruption very difficult, a notion to which we will return. For now, let's finally address the "magic" that traditional nonviolence wielded so efficaciously and that seems to evade the grasp of contemporary nonviolence practices.

NONVIOLENCE AS A STRATEGY OF CONDESCENSION

[I]n November, the day after Lieutenant John Pike of the University of California, Davis, put a name and a face on police barbarity with the pepper-spraying seen around the world, when Chancellor Linda Katehi left a public meeting where she refused to resign and walked to her car, thousands of students sat on the ground lining her route in utter silence—*unthreatening*, judgmental, bearing witness.

—Todd Gitlin, *Occupy Nation*[80]

In holding up the silent protest at UC Davis as the epitome of nonviolent protest, Gitlin makes an odd assumption: how is the presence of thousands of protesters, their glares just visible in the dark, with the trauma and rage of the previous day's police attack still thick in the air, to be read as *nonthreatening*? Indeed, Katehi's face in the video visibly trembles with the effort to maintain composure under the nearly unbearable encompassing gaze of silent rage. Is it not precisely

79   Lakey, *Strategy for a Living Revolution*, 82.
80   Gitlin, *Occupy Nation*, 155. My emphasis.

the imminent potential for overwhelming force against Katehi that makes the gathered crowd's refusal to carry it out so powerful? Would the statement have had anything like the same power if the number of students had been small enough to be demonstrably unable to inflict harm, or if, for example, they had all been safely isolated behind a fence? Contrary to Gitlin's reading, it is the contingency of the protesters' decision, the material performance of a refrained agency based on their *capability to be other than nonviolent*, that imbues the action with meaning and power. Gitlin's misreading is symptomatic of the discursive slippage of nonviolence, typical in contemporary discourse—both by its advocates and its critics.

The strangely magical eloquence of nonviolence works precisely through highlighting the presence of violence while pretending to speak of its absence; by being dramatically disavowed, violence is simultaneously foregrounded; it becomes present through denial. Gandhi acknowledged this dependency in axioms like "nonviolence is a weapon of the strong" and "the weak can never forgive, forgiveness is the attribute of the strong." It is not that nonviolence magically summons a strong subject; rather, a subject must be "strong" in the first place—that is, capable of *choosing* nonviolence among other options—before nonviolence is even an option. Martin Luther King Jr., in his early "Pilgrimage to Nonviolence," explains this quite explicitly: "First, it must be emphasized that nonviolent resistance is not a method for cowards; it does resist. If one uses this method because he is afraid or *merely because he lacks the instruments of violence*, he is not truly nonviolent. This is why Gandhi often said that if cowardice is the only alternative to violence, it is better to fight."[81]

King's admission that one must possess the instruments of violence to practice nonviolence should not be read figuratively as a simple restatement of not having a cowardly character. King's choice of "or" to set apart the conditions of nonviolence from the courageous character of its practitioners belies this reading, for the "instruments" are a thing apart from fearlessness; the lack of development of the "instruments of violence" phrase does not suggest any figurative interpretation, but only a quite literal one. As in his friendships and collaboration with Robert Williams and the Deacons for Defense, each of whom

---

81   Martin Luther King Jr., *Stride toward Freedom: The Montgomery Story* (New York: Beacon Press, 2010), 90.

espoused an armed approach to civil rights, King acknowledges the nondichotomous nature of non/violence just in the moments when he performs disavowal.[82] That King understood the immediate threat of violence as a necessary condition of effective nonviolence can be seen in his frequent pairings of disavowal-lamentation and presencing-warning, as for example in his telegram to President Kennedy in 1962: "I will continue to urge my people to be nonviolent in the face of bitterest opposition, but I fear that my counsel will fall on deaf ears if the federal government does not take decisive action. If Negroes are tempted to turn to retaliatory violence, we shall see a dark night of rioting all over the South."[83]

In "Letter from Birmingham Jail," King legitimizes his own campaign to his critics through the same, if retrospective, disavowal/presencing, invoking the "nightmare" of universal race war to demonstrate the power of his own approach:

> If this [nonviolence] philosophy had not emerged, by now many streets of the South would, I am convinced, be flowing with blood. And I am further convinced that if our white brothers dismiss as "rabble-rousers" and "outside agitators" those of us who employ nonviolent direct action, and if they refuse to support our nonviolent efforts, millions of Negroes will, out of frustration and despair, seek solace and security in black nationalist ideologies—a development that would inevitably lead to a frightening racial nightmare.[84]

The letter goes so far as to frame the violent power undergirding his own nonviolent persuasion as a threat that is foregrounded as it is denied: "If his repressed emotions are not released in nonviolent ways, they will seek expression through violence; this is not a threat but a fact of history."[85]

---

82 For King's friendship with Robert Williams, see Clayborne Carson, ed. *Autobiography of Martin Luther King, Jr.*, 317. For his relationship with the Deacons for Defense, ibid., 73.

83 Ibid., 166.

84 Ibid., 197.

85 Ibid., 198.

Even King's famous March on Washington speech contained a phrase quite close to a direct threat. King speaks with surprising aggressiveness, extolling "the marvelous new militancy which has engulfed the Negro community" and advising that "[t]hose who hope that the Negro needed to blow off steam and will now be content will have a rude awakening if the nation returns to business as usual."[86] Along with the speech's multiple direct indictments of institutional racism and police brutality, these words have been completely erased from public memory, perhaps because their relevance has not abated over time.

As political scientist and presidential advisor Harold Nieburg observed in 1969, the increase in rioting worked to bring King from a place at the margins to a place of central influence. "All of those many institutional leaders who refused to bargain with Martin Luther King Jr in the 1950s needed him desperately in their attempts to contain the eruptions of black militancy in the 1960s, and they had to meet many of his terms."[87] Nieburg also analyzes the logic of disavowal/ presencing in a passage worth quoting at length:

> The moderate leader is placed in a position of minimum risk and maximum effectiveness, that of playing the role of "responsible leader." He can bargain with formal authorities and with other groups of the society in this way: "You must accept our just complaints and you must deal with us; otherwise, we will not be able to control our people." While playing this role, the reformist leader may not be unhappy to have his prophecies fulfilled by a few psychotic teen-agers. Events which demonstrate violence, and thus induce other elites to make concessions, do not have to be planned. Once the emotions of a real social movement are churned up, the problem is to keep them from happening.
>
> The irresponsible elements are, of course, disowned, but the bargaining power of the responsible leaders is

---

86 Ibid, 225.

87 Harold L. Nieburg, *Political Violence: The Behavioral Process* (New York: St. Martin's Press, 1969), 58.

enhanced.... This is a healthy mode of exploiting the demonstration of violence without condoning it.... Most followers in social movements will follow responsible leadership through the give-and-take of compromise because they share the general fear of unlimited violence and counterviolence, which can bring unpredictable results and defeat all rational goals.[88]

Should we understand this disavowing-while-calling-to-mind of violence as simply hypocritical? The observation of the dependency of nonviolence on its purported opposite implies far more than mere "gotcha" demystification; indeed, just as violence threatens to "bring unpredictable results and defeat all rational goals," nonviolence, under the necessary conditions, is capable of enacting an unparalleled eloquence and power. Given certain conditions, Gandhi and King's performances of this disavowal/presencing multiplied the power of their organizing precisely by gathering and demonstrating a great deal of material rage and by going further to perform a very visible agency in *not* activating this rage—a potentiality eventually activated in the massive riots that resulted both when Gandhi and King were assassinated.

In Birmingham, King additionally acknowledged that riots worked very effectively to highlight the crisis of systemic violence, bringing about productive interventions. "Terrified by the very destructiveness brought on by their own acts, the city police appealed for state troopers to be brought into the area. Many of the white leaders now realized that something had to be done."[89] During the Birmingham campaign, when both King's hotel room and his brother A. D. King's home were bombed in the same night in an apparent attempt to disrupt the integration pact with local business leaders their negotiations had just brought about, King observed that

> [f]ighting began. Stones were hurled at the police. Cars were wrecked and fires started.... I listened as [A. D.] described the erupting tumult and catastrophe in the streets of the city. Then, in the background as he

88   Ibid., 128.
89   Clayborne Carson, ed. *Autobiography of Martin Luther King, Jr.*, 212.

talked, I heard a swelling burst of beautiful song. Feet planted in the rubble of debris, threatened by criminal violence and hatred, followers of the movement were singing "We Shall Overcome." I marveled that in a moment of such tragedy the Negro could still express himself with hope and with faith.

The following evening, a thoroughly aroused President told the nation that the Federal government would not allow extremists to sabotage a fair and just pact. He ordered three thousand federal troops into position near Birmingham and made preparations to federalize the Alabama National Guard. This firm action stopped the troublemakers in their tracks.[90]

The passage is complex.[91] Though vehemently distancing himself from the rioters by equating them with the bombers through the ambiguity of phrases like "criminal violence and hatred," "such extremists," and "the troublemakers," King also acknowledges through the narrative that federal military intervention—always one of his explicit goals—came about as a direct result of the rioting, and not only because of the pact. In order for the violence to be overcome and superseded in the indisputably powerful transformation heard over his brother's telephone, the violence had to have been performed in the first place.

In King's later years, his response to riots and other sorts of political violence deepened in complexity. In speaking of youth on the streets who had just rioted, King, while maintaining his disagreement with their acts, expressed a reluctance to condemn them: "Their questions hit home, and I knew that I could never again raise my voice against the violence of the oppressed in the ghettos without having first spoken clearly to the greatest purveyor of violence in the world today: my own government."[92] King expressed respect and even a bold

---

90   Ibid., 215.

91   As King's autobiography was compiled, and in many sections composed by Clayborne Carson, who was trusted with exclusive access to King's personal documents, the word choice in this passage may be more Carson's than King's. Unless otherwise noted, all other passages are direct quotations from King.

92   Clayborne Carson, ed. *Autobiography of Martin Luther King, Jr.*, 338.

sympathy with the rioters of Watts—if not actually commending the riots themselves, at least recognizing in them some of the same rhetorical mechanisms we will explore in future chapters:

> The looting in Watts was a form of social protest very common through the ages as a dramatic and destructive gesture of the poor toward symbols of their needs.... There was joy among the rioters of Watts, not shame.... They were destroying a physical and emotional jail; they had asserted themselves against a system which was quietly crushing them into oblivion and now they were "somebody." As one young man put it, "We know that a riot is not the answer, but we've been down here suffering for a long time and nobody cared. Now at least they know we're here. A riot may not be *the* way, but it is *a* way."[93]

That final line, in a voice simultaneously King's and not King's, acknowledges that riot plays a serious role in bringing about social change. King was still far from recognizing this role as necessary or preferred, but his criticism was clearly far more muted than most of those who now claim his legacy.

King was one of the first major public figures to express passionate opposition to the Vietnam War, even going so far as to express open support for political recognition of the Vietcong's cause.[94] In reference to the global wave of anti-imperialist revolutions, King avowed unabashedly, "[t]he shirtless and barefoot people of the land are rising up as never before.... We in the West must support these revolutions."[95] At the same time, King began to frequently speak of racism and the material conditions of Black communities as internal colonialism: "The Northern ghetto had become a type of colonial area. The colony was powerless because all important decisions affecting the community were made from the outside. Many of its inhabitants had their daily lives dominated by the welfare worker and the policeman."[96]

---

93   Ibid., 293.
94   Ibid., 111. "Beyond Vietnam" speech.
95   Ibid., 341. See also ibid, 111.
96   Ibid., 301.

King, losing popularity to the growing Black Power movement, continued to be critical of its approach at the same time that his language grew surprisingly similar to it: if armed struggles against colonialism abroad were justified and commendable, and the domestic situation was best described as internal colonialism, might King have been suggesting an eventual break with nonviolence under these new conditions? Near the end of King's life, he began to discuss "[n]ew tactics which do not count on government goodwill."[97] There is a frustration in his tone that simultaneously acknowledges that the tactics of the southern campaigns had stalled in the face of issues of northern poverty and foreign policy, and, astoundingly, that he had had previously depended too much on "government goodwill," clearly indicating an immanent break in some form with his previous approach. In any case, by the time he was murdered, King had certainly acknowledged that the form of nonviolence with which he was synonymous was in fundamental ways dependent upon conditions that did not transfer into his latest campaigns.

Leaving aside speculations concerning the political metamorphosis cut short by his assassination, I will now return to an analysis of nonviolence under those conditions in which it has undoubtedly proven effective. How might this pairing of disavowal/presencing, this strange magic that disowns at the same time it highlights its own context, bring about such powerful effects? If not mere hypocrisy, how does this rhetorical strategy work? To appreciate the specific efficacy of nonviolence, we should consider what Pierre Bourdieu calls "strategies of condescension,"[98] which he defines as "those symbolic transgressions of limits which provide, at one and the same time, the benefits that result from conformity to a social definition and the benefits that result from transgression."[99] Bourdieu came upon the concept in seeking to explain an odd occurrence in his home region in France. On the occasion of a public commemoration of the provincial region's most renowned poet, the mayor of the town delivered a speech to the crowd in the local dialect, Béarnese, an event widely remarked on with admiration in the national press. Why, Bourdieu asks, would a mayor (evidently a native speaker

---

97   Ibid., 348.

98   Pierre Bourdieu, *Language and Symbolic Power* (Cambridge: Harvard University Press, 1991), 68.

99   Ibid., 124.

of Béarnese) addressing a Béarnese-speaking audience about a Béarnese-speaking poet be so worthy of remark by Parisian journalists?

The answer, Bourdieu asserts, lies precisely in the disprivileged status of Béarnese, known to any member of the audience or reader of the article. Since a speaker *only* of the dialect could never hope to accumulate the social capital necessary to become an elected official, the mayor's use of Béarnese was performed before his audience as a situated *choice* over the normal use of standard (Parisian) dialect in which all official affairs were conducted. Such strategies, says Bourdieu, are "reserved for those who are sufficiently confident of their position in the objective hierarchies to be able to deny them without appearing to be ignorant or incapable of satisfying their demands," which echoes those "weapons of the strong" that King noted were not for those who "merely lack the instruments" of power.[100] Moreover, since the audience could figure out that the mayor was still able to speak fluent Parisian even when they only heard him speak Béarnese, his status as a speaker of the privileged Parisian dialect was actually enhanced by *not* speaking it. Were the mayor to be "suspected of resorting to the stigmatized language *faute de mieux*," that is, because he only knew how to speak Béarnese, he would have swiftly lost his job.[101] Rather, because the audience could be relied on to recognize his linguistic privilege in the very absence of its performance, the mayor's power was reinforced through the act of interpretation itself.

However much Gandhi spoke of the self-subsistent power of *satyagraha*, he could rest assured that his Indian, British, and global audiences would imagine the unspoken contextual power of Axis armies and V2 rockets raining down on London—as well as the closer-to-home growing popularity of emphatically violent nationalists like Bhagat Singh and Chandrasekhar Azad and the widespread anticolonial insurrectionary activity escalating across India. However much King insisted on the potency of his campaigns' own local performances of peaceful petition—even to the point of passively meeting the violence of batons, firehoses, and dogs with gestures of love—the audience can be guaranteed to ascribe a power of enraged violence to (in King's words) "the square blocks

---

100 Ibid., 69.
101 Ibid.

of Negroes, a veritable sea of black faces."[102] The rage and, not infrequently, the riots of ghettos across the country were always standing just behind King, and he was never slow to remind his audiences of this constant presence. The peaceable acquiescence to British police truncheons or Bull Connor's dogs only implied more and more clearly that such superhuman forbearance could not be expected to last long.

This pattern of ascription—a "strategy of condescension"—is precisely what is misrecognized as "strange magic" by many contemporary nonviolence advocates. They conveniently forget, when it comes to both Gandhi and King, to read the texts within their context of riots and murder, the centuries of insurrectionary violence and rage surrounding nonviolence's narrative like an overwrought baroque frame. When nonviolence lapses into mere avoidance of conflict and risk; when, contrary to Gandhi and King, it hopes to achieve its goals not as a *substitute* for imminent potentialities of violence but in the *absence* of such potentialities, it lacks any efficacious mechanism with which to make its appeal. Kenneth Burke accurately describes this sort of thinking as "magic, in the discredited sense of that term," which in his account involves the misapplication of symbolic resources outside of their appropriate conditions.[103] "The realistic use of addressed language to *induce action in people* became the magical use of addressed language to *induce motion in things* (things by nature alien to purely linguistic orders of motivation)."[104] Similarly, the strange magic of nonviolence outside of its felicitous conditions ritually mimics the effective performances of the past without the context of power—of potential violence—that imbued these performances with their meaning.

NONVIOLENCE AS CONFLICT AVERSION

Pacifism is hugely influenced by *conflict aversion*. It really shows its middle-classness in that way. There is a tremendous level of yearning for harmony because *many pacifists see conflict itself as the problem*. On the other hand, nonviolent revolutionaries welcome

---

102 Clayborne Carson, ed. *Autobiography of Martin Luther King, Jr.*, 213.

103 Kenneth Burke, *A Rhetoric of Motives* (New York: Prentice-Hall, 1950), 42.

104 Ibid.

conflict, depend on it, and see polarization as absolutely essential. Whereas most pacifists hate polarization, we welcome it as long as polarization happens in such a way that we're on the winning side! And then, of course, lots of pacifists are OK with capitalism, and nonviolent revolutionaries are not. They are strongly anticapitalist, and often antistate.

—George Lakey[105]

In November 2014, when a grand jury decided to not put white Officer Darren Wilson on trial for shooting down unarmed eighteen-year-old Black youth Michael Brown, and protests and riots in Ferguson quickly spread across the country and began to be called the Black Lives Matter movement, *Time* magazine ran a surprising article by columnist Darlena Cunha. Its title was "Ferguson: In Defense of Rioting." Among other insightful points, Cunha stated that

> [w]hen a police officer shoots a young, unarmed black man in the streets, then does not face indictment, anger in the community is inevitable. It's what we do with that anger that counts. In such a case, is rioting so wrong?
>
> Riots are a necessary part of the evolution of society. Unfortunately, we do not live in a universal utopia where people have the basic human rights they deserve simply for existing, and until we get there, the legitimate frustration, sorrow and pain of the marginalized voices will boil over, spilling out into our streets.... I would put forth that peaceful protesting is a luxury of those already in mainstream culture, those who can be assured their voices will be heard without violence, those who can afford to wait for the change they want.[106]

For those active with social movements before and leading up to the Ferguson and Black Lives Matter movements, such talk marked a stark break with previously acceptable ways of discussing protest

---

105 George Lakey, quoted in Andrew Cornell, *Oppose and Propose!*, 64.
106 Darlena Cunha, "Ferguson: In Defense of Rioting," *Time*, November 25, 2014.

repertoires. Here, in the pages of the magazine with the world's largest weekly circulation, recognized for nearly a century as perhaps the quintessential publication of "mainstream America," were words that flew in the face of what had been the unquestioned common sense around protest movements for at least forty years; perhaps the 1967 Kerner Commission Report was the last time a similar position had been voiced from the American center. Certainly, the 1992 Rodney King riots had never been defended in a similar fashion in any but marginal outlets, nor had the 2001 Cincinnati riots, nor any of the property destruction or clashes with police that had accompanied alter-globalization and antiwar protests in the US or around the world. This shift was particularly stunning when compared to discussions of tactics in the recent Occupy movement, when voices from the Progressive Left did not hesitate to label proponents of riot as "the Cancer in Occupy." As Chris Hedges, Rebecca Solnit, Todd Gitlin, and other well-known figures published such commentaries, local Occupy participants were quick to label any number of other protesters as "violent," often collaborating with media outlets, politicians, and police seeking to foster divisions within the movement. Without exception, these dismissals always went under the noble name of "nonviolence." Where had these voices come from in the first place, and how had they become so different from nonviolence proponents of the past?

In what Sharp refers to as "political jiu-jitsu," traditional approaches to nonviolence succeeded, in their day, by claiming the "moral high ground," evoking conflict, asserting "violence" as a central moral axis, and then positing themselves as the antithesis of the state powers that exercised violence against them. Gandhi arguably enacted the term's most significant discursive victory, when he reversed colonization's dichotomy of "civilized" and "savage" through globally distributed newsreels of British iron truncheons crushing the stoically ascetic skulls of *satyagrahis*. As noted in Chapter 1, however, the success of this performance depends on certain concrete social conditions, such as the presence of cameras willing to convey the images of sacrifice to a mass audience; this is what has been lacking in the plateau and denouement of recent movements. Consequently, without access to the set of resources that gave traditional nonviolence its power, but continuing to enact routines similar to those of their heroes of the past, activists who continue to define their approaches as nonviolent fall back on the only thing that remains: performances of disavowal. By the time of the Occupy movement, so little remained of nonviolence's traditional repertoires of power that it was reduced to meaning little other than "not those bad violent people," even when such violent people didn't exist. And even when no property destruction or notable conflict with police had occurred, many of those who identified as nonviolent resorted to enacting their difference from fellow Occupiers by conjuring a phantasmal violent Other.

In one example, the leader of the popular Occupy group "Occupy Seattle Nonviolence Working Group" explained his thoughts about the movement during a Seattle radio station interview.[107] Rather than focusing on the injustices that had brought tens of thousands out in the city or voicing criticisms to any of the numerous institutions targeted by Occupy in its local, national, or global manifestations, he focused on how the movement had been "obviously taken over by the violent pro-violence anarchy people and others who are sympathetic," and quite explicitly advocated a split—under his guidance.[108] At the time, no property destruction or particularly dramatic confrontations with police had occurred; thus, Anderson is forced to distance himself from the "violence" of what these spectral Others "say and think":

> **TIM:** Where I think we are going is a division of the movement between those who are open to being violent and those who are not.... [W]e're going to have to start a different Occupy, so we're going to have a choice, if you want to be with the [pause] violent people, that's great, and if you think that's the way to go, go there. And then we're going to have one that's going to get really big, because we're going to break free of the violence, and we're going to have hundreds of thousands of people.
>
> **INTERVIEWER:** *So what is that going to look like?*
>
> **TIM:** It's going to look like a picnic. It's going to look like a church service. It's going to look like a dance....

---

107 Tim Anderson, interview on KKNW, Seattle, November 16, 2011.
108 Ibid.

I mean I can't predict the future, but this is what, yeah, that's what we're looking for, like a giant movement, where everybody can come and be welcome, unless you're violent, and you wanna control things and dominate from the dominator culture—because whatever, you're hurt, because you don't remember that your dad molested you and so you're taking out that kind of anger. Or you may legitimately believe that that's the way to go, subvert us retarded, middle-class, bourgeois people who don't know that if we don't throw rocks we won't win. That's what they say and what they think.[109]

In the absence of immediate differences of approach, Anderson was not alone among proponents of nonviolence in resorting to condemnation on sheer hypothetical grounds. Another proponent asked those not willing to sign onto a nonviolence proposal to still join in the gesture of disavowal (and imputation) of absurd crimes, or risk being accused of them themselves. "I have not seen a list of tactics which are included in what people call a diversity of tactics, as I have requested. Let me list some possibilities: 1) Murdering an opponent, 2) Assaulting a police officer, 3) Throwing a brick through a window and running away from a crowd of protesters, 4) Spitting at a police officer, 5) Killing a police horse."[110] Another public figure made similar condemnatory demands: "For me, individually, *given what I believe is actually being planned by some people associated with* [Occupy Seattle], I would need OS to expressly disavow the use of violence against people or property, to be able to continue to work with and assist the movement/organization."[111] In the December 15 Oakland debate, one proponent voiced his concerns about the lack of "some principles to ground us," pointing out that "someone at the general assembly one night said, 'Does that mean we would endorse someone kidnapping, torturing, and murdering the children of corporate executives?' None of us, none of us at this table I'm sure, would advocate for that. But without some common understandings, we don't know how far we're allowed to take it."[112]

---

109 Ibid.

110 Personal correspondence (B).

111 Personal correspondence (C).

112 Positive Peace Warrior Network, "How Will the Walls Come Tumbling Down?"

No one in these debates seemed to acknowledge that noninjury was in play as a very clear de facto limit. Bodily harm aside, "nonviolence" advocates seemed unaware that the sort of redistribution of wealth demanded by *all* participants of the movement likely implied a level of conflict, rather than conciliatory communication, with elites. Social movement theory has long recognized elite defection as an important factor in systemic change, occurring under sufficient pressure as to motivate their investment in the success of a future order and their divestment from the present one. However, contemporary nonviolence advocates often lapse into speaking of elite defection as occurring automatically, without reason, simply through the acceptance of a friendly invitation. Such voices often equated violence with *any* level of conflict with, and even vocal disapproval of, authorities. Anderson clarified his own version of the social change process in his radio interview as not only nonconflictual but also even welcome by the elites it would displace:

TIM: Trying to find a way to make an offer to the 1% that they *really* are so happy to have received. I think the 1% are just as scared as we are.

INTERVIEWER: *Of course they are, probably even more so.*

TIM: They don't know how to get out of this mess. It feels like they were born with a silver spoon in their mouth and somebody has to have it and they're going to have it and there's no way to stop it. I think if we made them an offer which said something like, look: give us the keys to the army, we'll give them to all the moms, plus the Dalai Lama, they can take care of all the military and policing in the world. Something like that. What we'll give you, is your lifestyle, take a couple percentage of your money to have your lifestyle, you know when you're a billionaire, or a multimillionaire, you don't need much, you know most of your money is going into business, you can have your lifestyle for 10 generations, but you can't have all that military power, let us run the military and the economy and the politics.[113]

---

113 Anderson, KKNW interview.

One professional "Kingian nonviolence trainer" I spoke with went so far as to present social change as *granted* by elites like recess in a classroom, with such change being withheld because of the misbehavior of other social movement participants, in a sort of maximalist interpretation of disavowal:

> I just feel like, it's like in a classroom, when one kid is misbehaving, then none of you get to go to recess until they stop doing what they're doing. And then, we're in the middle of recess, we're sitting in our desks, and little Jimmy is still acting up, and you're just like, "Come on, Jimmy! If you just cooperate, then all of us get to go on recess!" That's what I feel like both sides felt like, if you could *just* join our side, we'd all be united…but I see what you're saying, that diversity of tactics maybe could involve some cooperation where some people are doing violence and others doing nonviolence, but the way that I see it is that, the whole classroom, in order for it to work, the whole classroom has to be playing that game. So that we can go to recess and then be free.[114]

Such thin analyses reveal that the conditions that made traditional nonviolence so powerful in its historical moment no longer exist; rather than setting out to force the hand of authorities by threatening legitimacy crises, contemporary nonviolence adherents must, in approaches such as those above, hope for their benevolence. As appeals of nonviolence devolve into moral cover for ineffectual conflict aversion, practitioners of traditional revolutionary nonviolence find themselves alienated from those sharing their symbolic resources, and more aligned with those who tend to reject them. Under such conditions, the goals and methods of "strategic" and, particularly, "revolutionary" nonviolence—with its commitment to disruption and risk, to actual change and not mere expression—begin to look oddly similar to those of riot. Only in rare fortuitous moments—moments generally arrived at only after a process of considerable violence, where "people's power" has rendered police force inutile, media distortions mute, and

---

114 Personal interview (H).

"progressive" institutions unable to manage dissent—are strategies of condescension still possible. The characteristic of such opportunities as moments in a larger process comes through eloquently in this testimony about the Occupy Oakland port shutdown march, where some tens of thousands succeeded in shutting down one of the West Coast's largest economic pressure points:

> I mean the port shutdown wasn't violence. If there was ever a time we were going to be on the receiving end of violence where we wouldn't really fight back, it might actually have been at that time, just because there was so many people. I mean, when the authorities had to reload, I think they would have been overwhelmed. It was like a zombie horde moving forward.... It became that situation where it's like, we're 40,000 people. We are pumped and ready to go, and we are choosing not to be violent and were not even preparing to do violence. No one was going to smash anything. And of course it's the one time when the police didn't provoke attack because they would have lost. That's the one time when nonviolence worked, backed with the threat of violence. Backed not even by the threat, I think the *potentiality* of violence.[115]

---

115 Personal interview (G).

CHAPTER 3

THE ELOQUENCE OF PUBLIC PROPERTY DESTRUCTION

Hours after Officer Darren Wilson gunned down Michael Brown in Ferguson, Missouri, the mostly Black residents had had enough of being considered routinely murderable. They came out into the streets of their small town, refused dispersal orders, and were met with tanks. Some rioted, damaging and looting businesses, and many clashed with police, at least in the sense of refusing to comply under threat of force. Indeed, such refusal became a major reason for coming out into the streets in the first place. Three months later, when a grand jury refused to even bring the officer to trial, the movement went national, with demonstrators in a number of cities blocking freeways, closing down commerce centers, and doing their best to disrupt business as usual. The next April, the violent death of Freddie Gray in police custody in Baltimore was met with large protests. After news and political agents completely ignored them for a week, the protests escalated into large-scale riots; the burning of one CVS pharmacy alone received more national attention than all of the previous protests combined, and six officers involved in Gray's death were indicted. As I write this, the movement continues to erupt city by city across the country; Black Lives Matter in Minneapolis, Chicago, and Detroit have all recently carried off large-scale actions in response to racist police murder. Although the scale of Ferguson/Black Lives Matter uprisings against homicidal police racism is unprecedented for the last few decades, rioting as a response to police murder or brutalization of Black youth had many precedents, even recent ones: 1992 in Los Angeles, 2001 in Cincinnati, or the 2009 and 2010 riots in Oakland around the brazen New Year's Day murder of Oscar Grant in a crowded subway station, a murder filmed by a number of witnesses. As one insurgent put it: "A week after the murder

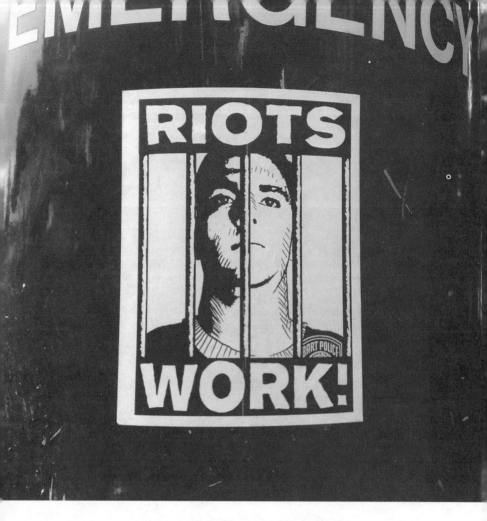

of Oscar Grant, nothing had been done. There'd been rallies, there'd been press releases, but nothing structurally had been done. And then, people who are not in this room went out into the streets and they smashed shit. And they set some stuff on fire. And they fought the cops.... The cop who killed Oscar Grant served a little bit of jail time. He would have served no jail time, had people not gone out into the streets and demanded vengeance."[1] The Oscar Grant riots in particular were a major influence on more radical tendencies in subsequent movements on the West Coast.

Aside from those bewildered by or attempting to dismiss the power of riots, most analysts who try to understand how they work represent

---

1   Personal interview (G).

them as creating material consequences that structurally force a change of policy by agents without other access to decision-making channels. Piven and Cloward explain this as a sort of social strike; just as workers' most powerful means of disruption lies in their withdrawal from economic production, so the marginalized urban poor have little else at their disposal than withdrawal of their roles as passive, peaceable citizens. The audiences of such activity are the policy institutions themselves and their supporters, and their characteristic affects—stern, hurt, and enraged—call to mind Langston Hughes's poem "Evil":

> Looks like what drives me crazy
> Don't have no effect on you—
> But I'm gonna keep on at it
> Till it drives you crazy, too.[2]

While I do not disagree with these analyses of riots, this focus perhaps neglects some of the more nuanced effects articulated by the rioters, the arguments put forward by their actions. In this chapter and the next, I will look at contemporary riot in more rhetorical terms, focusing on the arguments expressed by public property destruction (Chapter 3) and clashes with police (Chapter 4). Faced with the opposition of the neoliberal state and its ideological regime, these actions attempt to constitute powerful collective subjects by manifesting material antagonism to police and property relations. They address an immediate audience, disdaining mass publics, in self-conscious contrast to the mediations of institutionalized dissent. However necessarily material their means of argumentation, though, contemporary riots are always, like their historical predecessors, social appeals. As one Oakland resident clarified, material effects are not the only, or even the main, expression of riots: "[A]ttack on property [is powerful] even if it's symbolic…but *the willingness* to actually attack corporate property is one of the biggest taboos in this culture."[3]

By claiming that counterhegemonic public violence reveals new rhetorical logics in contemporary social movements, I am not claiming that it is the only tactic that puts these logics to use. Instead, rioting

---

2   Langston Hughes, quoted in Nieburg, *Political Violence*, 136.

3   Personal interview (J).

may be a rather tragic attempt to express values in very constricted conditions; a sort of condensation of the values more fully present when movements have more breathing room and can utilize a wider repertoire of action. Why bother focusing on it, then? For one, as a condensation, public violence may give us a clearer view of tendencies that exist more diffusely throughout the movement. Additionally, its ambiguous, in-between nature—not nonviolent *and* unarmed—may help us understand why dissidents have generally grown wary of nonviolence as an ethical and political keyword. For example, the West Coast port shutdowns were, according to most Occupy participants I interviewed, far more emblematic examples of unarmed insurrection than were the moments of riot; Black Lives Matter has generally been much quicker to blockade opera houses, presidential candidates, freeways, shopping centers, police stations, and airports than to resort to public property destruction or clashes with police. Yet no one identified with Black Lives Matter decried or sought to distance the movement from riots when they did happen; and little effort was made to identify the movement as "nonviolent." Rioting exists in a continuum with the disruptive approach of the movement as a whole, as it has in global movements at large since 2011, and broadly for much longer. Since riots are the disruptive activities most often dismissed as mute, irrational explosions of senseless violence, learning to hear their eloquence promises us a greater understanding of disruptive social movements under neoliberal conditions more generally.

Weeks after Michael Brown's murder, Kevin Sorbo, star of the *Hercules* television series, posted a repulsively racist Facebook status reacting to the protests, and limited rioting, in Ferguson. Though the conservative's tone was unusually brazen, the ideas expressed were not uncommon even among liberals: "Ferguson riots have very little to do with the shooting of the young man. It is an excuse to be the losers these animals truly are. It is a tipping point to frustration built up over years of not trying, but blaming everyone else, The Man, for their failures. It's always someone else's fault when you give up."[4] Eight months later, Sorbo repeated similar sentiments in

---

4 Quoted in Prachi Gupta, "Kevin Sorbo's insane, racist Ferguson rant," *Salon.com*, August 21, 2014. Accessed May 24, 2016, https://www.salon.com/2014/08/21/kevin_sorbo_writes_an_insane_rant_on_ferguson_calling_protestors_losers_and_animals/.

a brief, relatively restrained, but perhaps even more condescending post: "Baltimore..........MLK weeps."[5] Though the post was unusually abhorrent, the representation of rioters as mindless, tantruming animals is commonplace in mainstream American discourse. Three years previously, Oakland's supposedly leftist Mayor Quan dismissed Occupy Oakland in similar terms, saying, "It's like a tantrum.... They're treating us like a playground."[6] Even Martin Luther King Jr. drew on the same commonplace describing the Watts riots, "When people are voiceless, they will have temper tantrums like a little child who has not been paid attention to. And riots are massive temper tantrums from a neglected and voiceless people."[7] In King's case, the rhetorical deployment achieved contradictory effects: a belittling in order to gain a distance from and an attempt at control over the events, but also a parental recognition and kindness in response to the rioters' desperate intent. Nieburg, back in 1969, pointed out the theoretical immaturity of this explanation of political violence: "[T]he psychological *theory of frustration-aggression*...is frequently used to explain violent behavior. Frustration imposed by external sanctions or the physical world generates a cumulative rage that, at some point, breaks through in violent behavior. This theory is similar to the doctrine of repressed sexuality, but it broadens the range of drives that may be frustrated. One must be a very naive psychologist indeed to be satisfied with such a mechanistic explanation."[8]

I've already discussed some of the contemporary racial implications of "tantruming," and I'll address its gendered aspects in the next chapter. For now, let's consider the riotous eloquence of these moments—the forms of insurrectionary *defiguration*, which act to destabilize established ideological forms, objects, and subject positions, and free up discursive material to make new subjects. In this chapter, we will look at three rhetorical strategies: *forced comparison*, *desubjectification*, and *profanation*; each enacted through the embodied, material arguments of public property destruction.

---

5   Facebook.com/KevinSorbo, April 27, 2015.

6   Osha Neumann, "Occupy Oakland: Are We Being Childish?" *Counterpunch* website, February 3, 2012. Accessed May 24, 2016, http://www.counterpunch .org/2012/02/03/occupy-oakland-are-we-being-childish.

7   Clayborne Carson, ed. *Autobiography of Martin Luther King, Jr.*, 293.

8   Nieburg, *Political Violence*, 40.

FORCING COMPARISONS

You are suggesting broken windows are worse than broken spines.
—DeRay Mckesson[9]

In 2012, months after Occupy Seattle had fallen apart during debates about whether the movement should sign a "nonviolence agreement," I attended a public discussion in a local Quaker Friends Center, where an anarchist and a nonviolence trainer attempted to come to terms around the difficult issues of violence and nonviolence. At the outset, the anarchist tried to establish what must have seemed like obvious common ground: violence should be defined exclusively as harm or threat inflicted on living beings, not, for example, on inanimate objects. Audience members immediately interrupted his introduction, and the three-hour event never moved beyond this initial disagreement of definition, much to the dismay of the anarchist, who had prepared the points of a discussion that never even got going.

Puzzlingly, the experience in the Friends Center is far from unique. Nearly every time property is destroyed at a demonstration, the same conversation follows almost immediately: young radicals ask whether firefighters wielding axes to save babies from burning buildings should be called violent, while proponents of nonviolence invoke Kristallnacht and burning crosses. Why does this argument keep coming up? And why bother discussing the issue at all if it is destined to go around in the same fruitless circles?

Massimo De Angelis's concept of "value struggle" might help us understand what is at play in such debates. When an antagonism that was previously naturalized, invisibilized, or hegemonically fixed is suddenly made present and explicit, the values represented by the poles of that antagonism are called into question, unfixed, and relativized. They become options one might choose between, worthy of comparison and deliberation, rather than unquestioned premises. Describing a press conference given by the British minister of labour, De Angelis illustrates the difficulty of approaching questions about

---

9   DeRay Mckesson, interviewed by Wolf Blitzer about the 2015 Baltimore riots, CNN, April 28, 2015. The use of this quotation is not an endorsement of Mckesson's mayoral campaign or his efforts to speak on behalf of the movement in other instances.

the "economy" in the era of neoliberal hegemony, when the "freedom" of the market is presumed to be a matter of consensus:

> The Labour minister highlighted progress, winked at the critics and spelled out policies that, in the usual neoliberal style, are all geared towards and justified in terms of creating "effective competition", a condition, we were told, that is indispensable for fighting world poverty. When challenged to explain what happens when a country has an "absolute trade advantage", like China, and the consequence of that is, for example, the ruin of Bangladeshi workers in the textile industry and their communities, he explained that "competition is a fact of life". Right, I can imagine what a woman in the struggle in the 1970s would have said to a man claiming that patriarchy is "a fact of life", or a black about racism being a "fact of life", or a migrant about border control being a "fact of life", or a gay about homophobia being a "fact of life", or an indigenous person about privatised sacred land being a "fact of life". In all these cases, in a wide range of modalities, what these struggling subjects would have said and done is *to contest a relational mode they did not value*, indeed, that they abhorred. Yet, we seem to be speechless in relation to the dominant relational modes through which we articulate life practices and that we call "the economy". We seem to be paralysed before the domain of the relational modes implicit in "economics". And so, critics who feel there is something wrong with the way we live and operate on this planet emphasise the effects produced by these relational modes, such as poverty or environmental catastrophe, and their critical stance is focused on correcting the facts they are given and trying to uncover the "lies" of power. And this is of course very good. However, they seldom look at power in its "truth", that is, in the fact that it stands for something that we, the critics, do not. To do so would require measuring it with the yardstick of what we value, and

being reconciled to the fact that the borderline is a line of conflict, a front line.[10]

In the context of such presumed consensus, simply starting arguments can itself be understood as already a powerful rhetorical strategy. De Angelis's challenge to the claim that economic "competition is a fact of life," destabilizes the unspoken consensus on trade policy by making visible social relations and values that had appeared necessary and thus unquestionable; this is what makes up a *value struggle*. The anarchist's proposed definition of violence at the Friends Center, by similarly contesting the unspoken (and embarrassing) equivalence of bodies and commodities in the hegemonic definition of violence, inadvertently foregrounded a disagreement and produced "a line of conflict" over values where before there seemed obvious consensus. Both property destruction itself and the contentious conversation it produces assert a value struggle, a strategy to expose this hidden conflict over definition. When turned to the relative value of life and commodity, this rhetorical strategy highlights an essentially *embarrassing* inconsistency within liberal ideology's humanistic claims, one that challenges its very core.

As the intractability of positions in the Friends Center debate showed, such value struggles often change very little in the short term. However, bringing values and terms into question may have other, more long-term results. When I asked one longtime Seattle nonviolence trainer if she had seen shifts over time in how property destruction was regarded—particularly in the wake of the arguments started by the Black Bloc actions in the WTO protests of 1999—she indicated that a shift had indeed taken place, noticeable only years later in retrospect: "I think there may be more understanding of…a difference between property versus people being hurt.… [It's hard to say definitely,] but I think there's more openness to seeing violence more as against people. [But] it doesn't mean people approve of it, or like it. To say something isn't violent doesn't mean that you think it's a good idea to do it right in the middle of the march or something."[11]

In addition to simply making the natural and obvious unnatural and doubtable, the conversations triggered by public acts of property

---

10   Massimo De Angelis, *The Beginning of History: Value Struggles and Global Capital* (London: Pluto Press, 2007), xi–xii. My emphasis.

11   Personal interview (C).

destruction always inevitably involve *comparisons*. Not only do they bring the "facts of life" tied to naturalized practices into deliberation but they also invariably do so by dragging them into a comparison with invisibilized forms of violence that, though less remarkable, are of worse consequence. Such comparisons are not mere rhetorical opportunism that follows acts of property destruction; rather, *they are the meaning of the actions themselves*, often but not necessarily borne out in conversations and subsequent discussions of the events. The material acts demonstrate a sort of faith that the implicit comparisons will be unpacked in the inevitable ensuing arguments. For example, in one public debate in Oakland, occurring shortly after a breakaway march had smashed up a local Whole Foods and surrounding businesses, one woman on the panel made explicit the comparison of foregrounded and backgrounded violence implicit in the original acts of violence. "When you start thinking about violence and the first thing that comes to your mind is that fucking Whole Foods or that stupid ATM…. I want you to reconsider and think about the violence of the state, think about the violence of the police. If you can get so mad about this theoretical violence against a window, or against a newspaper stand, but you cannot actually muster enough energy to get that pissed off about the everyday systemic violence that occurs against my people, against your people, then you have no place talking about violence."[12]

Another speaker at the same event confirmed the contradictions of violence, in the service of power and against it, in another extended set of comparisons:

> Violence is when a mother is denied food stamps and it feels like she has no options left but to shoot herself and her two children. Violence is when the police beat and kill youth of color in Oakland. It is when immigrant families work three jobs to sustain themselves and their relatives abroad, when the military spreads democracy in Iraq and Afghanistan with stealth bombers and drones. Violence is the modern-day slave labor facilitated by the prison system. It is the slow insidious havoc that the court system wrecks on the lives of those who have the wrong skin color, or can't afford a

---

12 Positive Peace Warrior Network, "How Will the Walls Come Tumbling Down?"

good lawyer. But violence is also when we fight back. It is a tool to get what one wants or needs, one of the oldest and most effective tools. Violence can be an intense form of care and love, the material expression of our passion for freedom and each other.[13]

It would be naive for these speakers to expect an audience in the contemporary US to simply accept these claims, but sometimes merely starting an argument, and not winning it, is the point. Since the equivalence of commodities and bodies is foundational to the ideology of liberal humanism, it is often enough to get audiences to notice that it's there in the first place.

Stealing John Locke's Coat: How to Embarrass Capitalist Ideology

In Chapter III of his *Second Treatise of Government*, perhaps the most important text of classic liberal political thought, John Locke proposes that law saves us from the supposedly natural state of war famously described by Thomas Hobbes. It allows people to live together "according to reason, without a common superior on earth, with authority to judge between them." The law works to protect, in much the same way, bodies and commodities. "Thus a thief, whom I cannot harm, but by appeal to the law, for having stolen all that I am worth, I may kill, when he sets on me to rob me but of my horse or coat; because the law, which was made for my preservation…permits me my own defence…. Want of a common judge with authority, puts all men in a state of nature: force without right, upon a man's person, makes a state of war, both where there is, and is not, a common judge."[14]

What is in one sentence a possession—"my horse or coat"— immediately becomes "my own" self for "defence," an equivalence that can be seen in the original, etymological meaning of *proper/property*, still present in French *propre* or Spanish *propio*—that one's own self is interchangeable with what one possesses. (The word "own," as in "to one's own self be true"/ "certificate of ownership," also reveals these

---

13   Ibid.

14   John Locke, *Second Treatise of Government* (Indianapolis: Hackett Publishing, 1962), 15.

intertwined meanings in the same way.) To defend through murder one's horse or coat quietly claims the same right of law in Locke's words as "my preservation." That he constitutes his (masculine) physical self through an odd equivalence of body with coat or horse goes unremarked; rather than understanding this equating as an expressive act of description within the ideologically permitted premises of his day, we might see it as an assertion that actively works to construct a new liberal order. What seals this odd equivalence is not any explicit argument (which, in any case, might not be so convincing to people with bodies but few commodities to their name). Locke's equating of body with commodity in this passage occurs through the threat of violence posed to both, somehow in the same way. Tellingly, the terrible "natural" state of affairs—a Hobbesian "state of war"—is defined as the opposite of Locke's peaceful order under the liberal state, in which "all men" exist together in "a state of peace" under a "common judge with authority"; any possibility of basic inequality, of exploitation and slavery, that one man's "state of peace" might be based on another's existence in a "state of war," is precluded. Inevitably, speakers who challenge this equating or exclusion thus find themselves confronted with the idea of violence within liberal ideology as a foundational concept that conjoins bodies with possessions through its shared threat.

Ayn Rand, the persistently popular scribe of capitalist ideology, articulates this body/commodity equivalency through the algebraic property of equality: A=C (in the first passage below) and B=C (in the second), then A=B. In this case, the third term that mediates equivalence is "rights," first implicitly and then explicitly understood as a guarantor against the violence that threatens the existence of the body/commodity. "Just as man can't exist without his body, so no rights can exist without the right to translate one's rights into reality—to think, to work and to keep the results—which means: the right of property."[15] The "right" to capitalist property relations is equivalent to the right to bodily integrity—and both are equally necessary for a full existence. Just as a body permits "a man" to exist physically, capitalist property relations produce all other rights—that is, the space within which "man" can exist as a *social* and *political* being among others. Later, Rand goes on to use the notion of rights as an equivalency of bodily protection: "The only proper purpose of a government

15 Ayn Rand, *Atlas Shrugged* (New York: Random House, 1957), 977.

is to protect man's rights, which means: to protect him from physical violence. A proper government is only a policeman, acting as an agent of man's self-defense."[16] Her repetition in the two quotes of the blunt clause "which means," makes all rights essentially elaborations of property relations in the first quotation, while it defines all "man's rights," in the second, as essentially bodily protection against the threat of violence. Both the parallelism of the first quotation and the algebraic equating of the term "rights" across the two passages, posit body and commodity as equivalent through the potential of threatening "violence." Later, Rand affirms the equivalence of "men's [physical] protection" with property relations as "the base of a moral existence," under the threat of unspecified "destroyers," determining property relations to the sacred moment of money: "Money is the barometer of a society's virtue. Whenever destroyers appear among men, they start by destroying money, for money is men's protection and the base of a moral existence."[17]

Neither Locke nor Rand can simply come out and say that things and lives are of equal worth, that both are equally valuable "property." Given the humanistic claims that liberal ideology mobilized against the old order of feudalistic divine rule, such an admission would be entirely embarrassing. This is why these equations have to be so tortuously indirect; in the end, although the notion of "property" as a body/commodity equivalence is the cornerstone of the whole system of beliefs, liberal ideology doesn't want to talk about it. It is precisely this embarrassing equation that property destruction in anticapitalist riots attempts to highlight and destabilize. The fact that they do not always immediately convince their audience should not be taken as evidence of ineffectiveness. The discursive attempt to disarticulate property from bodies meets with resistance and often fails to take hold precisely because to accept it would entail rejecting, in Ernesto Laclau and Chantal Mouffe's terminology, the most basic "chain of equivalence" constituting liberal ideology, an essential aspect of the "superstructure" expressed by the "base" of capitalist property relations.[18] This is a very articulate disarticulation; it foregrounds and potentially

---

16   Ibid.

17   Ibid.

18   Ernesto Laclau and Chantal Mouffe, *Hegemony and Socialist Strategy: Towards a Radical Democratic Politics* (London: Verso, 1985).

demystifies beliefs that, like all ideological formations, remain un-questioned at the level of common sense. In this strict sense, drawing attention to the embarrassment of Locke's equivalence can be read as a powerful move of properly anticapitalist rhetoric.

One might well ask—as would orthodox Marxists who see discursive shifts as simple effects of material changes—whether rhetorical challenges to such core ideological elements are by their nature futile. Such claims against deeply entrenched ideologies, though sometimes slower to bring about any noticeable change, are necessary instruments for loosening the meanings of the present and making new meanings imaginable. Not only do such deep claims point out possible directions for future meaning, but they also aid more moderate claims by shifting the context, allowing previously marginal positions to appear as more reasonable. Schock terms this the "radical flank effect."[19] It extends the radical margins, shifting the center along with them. Martin Luther King Jr. himself highlighted the embarrassment of Locke's equivalence, giving voice to his own anticapitalist convictions: "We must rapidly begin the shift from a thing-oriented society to a person-oriented society. When machines and computers, *profit motives and property rights*, are considered more important than people, the giant triplets of racism, extreme materialism, and militarism are incapable of being conquered."[20]

The contentious and unresolved character of these arguments is a sign of their importance and of the necessity of *starting arguments* as useful means of persuasion. As one organizer for the Palestinian Boycott, Divestment, and Sanctions campaign describes that movement's productive and efficacious contentiousness,

> One of the more popular arguments against academic boycott, both during BDS in South Africa and with the Palestinian campaign, is that it's against dialog, that it's shutting down the conversation. The response that people were making was—listen, this is actually starting fruitful debate about what we actually believe, and how we're connected to what's happening in other

---

19 Schock, *Unarmed Insurrections*, 47.

20 Clayborne Carson, ed. *Autobiography of Martin Luther King, Jr.*, 340. My emphasis.

places. By definition, the debate has to be about themes
of complicity, about the definitions of academic freedom, what are our responsibilities to the world... I
don't think people have real conversations about places that feel far away. Those things don't feel urgent
enough for real conversations, unless it feels contentious. I also wonder if things are or feel contentious by
the same mechanism that they are relevant or urgent,
because debates around BDS get at the heart of...chal-
lenge their core values, things people believe they believe—that it gets at things people believe or feel about
other parts of their life beyond just how they feel about
Palestine or BDS, so it *has* to be contentious.[21]

This contentious style of address—whose purported incivility supposedly "shuts down the conversation"—is precisely what forces audiences to become aware of topics too implicated in their core values to
allow polite questioning, in particular topics that are both too painful
to engage and distant enough to avoid. Such forceful appeals are part
of what James Darsey calls the "Hebraic" tradition in Western rhetoric, which foregrounds topics precisely through nonidentification
with the audience, through jeremiads, accusations, threats, and general perturbations of the rhetorical status quo.[22] According to Darsey,
the importance of confrontational rhetoric is often forgotten under
the general dominance of the more civil "Hellenic" approach, which
attempts to identify with and kindly win over its audience. If the acceptable terms of the debate are themselves a matter of disagreement,
one's appeals must involve incivility in order to question these boundaries—since any "civil" claims are defined as such by their acceptance
of the terms of debate and willingness to argue within them.

Journalist and protest participant Emily Brissette poignantly con-
veys the sense of violation an audience experiences when its unquestioned presuppositions begin to unravel before public property destruction and urges her audience to accept this undoing:

---

21 Personal interview (K).

22 James Francis Darsey, *The Prophetic Tradition and Radical Rhetoric in America*
(New York: New York University Press, 1997).

That so many react with horror and outrage at broken bank windows is not, however, surprising. The capitalist system in which we live sanctifies property and personalizes corporations, while dehumanizing millions of people in the US and billions worldwide. To a very large degree these ideas suffuse our common sense; they are the taken-for-granted assumptions out of which our moral and affective reactions emerge. But if we are serious about transforming our society to put human need at the center of our politics and economic practices, then we need to attend to the way unexamined assumptions shape our interpretations of this moment, its pitfalls and possibilities, and the way forward. We must deny the existing system the power to define the situation for us. We must root out the ways it shapes our interpretations and reactions, by thinking deeply, probing our assumptions, questioning the origins of our gut reactions and the allegiances these express. We must have the courage to pursue personal transformation alongside, in conjunction with, and as mutually constitutive of the social transformations we seek.[23]

The debates with which she broaches the awkward subject of property relations are not simply *about* broken bank windows, but rather intentionally precipitated *by* the breaking of windows in the first place. That this is not accidental, but purposeful, is borne out in Brissette's language; such acts work as eloquent appeals, "probing our assumptions" and "questioning the origins of our gut reactions and the allegiances they express." Whether figuratively or quite literally, such unraveling of common sense is necessarily a violent process.

Arguing that property destruction should not be called "violence" is merely wishing the ideological challenge away by denying the equation still clearly at play within current hegemony. I am not claiming that "violence" *only* exists as a social construct under capitalism in

---

23 Emily Brissette, "For the Fracture of Good Order," *Counterpunch* website, November 4, 2011. Accessed May 24, 2016, http://www.counterpunch.org /2011/11/04/for-the-fracture-of-good-order.

order to establish a value equation between body and commodity. However, the way that violence is understood under capitalism is inescapably conditioned by the equivalence nested within the idea of "property," and calling attention to it works, in whatever measure, to destabilize the ideology built upon it.

DESUBJECTIFICATION

Marketing has become the center of the "soul" of the corporation. We are taught that corporations have a soul, which is the most terrifying news in the world.
—Gilles Deleuze[24]

While public performances of property destruction raise awkward questions about the relative values of life and commodity, they also call certain subjectivities into question. Examining this rhetorical mechanism in anticapitalist riot demands a brief trip into some counterintuitive corners of post-structuralist philosophy, where recognizable social roles—"subjects"—are constituted within discourse. These subjects are socially constructed in processes that are somewhat independent from the individuals speaking in those roles. Foucault defines a subject as an "enunciative modality," a certain way in which one can speak and be heard, while Louis Althusser talks of a "subject position," the place one can speak from and be understood as a speaker.[25] What matters here is that the place or way one can speak and be heard from is socially constructed and thus can be socially challenged and altered. For many political philosophers, this process of forming new subjects and abolishing old ones is necessarily a violent process. In his classic "Reflections on Violence," Georges Sorel put forward his notion of the general strike as a myth which condensed all of the desired political values of proletarian struggle; violence not only played an inevitable part of this confrontation with ruling powers but also in forming the new subject who would emerge from this conflict. In Sorel's

---

24   Gilles Deleuze, "Postscript on the Societies of Control," *October* 59 (1992): 3–7.

25   Michel Foucault, *The Archaeology of Knowledge* (New York: Pantheon Books, 1972); Louis Althusser, "Ideology and Ideological State Apparatuses (Notes Towards an Investigation)," in Aradhana Sharma and Akhil Gupta, *The Anthropology of the State: A Reader* (Oxford: Blackwell, 2006), 86.

words, violence "is assigned the important function of 'constituting' an actor."[26] Similarly, Fanon's *The Wretched of the Earth* declares that decolonization requires violence to be done to the colonizer's body in order to disprove and negate its sacred inviolability—antihegemonic violence actually creates the post-colonial subject through the act of violation.[27] Contemporary practices of public noninjurious violence, such as public property destruction, can be seen as discursive actions creating subjects in a similar way, while avoiding reinforcing the dehumanizing effects of capitalist society's inherent disregard for life. In the words of one anarchist I interviewed, "I think that property destruction has a good effect on those who carry it out.... I think most people need to unlearn submission and show themselves that they have the capacity to act for their own liberation. I think that when people burn cop cars, break bank windows, or blockade a road (thwarting the transfer of goods and/or law enforcement) they are also demonstrating to themselves some of the magnitude of their ability to resist."[28]

Seeing destructive acts as a way to "unlearn submission," reaffirms what many philosophers have claimed: subjectivity is in some sense a zero-sum game, and new places to speak from, or ways to speak and be heard, can only be won through the destruction of old subject positions. And these reconfigurations are inherently, unavoidably violent. According to philosopher Giorgio Agamben, "[a] desubjectifying moment is certainly implicit in every process of subjectification."[29] His words also remind us that the subjective "material" freed up by desubjectification does not necessarily coalesce into new subject positions in any straightforward way, and rioters are often too busy dissolving objectionable discursive targets to pay much attention to constituting new ones. What is certain, in all of these views, is that if new subjects are to be formed, old subjects must be *deformed*; their speaking voice must be removed from recognition, their modality of enunciation thinned or erased if another is ever to be heard.

---

26 Georges Sorel, quoted in Seferiades and Johnston, "Dynamics of Violent Protest," 6.

27 Frantz Fanon, *The Wretched of the Earth* (New York: Penguin Books, 1969).

28 Personal interview (L).

29 Giorgio Agamben, *What Is an Apparatus? And Other Essays* (Palo Alto: Stanford University Press, 2009), 21.

Violence is, in a certain sense, precisely this power to rearrange subjectivities. Lacan views the imposition and fixing of *any* symbolic order to be essentially violent, indeed the very meaning of violence itself. In fact, the idea that semiotic disruption requires violence is, for Lacan, a pure tautology: violence *is* semiosis—the making of meaning—just as semiosis is the very motion of violence. Susan Brison, in her unforgettable reflection on the role of narrative in "remaking a self" in the traumatic aftermath of rape and attempted murder, understands violence as that which undoes the Self, shattering the subject by introducing an intensity of the unspeakable.[30] Narrative, in its turn, offers a restoration by integrating trauma into a unity, one that might be considered a new subject in some senses. Koestenbaum, whose reflections I will analyze at length in the next chapter, asserts that humiliation, as it "observably lowers [its object] in status and position...represents *the destruction of matter.* Something once present—an intactness, a solidity, a substantiality—turns into tatters."[31] Humiliation, in this sense, is violent in its effect on the dignity of its object. That the redistribution of subjectivity inevitably relies on violence seems a dismal but unavoidable conclusion.

Sara Ahmed sees this process of destroying old subjective boundaries and establishing new ones as a physical act of *surfacing*, and hence necessarily a physical one. "Bodies surface by 'feeling' the presence of others as the cause of injury or as a form of intrusion."[32] Anticapitalist protest violence works to intensify and localize this surface, this boundary of injury and safety, without necessarily making other living bodies the excluded object of the process. Violence manifests as work that establishes a material boundary, reforming social space, *surfacing*, touching as it destroys—an exorcism that transforms a border into an object. Anticapitalist violence *objectivizes* property relations, materially humiliating the enunciative modality of the Other. Ahmed gets us closer to understanding how this works in her analysis of "words that wound," by looking at "the enactment of hate through verbal or physical violence." In Ahmed's analysis of the effects of violence,

---

30   Susan J. Brison, *Aftermath: Violence and the Remaking of a Self* (Princeton: Princeton University Press, 2002).

31   Koestenbaum, *Humiliation*, 10–11.

32   Sara Ahmed, *The Cultural Politics of Emotion* (New York: Routledge, 2013), 48.

[L]ived experiences of pain can be understood as part of the work of hate, or as part of what hate *is doing*. Hate has effects on the bodies of those who are made into its objects; such bodies are affected by the hate that it is directed towards them by others. Hate is not simply a means by which the identity of the subject and community is established (through alignment); hate also works to unmake the world of the other through pain. Or hate crimes seek to *crush* the other in what Patricia Williams has called "spirit murder".[33]

Despite her brilliant analysis of the subjective mechanics of violence, Ahmed falls into an easy liberal framing of the political-subjective effects of violence by typifying the process as hatred and by using only white supremacist and neo-Nazi discourse as examples of hatred and violence. This defaults to a politically limited framing of the political-subjective effects of violence. Ahmed's readership is obviously unsympathetic toward neo-Nazis, so the question of potentially emancipatory, counterhegemonic political violence (perhaps even *against* neo-Nazis) is forestalled. But aren't some worlds better unmade than left to be? Don't some traits deserve exorcism? Mightn't it be best to violently "surface" certain forms of otherness? If certain inanimate objects and social practices cause an unfathomable amount of suffering to the actually living, doesn't a passionate love for living beings entail passionate acts against the things that cause such suffering? It would, of course, be odd to call something like this "hate." Koestenbaum's analysis suffers from a similar selective range of examples to illustrate his supposedly universal claims regarding humiliation. Though he brilliantly analyzes the mechanisms of desubjectification, of violent undoing through humiliation and laughter, he can only imagine these as tools available to the powerful, and never as a tool of resistance:

> The humiliation of a derided performer on American Idol is immeasurably different from the humiliation of a Palestinian under Israeli occupation. One plight is chosen, the other is not. But isn't there present, in both situations, in the demeanor and behavior of the

---

33   Ibid., 58.

aggressors, an underlying coldheartedness, a rock-
bottom refusal to believe the worthiness of the person
whose reputation (or house, or land, or ego, or self-
esteem) is stolen, trashed, occupied, razed? Isn't there
present, in both situations, an underlying will to de-
racinate and desubjectify this other person? And, most
insidiously—isn't there an insistence on considering
this process of desubjectification (with my laughter
I take away your humanity) an entertaining process,
even a cathartic exercise, therapeutic and energizing,
like calisthenics? The audience at American Idol (or
so I hypothesize) experiences laughter as a cosmetic,
cleansing procedure—a cheerful exfoliation. I hate
group laughter. It is always smug and certain of its
position. Lynndie England's smile and the laughter
of the audience at American Idol display a callous,
morally deadening joviality. Any good soldier must
undergo—must grow inured to—this morally deadened state. We spread it elsewhere; we cultivate it at
home. Through the enslavement and abuse of African
Americans, and the genocide of Native Americans,
the United States honed its gift for morally deadened
cheerfulness. This self-assured laughter isn't solely
U.S. property. It grows elsewhere, too. But it has the
quintessentially American tone of mass-media confidence—advertising, commerce, McDonald's, slaugh-
terhouses, or what in the 1960s I learned to call the
military-industrial complex.[34]

Koestenbaum's unambiguous moral claim regarding humilia-
tion-as-desubjectification is that "moral individuals...should work
toward minimizing humiliation, toward not inflicting it."[35] But there
is something dubious about his examples, however well they describe
the genealogy of "morally deadening joviality" in the US. Do they
perhaps say more about which groups strike the author as typical?
Does his category of "aggressor" mask potentially relevant differentials

---

34   Koestenbaum, *Humiliation*, 37.
35   Ibid., 16.

of power beyond those his anecdotes suggest? Are Ahmed's implicit and Koestenbaum's explicit moral prescriptions as convincing if we imagine them applied *counterhegemonically*, that is, against the ruling systems of racism, patriarchy, and capital? Can't Palestinians, African Americans, Native Americans, or civilians on the receiving end of the violence of the "good soldiers" make use of the desubjectifying power of group laughter, if only for fleeting moments? True, these "jokes" command less terrain, but does that make Koestenbaum's presumptions of subject position, his habit of only attributing agency to the hegemonic, any less selective—however common they are among advocates of nonviolence? Indeed, if group laughter can constitute collective self-confidence, shouldn't he celebrate this power *for those who need it* rather than decrying it as necessarily "smug"? Aren't there as well certain types of humiliating humor, correlating to certain subjects, that are capable of being used against the status quo?

Anticapitalist public violence, unlike Fanon's anticolonial violence, or the daily hegemonic violence maintaining the status quo, distinguishes itself by primarily targeting inanimate objects, artifacts of state and capitalist power. By starting arguments that foreground hegemonic chains of equivalence, targeted property destruction insists that liberatory movements can make use of the means of humiliation and apply them to nonhuman targets in order to "observably lower in status and position" the very cultural nodes that re/inscribe antihuman value systems. Since such transgressions against foundational social norms are bound to be illegal, from a liberal perspective they could be considered "hate crimes against corporate personhood," examples of the "terrifying news" Deleuze describes above: that corporations have souls. What is missing from this definition—and this may be true of right-wing "hate crimes" as well—is that they might in no sense depend upon hatred per se, but rather on the political will to exclude, redefine, and redistribute subject positions in an immediate, localized sense that instantiates wider social visions in the here and now. Noninjurious anticapitalist public actions—in contrast to right-wing violence that, given the ideologies it works to bolster, *does* prioritize violence against bodies—commit violence against inanimate subjects not as an accident but as a claim against the subjectivity, the "soul" of corporations or wider property relations, against their propensity to be heard over the voices of the living.

PROFANATION

One young nonviolence trainer spoke to me with concern and incomprehension regarding the propensity of others to break the law during protests, seemingly only for the sake of breaking the law itself. "It skews the narrative," she said, "to have a couple of specks on the record where they were doing things that were [transgressive].… I totally believe in civil disobedience, but I don't believe that you should break laws that are tangential to the actual thing that you're protesting. Sit-ins were breaking the law because it was wrong—just sitting there was illegal, or kind of illegal, for African Americans to be there. But, sometimes, blocking traffic is not exactly…I don't believe it's our complete right to do that."[36]

It is true—traffic laws are not a frequent target of demonstrator grievance in the US. Nevertheless, the same cannot be said for capitalist property relations. Frequently, the depth of demands correlates with the tactics that seem appropriate to them. For example, for those who saw the Occupy movement as a plea to reinstitute the Glass-Steagall Act and to repeal Citizens United, or for those who understood Black Lives Matter primarily as suggesting reforms of existing police policies and procedure, "the message" indeed might be lost in the noise of unruly protest conduct. However, if policies and legislative acts are symptomatic of deeper social relations, seeing transgressive public acts as "tangential to the actual thing that you're protesting" misses the point. In a manner often unspoken but always articulate, these acts target social relations directly, not through the mediating intervention of state authorities. They operate through an interruption of the reproduction of property relations, through the immediate, empowering, rhetorical action of value struggles. As Piven and Cloward conclude, even reforms may paradoxically be won more effectively by threatening deeper, "revolutionary" challenges than by directly petitioning for those reforms. In any case, "the message" of disruptive protest acts is often much deeper than can be expressed in a placard or slogan. The above nonviolence trainer advocated in her interview that "we should all attack forces, not individuals; attack their behavior, not the person." Since the forces of capital are, in a very real way, materially manifest in commodities, riotous insurgents do just this, even challenging the mystique of the commodity form itself at moments.

---

36 Personal interview (H).

Property destruction targets not only the institutions that own the property but also the relationship of ownership that makes their existence possible. Although media reports frequently allege destruction of small businesses and highlight when public property destruction targets personal property, anticapitalist demonstrators are in practice generally scrupulous to target corporate property. Beyond the particular sins of these corporations, participants often indicate that the central appeal of these acts is how they call social relations into question. As a technique of value struggle, not only does targeted property destruction attempt to force comparisons about the relative values inherent in foregrounded and backgrounded practices; it also attempts to denaturalize capitalist relations themselves, bringing them into view as subject to deliberation, which implicitly asserts the potential of alternatives. Wacquant speaks of neoliberal society as regulated by the "sacralization of the market" and as "submitted to the joint empire of the commodity form and moralizing individualism."[37] Militant anticapitalist protesters mirror Wacquant's analysis; the uniquely sacred status of property relations is precisely what demands their being called into question, as with this anarchist I interviewed:

> As far as this violence against property…there is of course the ridiculous cases of people who don't believe in damaging property jumping on other people as they're trying to damage property and hitting them, choosing to injure another person who's damaging property in order to stop them…. Not even damaging their own property, mind you, but damaging corporate property, you know? To me that's just, that speaks to me about how especially in the United States, how deeply that deification of property, corporate property, is. And that actually, that attack on property even if it's symbolic, because obviously we are not doing enough damage to Wells Fargo to really damage their bottom line, but the willingness to actually attack corporate property is one of the biggest taboos in this culture. Historically, it would've been the equivalent of attacking the church or something, you know? If you think

---

37 Wacquant, *Punishing the Poor*, 23, 20.

about the Spanish Civil War, anarchists exhuming the nuns, and the firing squads shooting at the crucifix, and so forth, you know? This is essentially what we're looking at, symbolically, we're looking at attacking the only thing that is left that is holy in this culture, which is corporate property. It's not a surprise to me, but it is always fascinating to just, how much people freak out about stuff. And it just reinforces to me that that is actually an important statement to make.[38]

This theme appeared repeatedly in my interviews. Another person spoke of how certain protesters urged a graduated approach to the disregard of property, one that celebrated the sacrilegious, but was careful not to alienate fellow demonstrators:

The scale of property destruction, too, changes things a lot. Like, in [one march], there were anarchists that paint-bombed the Wells Fargo and the Bank of America on the way there, and there was this idea, probably, allegedly, that you have to ease into the idea, because *people are shocked by even the lowest level of property damage, because they hold property to be so sacred....* So paint-bombing, rather than smashing a window, is a way for people to celebrate how they don't, to celebrate an attack against the banks that's like, playful still, and is not seemingly as violent, and that maybe will later lead to more acceptance of more so-called violent things, like smashing windows or whatever.[39]

The general character of empowering transgression has been discussed elsewhere and is obviously a feature of any riot or counter-hegemonic performance, public or private, but here the public transgression specifically attacks capitalist relations themselves through a strategy of targeted property destruction. Notably, a more powerful instance of profanation described by the same speaker relied *not* on any destruction, but rather on simple violation, when two hundred

---

38   Personal interview (J).
39   Personal interview (L).

activists collectively occupied a long-abandoned warehouse in the center of Seattle's Capitol Hill for nine hours. Participants found this transgression especially potent—it released emotions and subjective potentials pent-up behind repressed fears. By violating deeply held norms around property, by profaning the sacred, people suddenly started to "believe in themselves" and to "dream so much bigger":

> The occupation of the warehouse at Tenth and Union...that detailed to me an example of radicalizing people, too, because it broke the myth. It was a process of breaking the myth of private property, or not the myth of it but the sacredness of it, and that was really important because I was sort of shocked, but also really happy to see so many people [with whom] I'd had really frustrating conversations about [how] the idea of illegality in any way was terrible to them. And now they're running around in an occupied warehouse! [Laughs] Talking about what they could do with it, and believing in themselves so much more than I thought, and dreaming so much bigger...[40]

Agamben traces the liberatory application of profanation to its Roman origins, oddly analogous to the warehouse occupation, as profanation seizes for use that which was set aside for only the gods to enjoy:

> According to Roman law, objects that belonged in some way to the gods were considered sacred or religious. As such, these things were removed from free use and trade among humans: they could neither be sold nor given as security, neither relinquished for the enjoyment of others nor subjected to servitude. Sacrilegious were the acts that violated or transgressed the special unavailability of these objects, which were reserved either for celestial beings (and so they were properly called "sacred") or for the beings of the netherworld (in this case, they were simply called "religious"). While "to consecrate" (*sacrare*) was the term

---

40   Personal interview (L).

that designated the exit of things from the sphere of human law, "to profane" signified, on the contrary, to restore the thing to the free use of men. "Profane," the great jurist Trebatius was therefore able to write, "is, in the truest sense of the word, that which was sacred or religious, but was then restored to the use and property of human beings."[41]

Agamben's definition of profanation as "restoring to use" that which had been reserved for the gods is also strikingly mirrored in the language of one statement released by the ACME Collective, a group of Black Bloc participants in the 1999 WTO protests in Seattle. It describes targeted property destruction in very similar terms, using a religiously laden vocabulary of "exorcism" and "spells":

> When we smash a window, we aim to destroy the thin veneer of legitimacy that surrounds private property rights. At the same time, we exorcise that set of violent and destructive social relationships which has been imbued in almost everything around us. By "destroying" private property, we convert its limited exchange value into an expanded use value. A storefront window becomes a vent to let some fresh air into the oppressive atmosphere of a retail outlet (at least until the police decide to tear-gas a nearby road blockade). A newspaper box becomes a tool for creating such vents or a small blockade for the reclamation of public space or an object to improve one's vantage point by standing on it. A dumpster becomes an obstruction to a phalanx of rioting cops and a source of heat and light. A building facade becomes a message board to record brainstorm ideas for a better world.
>
> After [these actions], many people will never see a shop window or a hammer the same way again. The potential uses of an entire cityscape have increased a thousandfold. The number of broken windows pales in comparison to the number of broken spells—spells

---

41   Agamben, *What Is an Apparatus?*, 17.

cast by a corporate hegemony to lull us into forget-
fulness of all the violence committed in the name of
private property rights and of all the potential of a society without them. Broken windows can be boarded
up (with yet more waste of our forests) and eventually
replaced, but the shattering of assumptions will hopefully persist for some time to come.[42]

As the ACME statement makes explicit, the actual "target" of the
property destruction was not the windows or newspaper boxes, but
rather the "spells," "hegemony," the "assumptions" of the potential
uses for these items, and particularly those who get to decide how they
are used. The making-available-for-use of property relations through
profanation brings the meaning of these items into a space of immediate public deliberation. And doing so in the middle of the city, on a
weekday morning, makes this profanation very much a public appeal.

What, then, is brought back into use through profanation? Other
than the banality of short-lived vents, blockades, and message boards,
what rhetorical purpose is served by "destroy[ing] the thin veneer of
legitimacy that surrounds private property rights"? If capitalist property relations—the commodity fetish's subsuming of use value under
exchange value—are themselves the last sacred things, what is made
available by bringing *them*—the values themselves—back into "use"?
What is the use of a value? By calling the sanctity of property into
question, acts of targeted property interrupt the everyday to ask, can
we talk about what this bank is doing? Can we talk about what goes
on in this agency? Can we talk about all those things that are off the
table? What is being contested is the nonavailability of these values
for deliberation; just as forcing comparison aims not to propose new
arrangements of hegemony but only to call values into question as
relative, so profanation makes values available and open to discussion.
It reminds the audience that values are produced and can therefore
be remade or replaced with other values, along with all their wider
ideological or hegemonic entailments.

---

42   Van Deusen and Massot, *Black Bloc Papers*, 45–46.

CHAPTER 4

THE ELOQUENCE
OF POLICE CLASHES

DISIDENTIFICATION

What we're really scared about is the uniform, more so than about the police. What's more scary is the uniform, not the person that's in the uniform. And I think people are mixing both of them. Yes, he's a human being, but it's the uniform that is telling you they have the power. And they're trained to think that they hold power, when in reality it's the people that hold the power.

—Nonviolence trainer, Seattle[1]

BEYOND THE STRATEGIES OF FORCED COMPARISON, DESUBJECTIFICA-tion, and profanation, which are rhetorical aspects of targeted property destruction, protesters also enact a number of rhetorical strategies when they clash with police. Given the central role of policing, incarceration, and the security state in the neoliberal order described, strategies that perform public antagonism with the police can be expected to play an important role in contemporary movements. Riotous subjects clashing with the police face a dilemma: protester hostility toward police must be manifested materially, like antipathy to property relations; however, as anticapitalist protest prioritizes the destabilization of Locke's chain of equivalence, such confrontations must generally avoid inflicting serious injury or death, or they risk summoning wider audience sympathy with the body in the uniform rather than

---

1   Personal interview (C).

gathering antipathy against the uniform itself.[2] However legitimate and justified such violence might be to the people that police are colonizing—those who Fanon says need violence in the process of decolonization—there are usually important audiences who might not see the police as an enemy. The latter still think of themselves and the police as part of a shared body politic and are likely to see such violence as a threat to themselves. Such mixed audiences might be what led one professional nonviolence trainer I interviewed to explain: "I do think that it's a fluid definition...there is a diversity of tactics and a diversity of things within nonviolence and within violence, so it's really hard to point out what is and what isn't, but the principles that I stick to in Kingian nonviolence are that we should attack forces, not individuals. Attack their behavior, not the person."[3]

What do protesters do, then, if these "forces" are intimately, materially bound to the "individuals" performing them? What if the "behavior" under attack is immediate and physical, such that attacking it risks attacking "the person" as well? The materiality of individuals enacting oppressive behavior isn't easy to divorce from the discursiveness of their role. One nonviolence advocate in the Bay Area tersely addressed this nonseparability in a debate with other demonstrators who insisted on publicly expressing antipathy with the police: "My question is for those who view police as the enemy, or as part of the enemy: What is your end goal? What would victory over the police look like? Does that mean we would lock them all up? Does that mean we would deport them all? Does that mean we would execute them all? When individuals become your enemy as opposed to the behaviors of those individuals and the injustice that they participate in, what does victory over them look like?"[4]

Although his words deny the possibility, public performances resisting the social institution of policing—without necessary focusing on individual police—have certainly been able to attack the role without eliciting sympathy for individual officers. If the institution hides

---

2   As this book goes to press, riots in France do seem to involve some potentially injurious attacks on the bodies of police. Should these persist and intensify, their very occurrence implies a wider legitimacy crisis of the state. For now, at least, such moments are unusual.

3   Personal interview (H).

4   Positive Peace Warrior Network, "How Will the Walls Come Tumbling Down?"

behind police bodies, how do protesters "do violence" to the institution without necessarily harming the bodies that enact it, even if such injury might entail unwelcome political and rhetorical results? How to materially enact this separation? The quotation opening this chapter posits just such a separation, what I term a *disidentification*, as essential to overcoming fear and reclaiming power, not only from the institution of policing but also between the institution and the flesh that momentarily embodies it. One veteran nonviolence trainer in Seattle observed how the tension between body and office might be lessened in actual practice:

> I don't know what I saw but I'm sure there were differences in attitudes around police. I definitely saw a lot of verbal abuse of police coming from some protesters, and pushing and shoving and stuff. I think for me, just personally, like, I know the police play such a repressive role, but to me, that's what I try to focus on, is the role. That's what we need to end, and I don't have any illusions that the police are our friends, or they're there to protect us. No, they're there to protect property and business interests and those kinds of things. But I try, I do believe in recognizing the human being, so attacking the role, challenging the role, but still acknowledging there's a person in there, who has a life and is doing a job that sometimes isn't easy.... I just try to keep in mind it's the role that I don't like, not them in particular—although some of them really are abusive.[5]

The *body* of police need not be the target of empowerment practices. As the quote opening this chapter suggests, fear and disempowerment in the face of neoliberal policing is itself a result of "mixing" the "uniform" or "role" with the human body inside it. People may position themselves differently in regards to non/violence, but the rhetorical performance of separation remains key. The opening quote prioritizes subject-formative empowerment in which the uniform allows a displacement of power: "It's the uniform that is telling you they

---

5   Personal interview (C).

have the power...when in reality it's the people that hold the power." Surrendering one's power and then attributing a "surplus agency" as an inherent quality of what you've surrendered to, recalls Althusser's term "misrecognition," which he considers essential to the constitution of all authorities, and which Bourdieu sees as dependent on a certain "code of gestures":

> What one might call the *liturgical* conditions, namely, the set of prescriptions which govern the *form* of the public manifestation of authority, like ceremonial etiquette, the code of gestures and officially prescribed rites, are clearly only an *element*, albeit the most visible one, in a system of conditions of which the most important and indispensable are those which produce the disposition towards recognition in the sense of misrecognition and belief, that is, the delegation of authority which confers its authority on authorized discourse. By focusing exclusively on the formal conditions for the effectiveness of ritual, one overlooks the fact that the ritual conditions that must be fulfilled in order for ritual to function and for the sacrament to be both *valid* and *effective* are never sufficient as long as the conditions which produce the recognition of this ritual are not met: the language of authority never governs without the collaboration of those it governs, without the help of the social mechanisms capable of producing this complicity, based on misrecognition, which is the basis of all authority.[6]

Public performances of antagonism with police disrupt the "ceremonial etiquette" that causes people to misrecognize their own power as police authority, and allows them to reappropriate the agency they surrendered. Just as profanation reverses the setting-aside mechanism of sacrament to return the object into use, so disidentification undoes the liturgical conditions of authority to return power to "the people." Even when the bodies of police are threatened in clashes, the common implements of those clashes—empty water bottles, paint

---

6   Bourdieu, *Language and Symbolic Power*, 113.

balls, marching bodies, naked arms, raised voices, and uncivil turns of phrase—generally carry little possibility of inflicting serious bodily harm. Even more serious implements rarely cause injury, given the stormtrooper-like gear with which most police enter such conflicts. Yet they are effective in humiliating the dignity of position and interrupting the effectiveness of the uniform. In situations where general antipathy against police becomes more common, attacks on police can become more frequently injurious or lethal, but they are generally rare, particularly within the US.

One slightly ridiculous but illuminating form of noninjurious violence against authorities is *pieing*. This tactic—hitting authority figures in the face with soft, messy pies—also separates body and position through a harmless but humiliating attack. As one nonviolence trainer I interviewed asked, "Is [pieing] violent or nonviolent? It doesn't hurt the person physically, but it hurts their dignity, it hurts their feelings perhaps. It embarrasses or humiliates them and preferably you're doing it with the media right there. So is that violent or nonviolent?"[7] Her description recalls Koestenbaum's insight that "[h]umiliation represents *the destruction of matter*. Something once present, an intactness, a solidity, a substantiality, turns into tatters"—in this case an authority's dignity.[8]

Perhaps the first and most famous instance of counterhegemonic pieing was the 1977 pie attack on beauty queen, country singer, orange-juice advertiser, and antiqueer activist Anita Bryant. Bryant had recently led efforts to repeal antidiscrimination ordinances in Florida, Minnesota, Kansas, and Oregon, and had just succeeded in prohibiting gay adoption in Miami-Dade County, a law only overturned in 2008. In the relatively tolerant 1970s, Bryant was visionary in modeling the future of right-wing punditry. *Advocate* editor David Goodstein bemoaned the pieing as betraying a lack of "professionalism" at the time; however, not everyone in the gay liberation scene agreed with his lament. One article, "Angry as Hell," from the *Gay Community News*, urged its readers, "Let's not feel awful about bustin' Anita's chops.... We can try to be cheap Christ imitators or we can be real."[9]

---

7   Personal interview (C).

8   Koestenbaum, *Humiliation*, 10–11.

9   Quoted in James Darsey, "From 'Gay Is Good' to the Scourge of AIDS: The

The moment Anita Bryant's haughty diatribe about "the homosexuals" is interrupted mid-sentence with a cream pie, her social position as antiqueer crusader is fatally injured and her glamor shattered, suffering in a public sense what Patricia Williams called "spirit murder." Bryant soon withdrew from public life, and she lives in retirement to this day. Even her attempt to gain the upper hand by using a common antigay slur—"At least it was a fruit pie!"—was rendered more sad than threatening by her pitiable condition. Bryant's voice becomes a personal voice, far from any misrecognized pride of place, reflected in the glittering shards of an enunciative position that had seemed so solid just moments before.

Identification with public figures generally relies on an unquestioned sympathy with the unified person, body, and persona. In the moment of the pie attack, a stark disjunction is introduced between the impervious haughtiness claimed by Bryant's social persona and the embarrassment of her pie-covered face. Notably, though, her face and body are not injured in any way, and the effect of the attack would have been quite otherwise if they had been. Her position as a social subject, defined by aggression against others, based on her apparently impervious position to attack and not even acknowledge vulnerability—an appeal to the powerful against the weak—could not accommodate the exposed vulnerability, especially a vulnerability exposed by those very subjects over whom she had always expected to remain powerful. Once the vulnerable has publicly produced even a momentary reversal, her discursive subject position collapses. Her appeal for sympathetic misrecognition with viewers eager to position themselves as impervious and haughty through her performance has collapsed. In the moment that the audience pities her, pity has already replaced deference. The reversal is hardly an adequate revenge, since the pieing seems rather insignificant compared to the harm Bryant has caused to countless queer lives. But it wasn't necessarily intended to be, despite being utterly effective in sabotaging her position to do further harm. This is an example of disidentification, since the previous process which drew audiences to identify with Bryant as a voice of antiqueer power has been disrupted, undone.

Evolution of Gay Liberation Rhetoric, 1977–1990," in Charles E. Morris III and Stephen H. Browne, *Readings on the Rhetoric of Social Protest*, 2nd ed. (State College, PA: Strata Publishing, 2006), 491–92.

Of course, disidentification attempts aren't always successful, and they often leave some audiences aside even in success. Koestenbaum, for one, fails to disidentify with Bryant; indeed, he sympathizes with her in the midst of his dislike:

> I'm no fan of Anita Bryant, who did harm to queers. But I cringe, watching the fruit pie slam into her un-suspecting face. Suddenly, she is no longer a wretched antigay activist. Suddenly, she is a victim, a woman physically assaulted by a male stranger. White cream, the pie's topping, covers her features; it resembles shav-ing foam or whiteface makeup. A few seconds ago, she was a wrong-minded, wrong-acting bigot, but now she has become a humiliated woman, crying in public. I can imagine how wretched I'd feel if someone threw a pie at me; in the capillaries of my cream-coated, hu-miliated face, I'd sense the aggression and hatred that motivated the pie-hurling hand. That's why I don't believe in capital punishment: any murderer weeping and shivering with humiliated fear at the oncoming electrocution earns my clemency. Anita Bryant put her orange-juice fame ("Come to the Florida Sunshine Tree") to noxious uses, but when the pie hits her face and she weeps, she becomes a horrifying, human spec-tacle, a white body smeared with white crap. During the awful instant when Anita Bryant breaks down crying, I suddenly feel guilty for my own aggression against her.[10]

Several complex features surface here. Koestenbaum begins to relate to Bryant through pity rather than resentment or fear, which suggests that, in some sense, the disidentification appeal of the pieing has partially succeeded. Bryant's power of place has certainly been transformed if her body and personal self, distinct from her office, is now available for pity. In another sense, though, Koestenbaum's response means the action was a failure, insofar as he is supposed to be its audience. Though the pie in the video is clearly a *cream* pie,

---

10   Koestenbaum, *Humiliation*, 78–79.

Koestenbaum *accepts* Bryant's antiqueer redefinition of it as a *fruit* pie. By sympathetically allowing her to define the situation, he has already reproduced a moment of antiqueer designation. For Koestenbaum, the genders of Bryant and her assailant gain sudden priority over their sexualities; both are copresent, but in Koestenbaum's reading of the moment, Bryant's femininity (before her assailant's masculine aggression) takes precedence over her antiqueer presence (faced with queer vengeance). In one sense, Koestenbaum identifies with the humiliated Bryant against her attackers, citing the "aggression and hatred" of the assailants as reason for his being unable to identify with them. In another sense, he does identify with the assailants, but only through the guilt of their masculine assault on Bryant's feminine body. There is obviously complex, hegemonic male-on-female violence at play here. But why doesn't Koestenbaum identify more with the attackers than with Bryant? In my research, the attacker's names and stories seem to have been lost to time; certainly Koestenbaum doesn't think to mention them in his analysis. Is it possible that Koestenbaum might feel more sympathetic with the attack if the assailants' figures were in frame, if their stories and reasons and trajectories of humiliation and dignity laid claim to the title bar, their lives present as more than merely Bryant's assailants? The camera frame recording the pieing remains the analytical frame of Koestenbaum's analysis, and the dignity and daily humiliations of the assailants, their subjectivities, remain utterly out of view, even as the author espouses a common sexual identity with them. The fact that Koestenbaum cringes and feels guilty in the face of the *surprising* moment of humiliation reveals a tacit acceptance of the *unsurprising*, systematic, and socially unremarkable humiliation that Bryant caused millions of people in the years before the pie attack. Elsewhere, the poet perceptively calls such everyday humiliation "the background music to our lives" but here allows himself to only see the foreground.[11]

A few pages later, the author confesses his analytical basis for his rejection, and it sounds very much like the objection of nonviolence advocates to the public rage of demonstrator clashes with police. "Aggressive public speech," he says, "humiliates the mouth that utters it, or the hands that type and transcribe and publish it."[12] Consistently

---

11   Ibid., 63.
12   Ibid., 88.

with his guilt about the Bryant pieing, Koestenbaum attends only to the visible instantiation of aggression itself, and never to the place of the aggressive speech within a possibly less visible context of tension, conflict, and power. In his frame, aggression is ahistorical and decontextualized; it remains outside of any network of power relations, the relative positions of subjects and objects of anger, and the differences between hegemonic and counterhegemonic flows of power. It is not, finally, the gendered nature of the Bryant assault that upsets him, but rather public aggression per se, which he frames as exceptional, isolated and excluded from the vast reaches of violence that surrounded it and gave it meaning. Koestenbaum blames humiliation on "aggressive public speech," but what if the regular *silence* of a subject position is always already its humiliation? Wouldn't its aggressive speaking constitute an act of dignity? For so many, daily humiliation lies precisely in patience, in habitual vulnerability and receptivity, in habitual and habituated love for one's abuser. The negation of humiliation, the interruption of its hegemonic reproduction, requires rage, making anger public and material, the opposite of humiliation.

As Koestenbaum reveals, disidentification's audience is never universal; he and Goodstein, in very different ways, elect to sympathize with the humiliation of the hegemonic subject, while the *Gay Community News* and others celebrate "bustin' Anita's chops." A century earlier, proponents of anarchist "propaganda by deed," like Emma Goldman and Peter Kropotkin, noticed a similar effect: "the people," whose interests seem to obviously be opposed to dictators, presidents, and Wall Street bankers, also, were unpredictable in their sympathies in the face of terroristic deeds. Assassinations and bombings tended to establish identification with the powerful *as living bodies*, rather than disidentification as powerful social entities (and enemies). Anarchism became widely identified with terrorism, and in the United States, the FBI was formed, the Palmer Raids enacted, and Goldman deported under the excuse of responding to such attacks. Goldman, Kropotkin, and others recognized the problems with "propaganda by deed" attacks as they came to appreciate the ambivalence of publics. Contemporary rioters are faced with similar ambiguities: police clashes certainly alienate certain audiences, but without reliable metrics to measure such responses, the dilemma persists. Disidentification relies on a shifting *imbalance* of sympathy, for those who firmly sympathize with hegemonic positions are unlikely to completely abandon their beliefs, and even those not sympathetic with such positions might require more direct experience if their own sense of self is to turn against status quo powers.

DISINVESTMENT

While disidentification challenges sympathies and identifications with powerful public figures, other rhetorical strategies work to disaffiliate certain subjects from *their own* position of power. Some people I spoke with made repeated reference to having disaffiliated from their own privileged positions, which helps to answer the obvious question: if the privileged are averse to disidentifying with power because of their own subjective commitments, how can antagonistic politics establish distance *within* individuals from those commitments themselves? Following George Lipsitz, who sees allegiance to privilege less as a state of belief than a subjective *investment* in hegemonic power structures, I see this internal disidentification from one's own privilege as *disinvestment*.[13] The significance of this process for social change is laid out by one nonviolence trainer:

> It just makes me think that police training should include, it really needs to include, more information about their role, and the oppressive role as well as the other roles, so that they cannot take it personally when people do certain things to them. They need to make that distinction. And anyone with privilege needs to do that. So, as white people, we need to recognize that when we're treated in certain ways, it's not because of *us*, it's because of the role of white people. We all need to get better in the areas where we're dominant, or privileged or whatever—at recognizing that difference, and then learning from it, and then not taking it so personally. So, hopefully politicians and CEOs and all those other people…would recognize that.[14]

---

13   George Lipsitz, *The Possessive Investment in Whiteness: How White People Profit from Identity Politics* (Philadelphia: Temple University Press, 2006).

14   Personal interview (C).

In some sense, her personalistic discourse is not the rhetoric of unarmed insurrection. She imagines police training as a potential site for disinvestment, whereas others might respond that police training is expressly for *preventing* this very process—as intensive conditioning in getting police to perform and embody their role, police training must get them to "take it personally." The same could be said for graduate studies and other forms of professional enculturation that produce "politicians and CEOs and all those other people."[15] On rare occasions, police officers *have* turned against their office, as for example in Wisconsin in 2011 and Thailand in 2013. Such instances are frequently espoused by nonviolence advocates as *the* central process of systemic social change as a whole, despite being exceedingly rare. Two things are worth noting here. First, nonviolence advocates often make instances of police defection seem more common by conflating them with defection of *soldiers*. Though the two might initially seem analogous, the institutional differences between policing and the military make them nearly opposites. A thorough comparison of the two institutions would be illuminating, but for now, it's worth emphasizing that soldiers are indoctrinated for confrontation only with foreign Others and historically have allied themselves with domestic populations *much* more frequently. Police, by contrast, are trained and enculturated to manage precisely those populations nonviolence advocates hope they will join. Some proponents of insurrectionary politics I interviewed described the moment when the army refuses to come out against its domestic population as the true limit case of revolution—which is to say that they define revolution through the very contrast of army and police. Secondly, antagonism can inspire sympathy as well as antipathy; in the rare historical instances of police defection, it was often because of, rather than in spite of, protester antagonism that individual police and other status quo subjects became sympathetic. The Tupamaros guerrilla movement of Uruguay, for example, did not avoid conflict with police or army forces but nonetheless found many supporters within their ranks.[16] The guerrillas often robbed banks, not only to finance their actions, but also as a

---

15   See Jeff Schmidt, *Disciplined Minds: A Critical Look at Salaried Professionals and the Soul-battering System That Shapes Their Lives* (Lanham, MD: Rowman & Littlefield, 2000).

16   Alain Labrousse, *The Tupamaros* (New York: Penguin Books, 1973).

challenge to the legitimacy of capitalist relations and to highlight the root causes of economic turmoil. Perhaps surprisingly, "[a]mong the lower middle classes, the Union of Bank Employees contains many supporters of the Tupamaros."[17] Despite its somewhat macho logic, perhaps there is some truth to the idea that sometimes the only way to acknowledge another's humanity is by fighting them.

It is through *investment* in privilege, rather than the mere cultural-material fact of one's status, that most subjects remain hesitant to engage in systemic change. The people who described to me going through a process of disinvestment, saw it primarily as a transfer of emotional commitments rather than a matter of intellect and opinion. "I guess you could say I went from having opinions and feelings about politics, to having political opinions and feelings. In some way, politics became much more vital and present to me, and I started to think of my political beliefs primarily in terms of ethics as opposed to analyses. Of course, I wouldn't say that my basic framework for looking at the world has changed, but the way I *perceive* the world, in relation to myself, has deepened a lot."[18] As we will see, disinvestment nearly always involves both concrete, emotionally intense experiences and a context of conversation to solidify these shifts.

One young Black woman told me how, before Occupy Seattle, she had never known how to respond to displays of racism, however much she understood them intellectually. Even within the Occupy camp, "I would hear [these people who] would talk and say derogatory things about the people of color caucus.... I hear that, I'm hearing them say that and I just like have this gut reaction that's so fucked up. Like, I can't figure it out and I don't know really why."[19] Then, one night in a large general assembly, a police officer insisted on standing in the middle of a meeting, and a heated confrontation ensued around whether he should be allowed to remain. The People of Color Caucus of perhaps one hundred people broke with the main meeting, walking away in mass as an expression of refusal to interact with the police. "As soon as that happened, and I went over and I was with the people of color caucus and they were talking. *I finally fucking got it.* It was really empowering, in a sense; it was really encouraging, and it just, I

---

17   Ibid., 118.

18   Personal interview (D).

19   Personal interview (M).

dunno, it just really woke me up to a lot of shit that I had been part of being silent about…before, but not really knowing. And part of that is my fault for not trying to figure it out, because I *knew*."

That this experience involved both conversation and an emotionally intense immediacy of physical confrontation with power is typical of the disinvestment narratives I heard. Language is a medium, perhaps the archetypal medium, of meaning making, but the immediacy here indicates the importance of a catalytic nonlinguistic event to distance the subject from their privileged investments. Asked to narrate his own disinvestment process, another protester described a central moment in his transformation. He had just been released from jail for a nonviolent civil disobedience action and describes catching up to friends in a march just in time to get caught in a conflict:

> Right when we get there we see one of our friends, who had been outside the bank with us, and he was trying to help somebody up, and this *huge* guy in a ski mask jumps him and tackles him to the ground. I thought it was [another protester], over some disagreement, so I ran towards them to break them up. All of a sudden, we're surrounded by cops. The cops are establishing a perimeter, very, very fast, very, very forcefully, and I'm still going towards them and one of the cops just grabs me and throws me and he's hitting me with his baton, throwing me back. Then I realize that my friend is now being turned over and handcuffed and that this guy is an undercover cop. All things considered, I was fine out of that, barely bruised, but *the immediacy of that was very shocking*. My friend gets up and he's screaming, blood pouring out of his mouth.[20]

That a measure of emotional intensity might be necessary to rupture one's investment in privilege is not a new idea. As Arthur Koestler says, "To unlearn is more difficult than to learn; and it seems that the task of breaking up rigid cognitive structures and reassembling them

---

20   Personal interview (D).

into a new synthesis cannot, as a rule, be performed in the full daylight of the conscious, rational mind."[21]

This immediacy is experienced as an unavoidable, sudden presencing of usually hidden everyday violence. The very intensity of risk—and risk shared with others—can work to destabilize the distance that keeps subjects attached to their own privilege. The same protester continued, "All my life it's something that's happened to somebody else, that I've always been very sheltered from—and all of a sudden there was the possibility that some cop would feel that it was really necessary to swing his night stick at my head, shoot a pepper ball at me or whatever, you know? It didn't happen, but stepping even that tiny little bit outside of the acceptable ranges of behavior meant that all of a sudden I was subject to that possibility."

What began as moments of fear is suddenly embraced as a consequence of risk. Instead of taking shelter within an involuntary privilege into which one was born, the subject experiences an intimacy of shared risk in the choice to remain present with others. The privilege that previously elicited comfort soon coalesces into something repulsive, offensive, threatening. People who may not have noticed their privilege, or who viewed it only intellectually, or with guilt as something they are stuck with, begin to see it as something external to their deeper selves, an outside threat embodied in the violence of the brutal agents of the status quo. Attachments and investments suddenly become visible and repulsive, attachments expelled in a sort of antibody mechanism that seeks to rid the body of institutional affiliations as actual threats:

> I was at the time actively engaged in something that I was fully aware that the police and the government did not want me to do. So that, in and of itself, gave a slightly different context than a university classroom or an AmeriCorps team meeting, which is where I did a lot of antiracism training and education.... So, I mean, it was already at this point, obvious the police are not allies, the city government is not an ally here—I'm not going to be protected by them, and that's one thing, right? I guess on a psychological level not having that

---

21   Arthur Koestler, quoted in Nieburg, *Political Violence*, 18.

protection means that I also am not going to protect them…I never thought about that, but, at this point, there were cops lining up with mace and shit, to stand there and fuck with us. *They are clearly not there to protect me, so* [laughing] *why am I going to protect them?* [22]

Of course, such intense conflictual moments do not *always* result in disinvestment—sometimes, a visceral repulsion can take the place of a privileged affiliation but result in a simple individualized trauma. Personal repulsion does not equal political disinvestment; if people don't learn to extend their repulsion, they may wind up either repressing the experience or receding into lonely isolation of anomie and horror. For disinvestment to carry through and create subjects willing to challenge the system from which their own privilege derives, an extension beyond the isolated self must take place through what we might call analogies of repulsion. The same protester eloquently narrated this stage of his disinvestment process, his repulsion viscerally and sympathetically expanding into others' situations, as he saw with new eyes the criminal justice process while awaiting his trial:

> By US standards and by world standards, I'm extremely well educated. I've gone to very good public schools my entire life. Raised on a culture that basically the education system and the criminal justice system are both built on, I would consider myself relatively intelligent, and yet, I sit in these courtrooms and I have no idea what's going on. I mean, if I didn't have a lawyer, I would just be completely lost. So if *I* don't understand it, you take any of those elements of *my* background away, and anybody who doesn't speak English, who's from another country, who didn't go to college, didn't graduate high school, didn't have a lawyer, is just from another culture—I mean, they are completely *fucked*, they have no hope. The first time I went in for a pretrial hearing, we sat in the courtroom for like an hour waiting for them to call our case, we

---

22 Personal interview (D).

watched six, seven cases come before us, about half were in prison jumpsuits, so they were coming out of being locked-up. I think out of six cases before us, five people were people of color, all of them were pretty poor, all of them were just listening to what their attorneys told them and basically just saying, yes, sure, and there's a judge sitting at the front of the room deciding what punishments these people merit, what's going to happen to them, what their lives are going to be like for the next 60, 90, 120 [days], a year, and like, all they could do is sit there. One guy started crying because he didn't understand what was going on, you know? And that shit is just sick. You can read all the statistics you want, and I mean, that's like the tiniest sliver, but, [you have] no choice at that point, you know? It goes against so much of what I was raised to believe about this country, or maybe it doesn't, but the immediacy of it made me think, made me reconsider a lot.[23]

In order to stabilize as political, the disinvestment process requires comparisons that separate the unavoidable *availability* of privilege from the avoidable but difficult refusal to take a privileged *stance*—a distinction that ultimately depends as much on the mediation of language as on the immediacy of repulsion, pride, and shame:

I have a totally sweet life, realistically speaking. I live in a nice house with good people that I care about. I have a job that I enjoy doing that more or less pays my rent most months. I can sit in a nice little yuppie bar with you and have abstract conversations about violence.... But knowing that all of that is predicated upon really horrible shit that I would never be able to watch being done to other people somewhere else. I mean, here, but somewhere else even here, for my benefit and with my assumed consent, is sickening.... I don't know exactly where to go with that in my life,

---

23 Ibid.

but I'd be really ashamed of myself if I ever turned my back on that. [24]

His involvement in protest leads to a sort of subjective extension; his immediately personal life is still privileged, but his selfhood, his social self, has reached beyond the protected sphere of his own physical life. What is needed for this to happen? An immediate intensity destabilizes and opens up the self, but then a new self is constituted through social networks, reflection, and discussion. In another protester's words,

> I think experiences are more powerful, for sure, but I think that they work together too…. Let's say that, someone was in the anticop general assembly, talking about it, and they didn't really agree, but they heard some people crying or talking really powerfully about why they're against the police, in a sort of really personal way. And then this person is sort of like, well that's heartbreaking, but it's just a few bad apples. But then they're at a protest and they get pepper-sprayed and all of sudden they're like, wait a second, this is fucked up. And it's a combination of both. One reinforces the other. [25]

Shaken by a moment of danger, the privileged listening subject is less able to ignore the narrated traumas of others or devalue them with naturalizations and justifications. "Stories that might have kind of bounced off some layer of armor at another point in my life just went straight in." [26] This listening, in turn, provides rudimentary discursive trails that the tender feet of the newly disinvested begin to walk with their own experiences:

> Some of the people of color that I've had really long conversations with have been really radical people, and it's been really deep for me to see how, in so many ways

---

24 Ibid.

25 Personal interview (L).

26 Personal interview (D).

we actually grew up living in totally different worlds. In some ways, that's one of the most important things… that it gave us this space to cross paths and start talking, when we would never have before. It's pretty hard to argue with a lot of people's experiences. People telling me about getting radicalized in prison, or prohibited from leaving the country. Watching somebody get shot in the chest with a tear-gas canister in Palestine and die— each one of those is a real story that someone's told me. I mean, how do you argue with that, honestly? How could you possibly? I guess I always knew, theoretically on some level, that the exercise of authority depended at root on violence, and not abstract violence, but people getting hit and beaten and tortured and shot…. I mean, I haven't seen anybody get beaten or injured or shot, but also the effect of seeing how ready the police were to do that, if they were ordered to or if the situation got out of control…they could be literally smiling and joking with someone [one moment] and turn around and pull their guns out and shoot them the next.

These spaces of transformation do not work primarily at an individual level; they are not only a movement of intensities within bodies in time but also between or across them. This "communism" of emotions recalls Ahmed's insight that affects are essential social material, more like *drives* in circulation across permeable boundaries of self than psychological emotions confined in an individual mind:

Well, because it was really personal, too, and people were crying, talking about their personal accounts, I think that, I have to believe that some of these people that were…for example were pro-cop or whatnot, had probably not even thought about police terrorizing immigrant communities. Or if they had, they don't think about it, because it's not part of their life. And that these sort of personalized experiences…[you] can't discount the raw emotional element of it.[27]

27 Personal interview (L).

These affects are relations rather than substances. When one protester explained why she previously hadn't gone through the process of disinvestment, she said it was "because I didn't have relationships with people who had experienced violence. Because I wasn't confronted with it in a very obvious way."[28] These circulations occurred not only between individuals but also across differentials in social power, which is exactly what made them startlingly effective, at times unraveling discursive formations centuries in the making. Suddenly, what had seemed natural and unquestionable was open to question, as in this description of conversations in protest situations: "White people probably never really thought about [it]…they maybe thought about genocide, but not about the land they're standing on as stolen indigenous land, those kinds of things. Real conversations that were emotional accounts from people who have a much different position in society from most other people—they don't ever have to hear things like that."[29]

We must not forget that these extraordinary spaces of transformation, where actual communication takes place across the divides that rule our society, did not exist in the absence of violence; indeed, in some way, they existed *because* of it. In the testimonies of many of those I interviewed, it was precisely shared antagonism with the police that opened up these spaces. Since it is the place of police to reproduce and instantiate the social relations of privilege and inequality with their very presence, potential or actual, such moments of temporary equality depended on the absence of police. And, since it is the primarily role of policing in neoliberalism to perform omnipotence and omnipresence in control of public space, this momentary absence of police always already constituted an antagonism, a clash.

EMPOWERING REVERSAL

While disinvestment works to distance a subject through his or her own previous position of privilege, one can certainly have a recognition of distance from privilege without having any idea or inclination to act. To act against one's privilege, people have to go beyond mere knowledge of injustice and somehow come to feel their power

---

28 Personal interview (M).

29 Personal interview (L).

to fight it. In overcoming the incapacitation by which dissent has so long been managed, one must know one's own capacity to affect the world—the fear has to break. In an extended example, one member of Occupy Patriarchy, a bloc of radical queers and feminists in Oakland, sat up as she heard one speaker assert during a 2012 public debate on non/violence that "I totally think the black bloc and property destruction is violent, that's what we're playing with. We're playing with scaring people; we're playing with intimidation. Intimidation is violence."[30] Her reaction encompasses what we will call the rhetorical strategy of *empowering reversal*, frequently and consciously enacted during contemporary riots, particularly in terms of destabilizing gender hegemony:

> I was like, oh, you're totally right. It's easier to constantly think about, "You guys, it's trashing a Starbucks window—what are you guys complaining about? It's not violence; what about all the violence in the world?" But I think the other very real thing is that, tiny folks from Occupy Patriarchy with the shields, you know, me, whoever, what we're playing with is violence.... We're scared all the time and we want to be scary too. You know? We're scared of you; we're going to tell you we're not scared of you anymore. We wanna take on feeling tough because we're constantly intimidated by the world in yay number of ways. I think that that's really real. And people are playing with it, and people are experimenting, people are *trying on* being violent, or being scary, you know? Because, at least any female person has the experience of being scared a lot. Whether we feel that way on a day-to-day basis as an adult, we've felt that way in our life, we've felt physically intimidated by people. So it's like, oh! I have in my life felt physically intimidated by people, what would it be like to physically intimidate someone else? And I don't think that's a bad thing.[31]

---

30 Positive Peace Warrior Network, "How Will the Walls Come Tumbling Down?"

31 Personal interview (O).

Another Occupy Patriarchy militant discussed this rhetorical strategy as analogous to reclaiming agency through resignification of sex work and domesticity practices. Though the spheres of sex work and domesticity are often the *terrain* of patriarchal power, the "spaces that have formally been used against" women, empowerment may take the form of appropriating and repurposing, rather than ceding, this terrain:

> I feel like a lot of my friends who are radical and also do sex work have a very similar understanding [to rioting] of the work that they do.... You can't go back into this space without necessarily feeling this stuff, but...you can actually, like, use your trauma and use these spaces that have formally been used against you to actually undo them, and watch them unravel. I've been really into women's weaving words as of late to describe revolutionary tactics. I feel like since the '70s, there hasn't been this whole, like, the women's peace actions in the early '80s, late '70s, where they wove the doors of the Pentagon closed...and I was like, oh man, I was never there for those but, I wish I had been, talk about fucking embracing domesticity and making it radical as fuck, like yeah, let's go weave the doors of the Pentagon shut![32]

The idea that police clashes could be opportunities for empowering reversal for women and queers runs squarely counter to the gendered and racialized dismissal of protesters as "tantruming" white male anarchists; it delegitimizes, invisibilizes, and in the terms of my analysis, *contains the transgression* of queer/feminist riot. A second member of Occupy Patriarchy explained,

> The problem is that it kind of becomes reified because so many people are talking about, "Oh it's this bunch of white male punk dudes that are doing all this shit."... What gets obscured when you start talking about, or when you start whitewashing the black

---

32 Personal interview (B).

bloc first of all—which in Oakland is, absolutely not true—and you start making the black bloc as a gendered thing is, not only do you not see that…[but] there have been radical feminists that have *always* been violent according to this narrative…like, the first gay pride was a riot. You know? Queers have always been violent, feminists have always been violent, and what happens when they control that narrative about who the black bloc is…it disempowers everyone that has been doing all of this work.

Discourses about riot can do complex work: the same indexes of disprivilege that mark riots as authentic also mark them as transgressive. Narratives about tantruming white boys that, as we have seen, delegitimize in racial terms ("white" as inauthentic), simultaneously work to *contain* transgression in gender terms ("male" rioters are expected, thus not threatening to hegemonic roles). In the contemporary American imaginary, young Black males are the subjects of riot; simultaneously disprivileged, heteronormative, and hypermasculine. However terrifying the notion of Black male riots are to the suburban white imaginary, they can be said to "make sense," even to reinforce the racist symbolic order, which legitimizes systemic violence against Black men by marking them as inherently criminal and dangerous. It is precisely for this reason that Katz's logics of containment, management, and repression, what recent scholars have termed "counterinsurgency," focus on Black males as their primary targets.[33] Contemporary riots have recognized this threat by diversifying in gender terms, if indeed they were ever even male in the first place: photos of the Oscar Grant riots in Oakland, for example, reveal them to have a considerable proportion of female participants. Indeed, the disruptive genius of Black Lives Matter has been led primarily by queer Black women, insofar as it has been "led" at all. Describing any of these disruptive actions, including moments of riot, as somehow inherently macho and masculine reveals only the total ignorance, or the bad faith, of the speaker.

When I asked the demonstrator above, referencing King's "the voice of the voiceless," whether people riot just because they can't be

33 Williams et al., eds., *Life during Wartime: Resisting Counterinsurgency* (Oakland: AK Press, 2013).

heard, she responded in frustration, insisting on the complexity of these moments where emotions become material, which gets lost in the Oedipal drone of "tantruming" claims. She described such claims as not only wrong, but painful and offensive:

> There's a lot of pent-up emotion for a lot of people in those moments. With that question, I wonder what that means. Does that mean that we are inarticulate, does that mean we have no other venues to express ourselves adequately at all?... I mean, I feel like there are things that can be expressed emotionally through fighting the police, that other ways of expressing them are not as satisfying.... [T]he classic cliché of, like, we're just a bunch of people regressing into, like, rebellious boys fighting the stern father.... It's just like, fuck you. It's horrible. It's just so boring.

What are the stakes here? If tantruming is *male*—which fails even as a metaphor; female children are just as likely to throw tantrums!—the potentially counterhegemonic, transgressive meanings of a feminist/queer riot are foreclosed. This demonstrator went on to explain this as *fear* of any interpretation, of riot that breaks with preexisting, heteronormative, hegemonic categorization schemes:

> If it becomes feminists and queers rioting in the streets, then everything is over. [Laughs] That's the end right there, that's really what people really are scared of. And women particularly, if you look at queer liberation or feminism, there is this terrified portion of American society that's just, like, radical women out in the streets fucking shit up? That really, really scares people. Whereas a young white man in a mask, that's something that they almost can, they have a place for it in their heads. Whereas if you're coming from this background where women are supposed to inhabit this role, to not only break out of that role but to break out of it in a way that's deemed violent—it's terrifying to people.

While the same actions carried out by straight white males might be equally *illegal*, the need to translate the queer/feminist riot into a bunch of boys reveals the extent to which feminist/queer violence is profoundly more *disruptive*—not only of state power but of the heteronormative-patriarchal complex on which it rests. The destructive power of subjects presumed to be passive, who take violent agency in the face of the very figures possessing Weber's "legitimate use of physical force in a given territory," is too powerful a semiotic disruption to gain space in representation. Indeed, its power can be measured by the extent to which dominant discourses try to hide and deny it. When it succeeds, such reversal makes manifest the patriarchal mechanism that covertly legitimizes only men to employ force.

If empowering reversal primarily seeks to catalyze new subjective possibilities through mass media, the strategy usually fails. For the most part, only those actually present at these riots were even aware of their gender demographics. But if it fails as a mediated appeal, what *does* it do? The people I spoke to indicated not only that they didn't really know what wider publics had to say about the actions, but often that they had not even thought about it before. Their focus on engaging the direct *demos* of women/queers was a new form of that most feminist of commitments: "the personal is political." One demonstrator described her sense of what happened when people battled the riot cops who (successfully) stopped a march of thousands who were heading to occupy a building in downtown Oakland:[34]

> I wanted folks to have some type of satisfying display of how they felt. I think that really is a big deal. Standing there impotently, we feel like, ugh! People don't feel proud; they feel weak, they feel helpless.... You know, when Oak Street happened, people felt proud, they felt inspired, they felt unified, and those are all important things to feel somehow, right?.... I just hoped people would have that opportunity that day because, well, we didn't get to [occupy the building] which would have been one way of physically manifesting,

---

34 For more on this action, see *The Battle of Oakland*, a 2012 film by Brandon Jourdan and David Martinez that is available at http://www.globaluprisings.org /the-battle-of-oakland.

physicalizing our emotions and our dreams and as-
pirations—which was taking a building, also totally
symbolic. So fighting the police is also symbolic, and
physical....

A bunch of people from Occupy Patriarchy took
the shields and they were like the rowdy people on the
front lines of Oak Street. I remember walking down
that line of people with a bullhorn and, like, "You guys
ready? You want to go up again?" And they were, like
[in a high-pitched voice], "Yeah! Yeah! Yeah! Yeah!"
[Laughs] They were *so excited*. And they were so unified.... I think this is a very common experience, and
certainly, from the meetings I've been in with Occupy
Patriarchy, it's a lot of women and queer people, and
they *want* to be militant. And because of what that
means to them, they want to be tough and radical, and
they want opportunities to practice this, to work it out
with other people. To practice this and get better at it.
And the fact was that on that particular day, whatever
fuckups happened, they got to feel tough and bad-ass
and militant, and unified. It was really awesome.[35]

The importance of such reversals for transforming disempowered
subjects is hardly a new observation. Brison makes the same point
while recounting her long recovery from the trauma of being brutally
raped and nearly murdered. She makes the mechanics of this process
clear, suggesting as well that the feminist/queer counterhegemonic
riot seeks to not simply limit and dismantle the space of heteronor-
mativity and patriarchy but also, in doing so, to create public spaces
for intimate healing of the self:

The incompatibility of fear of my assailant and appropriate anger toward him became most apparent after
I began taking a women's self-defense class. It became
clear that the way to break out of the double bind of
self-blame versus powerlessness was through empowerment—physical as well as political. Learning to fight

---

35   Personal interview (O).

back is a crucial part of this process, not only because it enables us to experience justified, healing rage, but also because, as Iris Young has observed in her essay "Throwing Like a Girl," "women in sexist society are physically handicapped," moving about hesitantly, fearfully, in a constricted lived space, routinely underestimating what strength we actually have. We have to learn to feel entitled to occupy space, to defend ourselves. The hardest thing for most of the women in my self-defense class to do was simply to yell "No!" Women have been taught not to fight back when being attacked, to rely instead on placating or pleading with one's assailant—strategies that researchers have found to be least effective in resisting rape.… The confidence I gained from learning how to fight back effectively not only enabled me to walk down the street again, it gave me back my life.[36]

In *The Will to Empower: Democratic Citizens and other Subjects*, Barbara Cruikshank provides a trenchant critique of contemporary empowerment projects and discourses, which frequently *subtract* agency from their subjects as they attempt to form them in ways capable of access to existing channels of power.[37] Many people I talked to demonstrated a similar reluctance around the term, all too aware of its implications of institutional recuperation. Yet they often returned to it, padded with apologies and hedge words, as an essential category in their repertoire. "I think that people need to have a sense of agency if they want to engage in any sort of revolutionary movement.… For themselves and for their movement to be sustainable, people need to feel…I don't know another word for it…*empowered*, or feel like you're relevant, and that you're doing something and changing something."[38]

Another person gives a powerful account of counterhegemonic reversal that turns primarily on a reluctant dependence on this sometimes degraded but unavoidable term:

---

36 Brison, *Aftermath*, 14–15.

37 Barbara Cruikshank, *The Will to Empower: Democratic Citizens and Other Subjects* (Ithaca, NY: Cornell University Press, 1999).

38 Personal interview (A).

[We] went to the range on Valentine's Day, like we do every year. We shoot up paper, heart-shaped doilies. It's our Valentine's Day trip. But I took this person who'd never gone before and afterwards I was driving them home, and they just started crying. They were, like, that felt [pause] *empowering.* [Laughs] And they were talking about what it meant to have something to do on Valentine's Day when they're single and isolated. But they were just, like, I have never shot a gun before that felt...em...powering. And I said, that's what we're trying to do. And it's just, like, that is a person who doesn't have much at all that gives them joy in their life right now. And they did something—it was exciting, obviously it was about having a specific kind of violent power. I think it was about being able to defend one's own perimeter in a certain way, express oneself in a certain way, and you know they just started crying. They were, like, that felt...I don't think it was a word that they were particularly comfortable with, that they don't use very much either, but they were, like, that felt...what's the word? [Pause] Empowering. I was, like, that's why we're here, that's why we do this. And it's just about, like, things that make you feel comfortable in your own skin, things that make you feel like you can stand up to other people, all that.[39]

Both speakers are negotiating the different, and very charged, senses caught within the word—the institutionally recuperated "empowerment" of inclusion and access, in tension with the empowerment of counterhegemonic reversal. They first offer somewhat guilty apologies, and then they move beyond their hesitation to offer their own reclaimed usage, providing enough detail to establish that their definition is *not* the recuperated dissent Cruikshank describes. Rather than a process aimed at inclusion in current social structures, it develops capacities of subjectivity and affect quite at odds with them. Radicals can be very clear about this distinction:

---

39   Personal interview (O).

When I was in high school, I was organizing with queer youth empowerment organizations. Their whole thing is: we want to empower you, but we're doing it through this hierarchical process. We're a nonprofit and we're getting funding from these people, and we're going to give you. We're going to let you guys organize yourselves, but we're going to *let* you do it. It's not like you *can* do it, and you *should* do it, and you should be doing it anyway, and you should just be expropriating the stuff that you need, instead of relying on nonprofits to serve you.

This is something that a lot of queer youth experience through the nonprofit industrial complex, of getting queer assistance from any of these nonprofits that operate in the city. It's a survival thing, but it's also incredibly disempowering, because it's coming from this hierarchical institution, necessarily. And so you don't [get] the understanding early on that we have fucking power, and that our power is not something that needs to be asked for, it's there already, it's ours already. We just need to reach out and grasp at it and hopefully get it in the palm of our hands initially. And if not, then, well, keep grasping. If I'd seen that shit when I was in high school, I would have been, I mean, I definitely would not have tried to kill myself a whole bunch of times. I definitely would never have run away from home. I never would have had these really traumatic experiences that are all byproducts of capitalism: living in a shitty home, coming from a working-class background where everyone is fucking miserable and nobody has the capacity to break out of the environment that they are [in]…. I really wish that I had had that when I was younger…. I look back on how awful it was to be a teenager and am, like, man, if I'd seen that kind of stuff, just, you know, yeah, in the media—if I had seen pictures of queers rioting in the street and just being, like, fuck you, patriarchy! Fuck you, compulsory monogamy! Fuck you, all this shit! Man, it would have been a whole 'nother thing.[40]

---

40   Personal interview (B).

In the struggle over meanings of empowerment, radical subjects reveal their dependence on the deep rhetorical power of strategies of reversal. The recuperated inclusion fostered by the nonprofit sphere pales before the counterhegemonic rioter's material, embodied, and immediately liberatory transgression, one whose power persists even when the media attempts to present it as unexceptional "tantruming."

BACKLIGHTING

I would say that property destruction is an important tactic in the fight against capitalism.... For one, it solidifies for us and reminds us that the powers we fight are not abstract and insurmountable. They are vulnerable to attack.

—Kerry Cunneen, speaking from hiding as she avoided a federal grand jury subpoena for alleged involvement in the 2012 Seattle May Day riot[41]

Possibly the most obvious and widespread rhetorical strategy at play in the noninjurious violence of contemporary protest, in acts of both targeted property destruction and clashes with police, is what I call *backlighting* the state. I've explored some of the relevance of this strategy under neoliberal conditions in Chapter 1: backlighting embarrasses what Wacquant calls the "grandeur of the penal state" by challenging the state's monopoly on violence. Backlighting shares discursive, rhetorical approaches with guerrilla warfare, but not material ones: it seeks to trip the state up in a situation of asymmetric conflict but does not seek to "seize power," or "break the back" of the state, or to directly make its function *materially* impossible outside the moment of performance. Like the strategic nonviolence of Sharp and Lakey discussed in Chapter 2, backlighting relies on the "political jiu-jitsu" and "dilemma demonstrations" evoked by shows of public rage rather than force of arms; it seeks to publicly perform collective potential, to "open space" for resistance which, in the minds of some practitioners, itself presents an insurrectionary undoing of status quo regimes of power, sometimes gradual, sometimes decisive.

---

41   Kerry Cunneen, "Interview with Kerry Cunneen," *Finn's Revolution* radio program, WUSB, January 22, 2013. Transcript available at https://nopolitical repression.wordpress.com/2013/01/24/radio-interview-with-kerry-cunneen.

Forced comparison, desubjectification, and profanation revolve primarily around targeted property destruction, while disidentification, disinvestment, and empowering reversals emerge from clashes with the police. Backlighting happens in both. Protesters, for instance, carry out "spray painting and breaking windows for the purpose of claiming space and showing that you're not in control, "you" being the police."[42] Property destruction as claiming space and taking control is inherently a rhetorical clash with the state, designed precisely to show the limits of state power. For a moment, it might be helpful to compare backlighting to previous strategies. Backlighting does not attempt to erase its subject (as desubjectification does), but to situate it in a finite, thinkable matter; to delineate the infinite; to demonstrate the contingency of that which claims to be absolute; and, in an often indirect correlative, to form new subjects who assume the space made available in this retreat of the infinite. In contrast to disidentification, backlighting does not presume to sever identification with a powerful subject, nor is it immediately concerned with transforming the subjectivity of its practitioner as are disinvestment and empowering reversals, though this is certainly a desired consequence. More akin to the discursive mechanisms of comparison and profanation—although while these two strategies contest the arrangement, equivalence, and ranking of *values*—backlighting seeks in particular to point up new configurations of *potential* and *foreclosure*, "making space" for the former through the public rolling back of the spatial claims of the latter.

After the WTO protests in Seattle, one group celebrated the end of decades of "disruptive deficit" and the institutionalization of dissent by boasting, "Again the poor and working class the world over were reminded that the ruling class is not *omnipotent*, not even in their primary home nation."[43] Six years later, after the dismal period of George W. Bush's first term, the September 11 attacks, and the onset of the Iraq War, another group traveled from West Michigan to Bush's inaugural procession and used similar language to describe the experience, ebullient in the momentary rupture of the era's stifling fear (protesters nearly stopped the presidential procession at several points): "In an environment of domestic war and increasing repression of dissent, we came and confronted the power of the state and dared to act for what

---

42   Personal interview (J).

43   Van Deusen and Massot, *Black Bloc Papers*, 41.

we dream. This was the first successful unpermitted mass action since 9/11, reinvigorating a culture of direct action and moving away from liberal coalitions that are content with sign-waving in pig-pens.... Despite the gallons of pepper spray and repressive tactics of the state, most participants came away from the action feeling positive about it.... *We proved to ourselves that the state is not all powerful and we have the power to challenge it."*[44]

One person I talked to clarified the importance of the emotional and subjective aspects of backlighting, of how "physicalizing their anger" can open spaces made available by the temporary retreat of policing powers, and by the act of forcing this temporary retreat:

> I would say, the moment when people start fighting the state physically—when people start physicalizing their anger, start striking back at corporations, at symbols of the state, and obviously the police, who are the human element of the state—all that tension, all that violence becomes immediate and becomes visible, and becomes physical, and I think that's not to be underestimated. The chance to be able to *physically express and feel that rage*, because there's not a lot of ways to do that....
>
> [S]houting "Who's streets? Our streets!" when you have police on either side of you and in front and back of you, and you're walking down the street, just has to be irony. You know? There's really no other way to see that. Because they're not our streets. The police are there to make sure that those aren't our streets. On a day-to-day level, not even just within a demonstration. And the moments when we are willing to fight for the streets and take them, is as close as I've ever felt to actually having the streets. And that may only be five minutes, that may only be ten minutes, that may be a few hours, but it is in that struggle, I think, that we come the closest. I honestly don't want to say that that's the only real form of political expression, that is really not what I'm saying at all, but it is a unique form of

---

44 Ibid., 334.

political expression that brings its own rewards, which
are very different than other forms. It has its own risks,
it has its own problems, just like all forms of political
expression.[45]

This person is pointing to backlighting's power to force comparisons, to make "immediate," "visible," and "physical" the implicit
violence of the everyday; by making obvious the backgrounded,
the limited and still large potency of the status quo is made relative
to its challengers, no longer absolute. Standing before the concrete
manifestation of systemic violence—for example, a line of riot police or soldiers lobbing tear gas and wielding batons and less-lethal
weaponry—the protester has little choice beyond fight or flight.
They can seek escape because they fear for their safety or that of
other members of their ephemeral community. Or they can give
themselves over to impudence, insolence, anger. The latter choice,
in Brison's description of her recovery, is already empowering in
itself, replacing a subordinate position with a more level one: "I
found it almost impossible to get angry with my assailant. I think
the terror I still felt precluded the appropriate angry response. It
may be that experiencing anger toward an attacker requires imag-
ining oneself in proximity to him, *a prospect too frightening for a
victim in the early stages of recovery to conjure up.* As Aristotle observed in the *Rhetoric*, Book I, 'no one grows angry with a person
on whom there is no prospect of taking vengeance, and we feel
comparatively little anger, or none at all, with those who are much
our superiors in power.'"[46]

The unyielding "grandeur of the penal state" presents its own vulnerability—it trips to cover up the ease with which it might be punc-
tured and prodded, and *mocked*. The farcical character of backlighting
is always close at hand. Communication scholar M. Lane Bruner con-
tends that "humorless" tendencies of the state leave it particularly vulnerable to destabilization through the public humor of carnivalesque
protest, particularly when "those benefiting from rampant political
corruption lose their sense of humor, [and thus] become ridiculous
in their seriousness, but are incapable, for one reason or another, of

---

45   Personal interview (J).

46   Brison, *Aftermath*, 13.

silencing their prankster publics."[47] In Bruner's theory, social movements often seek to create and define social environments of public transgression and destabilization of meaning, precisely because the state, constituted as serious and somber, is incapable of negotiating such semiotic terrain.

The cover of the Seattle anarchist journal *Tides of Flame*, in its first issue after the May Day riot, bears out Bruner's claim. It depicts two holes shattering what might be a pane of window glass (a clear reference to property destruction) overlaid, in absurdly bold, large letters, with the words, "HA HA HA." Although the list of contents below the image mentions May Day and violence, the image seems to stand on its own. In the face of official interpretations of the May Day events as sullen, threatening thuggery and brute explosions of pent-up unconscious frustration, the juxtaposition manifests the core claim of backlighting: "We got away with it, so there!" Rather than speaking truth to power, backlighting might be said to talk shit to power. In a moment rife with desubjectification and disidentification, guiding their audience away from the point of view (invariably represented in media coverage) of the business owners and representatives of state agencies whose windows were broken, the image invites spectators (frustrated by a lack of agency) to identify with the antagonistic subjects who, for a moment, perform their power in calling the bluff of neoliberal policing's claims of omnipotence.

In another image that has become an iconic representation of the May Day riot, Assistant Police Chief Mike Sanford trips and stumbles as he rushes out from police lines toward a crowd of Black Bloc demonstrators. The photo might have been one of Sanford's renegade

---

47 M. Lane Bruner, "Carnivalesque Protest and the Humorless State," *Text and Performance Quarterly* 25, no. 2 (2005): 136.

Photo credit: Alex Garland

heroism, a passion so great as to drive him to risk his personal safety in order to take a stand—the bureaucrat-turned-hero. But, catching the cop in awkward mid-stumble, the image becomes slapstick. The black-clad protesters, far from threatening, all seem to be moving backward or aside, trying to get out of the way of the blundering bull. They seem hesitant and concerned. Sanford, the official tasked with reforming the Seattle Police Department at the time, was not rewarded for his tragicomic heroism, but severely sanctioned. As an artifact of successful backlighting, the photograph excels: it perfectly captures the indignity and disgrace of the state with a fumbling Keystone-Kop tableau of powerful eloquence.

What the neoliberal state lacks in flexibility, it attempts to compensate for in force. The dual nature of the neoliberal state as both a security state and a penal state is expressed by its two modes: the preventative and the retributive/punitive. If prevention fails or is transgressed, the punitive aspect appears with special zeal to repair the punctures and gouges in the smooth surface of power. One example, brilliantly analyzed in *Afflicted Powers: Capital and Spectacle in a New Age of War*, is the "War on Terror," which can be understood as a discursive or "spectacular" presentation of an image of power to compensate for the vulnerability expressed in the attacks on the World Trade Center twin towers, rather than as any rational exercise of power in material terms.[48] The torture images leaked from Abu Ghraib, the clouds of flame raining over Baghdad's skyline, and the mutilated bodies of Afghanis and Iraqis piled as evidence of savage rage, as the US empire tried to modify its image into one of vengeful invulnerability.

But this two-faced slippage also presents two cheeks asking to be pinched. Social movement participants attempt to interrupt this chain of consequentiality, the supposedly inevitable horrors of spectacular revenge. Humor surfaces in the figure who "gets away with it" in the face of neoliberal state threats of retribution. There is, for instance, Colton Harris-Moore, "the Barefoot Bandit," who in his teenage years freely commandeered a series of planes and cars and ate uninvited from scores of private refrigerators for his own personal traveling pleasure. Moore evaded capture for several years before police shot out the engine of his stolen boat in the Bahamas in 2010, and he has remained a sort of casual saint among some young radicals ever since. That the seemingly impossible can be so easily achieved despite a discursive hegemony of apparent universal administration is inspiring and, at times, funny—in spite and because of the potentially disastrous consequences. The fear imposed by seamless impossibility suddenly shatters in surprise at an unforeseen fission of potential, and a sudden shocking relief expresses itself through laughter, which always includes a note of derision for the lost supremacy of the forces overcome.

The eloquence of backlighting events should not necessarily be seen as an excuse for the context in which they occur. Even those who enact these strategies find themselves frustrated by the *stupidity* of riot. People I spoke with often praised *moments* of effective backlighting within overall situations that they recognized as disastrously ill considered, unstrategic, context-ignorant, and irresponsible. One example was a badly botched attempt, on the evening of Occupy Oakland's general strike, to occupy a vacant hotel bordering on the camp. Instead of covertly taking the hotel, a number of participants lit a large dumpster on fire, ostensibly to repel clouds of tear gas, and then quickly ran away. The woman I spoke with praises the effects of backlighting but does not spare criticism of the Occupiers conduct, or their follow-through:

---

48   Iain A. Boal et al., *Afflicted Powers: Capital and Spectacle in a New Age of War* (New York: Verso, 2005).

The police came, and they walled off the street. They were kicking the shit out of people, shooting a lot of tear gas, and people were charging them for a minute. And that part was spectacular. I'm like, please! You're not going to win, but go for it! Like, please, show them that they don't have power beyond their brutality. Do that. Make that real. Because half their power is the fact that they can actually destroy your life, and the other half is power we give them. So take that back. That's thrilling.

But people did that for twenty minutes, lost interest, or knew that wasn't going to end anytime soon, and ran away. And what that left was a ton of folks in the park, mostly folks who were homeless who needed to live there anyway and happened to be getting kind of sheltered by Occupy still in the park, many of whom had a variety of disabilities, getting the shit kicked out of them by the police because the Black Blockers all ran, and the police came and swept; so at that point we did a two-block carry on this dude who got shot in his bad knee, who was a Vietnam War vet. We had to carry him two blocks to where the ambulances would come....

It was all this thing where I was like, you have to walk the walk, dude. You can't just charge the police—which I think is really important—and then leave, you have to hold the line, or you have to get people out, or you have to then move away from there. You can also light that fire all you goddamn want, [but] not a quarter-block from all the people who are not up for that and don't have the capacity and have not given their consent. So it's just this intense situation where I'm really tired of the conversation, I do think it is obstructive of the conversation, between violence and nonviolence, because it's about strategy... [Abstract debates of violence versus nonviolence are] about "should you or should you not." That's not real. What's real in the world is what works, and that means that everything is on the table every time that a new situation arises, and you pick the thing off the table that is the correct thing for that moment, that works best. And when it doesn't work best, you don't have crazy fallout, you learn your lessons, and you heal your wounds, and you try again.[49]

Riots don't work by magic, any more than nonviolence does. The public destruction of economic and political targets and clashes with police certainly do not guarantee the success or failure of a social movement. The performance of riotous rhetorics are not in themselves a self-sufficient political formation. Nor, despite what some strands of militant discourse claim, can their subjective, emotional effects substitute for the dissensual collective deliberation of politics, that wide arena of conflict that results from what Jacques Rancière calls "the presupposition of equality."[50] The powerful appeals of riot do not exempt its participants from the need to make common cause across demographic, cultural, and ideological differences; to have patience before awkward lapses, misunderstandings, and insults; to listen in good faith and explain in humility, however smashier their preferred means of action might be. Otherwise, riot, lacking incentives and mechanisms of contagion with which to generalize and escalate into a wider insurrectionary movement, degenerates into a mere pastime: a low-risk, nonthreatening, self-congratulatory, self-incapacitating hobby, useless for any end but personal expression and identity marking. Like progressive nonprofits, fetishists of riot lay claim to the prestige of risk-taking without actually taking real risks; that is, without threatening any social transformation that might make elites uncomfortable, any social significance that might actually invite repression. They are generally free from the inconvenience of having to confront any real measures of counterinsurgency; in the exceptional cases where they do invite real repression, it is because they have ended up socially significant despite the intentions of their practitioners.

Riot aims at particular rhetorical effects that may succeed or fail. Riot is no more above or beneath its conditions than is any other

---

49 Personal interview (A).

50 For a good introduction, see Todd May, *The Political Thought of Jacques Rancière: Creating Equality* (University Park, PA: Pennsylvania State University Press, 2008).

rhetorical assertion. The fetishization of riot in both negative and positive terms may be the central distortion in the applied analysis of social movements in our era. Conversations both analytical and propositional would far better be focused on contextual conditions of strategic effectiveness and outcome than on the inherent holy or satanic nature of the strategy. If I have focused more on critiquing the demonizing dismissals of riot than its sanctifying exaltation, it is because these dismissals condemn precisely those strategies that have been so strikingly powerful in their rhetorical and material effects. These dismissals were also instrumental in the discursive practice of distinguishing "good protesters" from "bad protesters"—a "respectability politics" that has been hugely useful for authorities in forcefully tearing movements apart.

It is important to remember that riotous strategies need not always exclude broad publics, even if, as we saw in Chapter 1, they do generally preclude appealing to "masses" already constituted by the symbolic and organizational order the rioters are targeting. Rather than quibbling over the supremacy of "deep" versus "wide" appeals, movement participants and theorists increasingly speak of fostering *complementarity* among differences, multiplying rather than subtracting the strengths of different approaches.[51] At first glance, the tactical dichotomy seems ubiquitous: progressives like Hedges decry "militants" as a "cancer" for disturbing an ideal constituted only in his imagination, a consensus that could never include those not invited to his utopia. At the same time, some militants cite "diversity of tactics" as a way to avoid discussing the place or logic of their actions; they might even reject the notion of utility altogether, in an individualistic and nihilistic stance that closely resembles right-wing "freedoms" at the cost of the welfare of others. However, one Egyptian revolutionary I interviewed suggests that such binaries can be transcended: "In Tahrir, every morning we would make it very clear that it was a peaceful protest, which was very important, because we needed *everyone* out on the streets for it to be a popular revolution—women, older people, children, everyone. And then, the sun would set, and every night, the *shebaab* [youth] would go out and fight with the police, set police cars on fire, burn down police stations and the offices of

---

51 Amster, *Anarchism Today*, 60–62.

the ruling party. And we needed that too. We needed both, having both was essential."[52]

As Luce Guillén-Givins argues, "diversity of tactics" was originally a trope meant to stimulate discussion and seek out moments for complementarity within difference, rather than a way to end conversation by asserting the superiority of one approach.[53] Bearing in mind the necessity of such complementarity for maintaining the internal differentiation of movements, we can begin to look for emergent common characteristics within wider contentious approaches and, perhaps, for what might characterize movements to come.

---

52 Personal interview (P).

53 Luce Guillén-Givins et al., "From Repression to Resistance: Notes on Combating Counterinsurgency," in Williams et al., eds., *Life during Wartime*.

CHAPTER 5

THE CHARACTERISTICS OF MOVEMENTS TO COME

WHICH PEOPLE ARE THE PEOPLE?

And then we're going to have [a protest] that's going to get really big, because we're going to break free of the violence, and we're going to have hundreds of thousands of people. It's going to look like a picnic. It's going to look like a church service. It's going to look like a dance.

—Tim Anderson[1]

This is a struggle to win the hearts and minds of the wider public and those within the structures of power (including the police) who are possessed of a conscience.... The continuing attempt by the state to crush peaceful protesters who call for simple acts of justice delegitimizes the power elite. It prompts a passive population to respond.

—Chris Hedges[2]

---

1   Anderson, KKNW interview.
2   Hedges, "The Cancer in Occupy."

I feel like when we feel like we're winning, even in the short term, that's also something that brings people out. And that doesn't really look like people getting hit with batons on TV and then [you] feeling sorry for them and going to support them for one march or something.... I think when it looks like we're winning more, and we're actually making gains in the streets and taking more space, that's gonna draw more people out. Because I've talked to so many people who are just, like, they are really hopeless and for good reason. That's a reason they don't come out, not because they're morally opposed to violence, or this, or that.... Like if we made anything that resembled [the 2006 teacher's strike and occupation in] Oaxaca, or something, I bet we'd be seeing thousands of people, or at least hundreds more, than we've seen before. Because it's exciting, and its new, and a lot of people do feel discontent, and also alienated in this society, and they need to feel inspired. It's gonna have to look like something new that America never really sees. And it's not gonna be a police baton in the face, because we've all seen that before.
—Anarchist demonstrator, Seattle[3]

---

3   Personal interview (L).

IN HIS CLASSIC PAPER ON SOCIAL MOVEMENT RHETORIC, RICHARD Gregg reminds his readers that social movements are often more concerned with "constituting selfhood through expression" than with appealing to authorities.[4] Such characteristics hold particularly true of those movements whose militant rhetoric might seem irrational if petitioning powers for policy changes is the measure. Herbert Simons similarly observes a functional dichotomy in social movements, between a co-constituting "militant" rhetoric more concerned with developing oppositional subjects and posing challenges and a "reformist" one that translates the movement's aims and semiotic advances into terms legible to existing institutions.[5] While these observations are true and helpful, what scholars of social movement rhetoric, and movement participants alike often fail to appreciate is that, in the absence of a unified, already coherent political subject known as "The People," "militant" and "reformist" rhetorics attract and mobilize very different demographic sectors of the larger population—they constitute very different selves, in Gregg's terms. These sectors in turn bring differing priorities and characteristics to the movement they join. For this reason, questions about *how* a movement articulates itself are always at the same time questions about *who* it's talking to.

The issue becomes acute in the absence of central leadership—a shift that clearly characterizes contemporary social movements. Martin Luther King Jr., for example, could personally mediate tensions internal to his movement to some degree. He could address the characteristic sentiments and expectations of different audiences and participants, as when he urged his listeners to act in a dialect of outrage and conciliation, stating that "if they accepted such injustices without protesting, they would betray their own sense of dignity.... But I would balance this with a strong affirmation of the Christian doctrine of love."[6] Today's movements, in the absence of a sympathetic mass

---

4   Richard B. Gregg, "The Ego-Function of the Rhetoric of Protest," in Morris and Browne, *Readings on the Rhetoric of Social Protest*, 45–58.

5   Herbert W. Simons, "Requirements, Problems, and Strategies: A Theory of Persuasion for Social Movements," in Morris and Browne, *Readings on the Rhetoric of Social Protest*, 35–45.

6   Clayborne Carson, ed. *Autobiography of Martin Luther King, Jr.*, 59. Of course, the movement in King's time was not unified either, and can only be claimed to have been through amnesia. King's often tense relationship with Ella Baker, for

media that might constitute any sort of unitary audience for them, often rely instead on social media, a platform that inherently produces fragmentary, evanescent identity formations.[7] Critics accustomed to a more traditional, centralized style of protest may bemoan the lack of "principles" and "leadership," scapegoating protesters who have little influence in the matter. In the absence of figurehead person- alities or a mediating center, movement tensions get displaced onto disagreements over what the movement is supposed to mean and how it expresses itself, onto debates around the legitimacy and place of different "messages" and "tactics." In essence, this becomes an intense, volatile, and shifting effort to define the movement's internal and ex- ternal characterization and appeal.

In the quotations opening this chapter, nonviolence advocates Tim Anderson and Chris Hedges appeal to a "wider public" and "pas- sive population" of "hundreds of thousands of people," each of whom is defined (and presumably attracted to participate) only negatively, by their aversion to "violence." This is a perfect instance of classic liberal ideology's often criticized idea of universal humanity. What human characteristics become norms when someone asserts that "re- ally, deep down inside we're all the same"? What characteristics are declared exceptions? Which humans get to be typical, which ones are aberrant, and what are the consequences? "The People" is always a choice among different demographics, a point that gets obfuscated in universalist discourse. Most of the time within movements, like appeals to like—participants frequently view their own demographic networks, whom they may be struggling to mobilize, as the default audience. There is nothing "universal" about it.

Notably, the anarchist whose quotation follows Anderson and Hedges above is more careful to qualify her evocations—"more," "many," "a lot of" people, who number more humbly in the "thou- sands…or at least hundreds." Speaking from marginal subject posi- tions, and frequently espousing positions affiliated with critiques of

example, or the student leaders of the sit-ins who very consciously turned their back on national leadership, remind us that such questions are not entirely par- ticular to our time.

7   Kevin M. DeLuca, Sean Lawson, and Ye Sun, "Occupy Wall Street on the Public Screens of Social Media: The Many Framings of the Birth of a Protest Movement," *Communication, Culture & Critique* 5, no. 4 (2012): 483–509.

universal humanism, militant discourses would sound strange claiming a unified subject. They tend to speak as one position among others, rather than claiming to be the only possible position. Militant disruptive repertoires of protest may indeed have a lesser appeal in sheer numbers, but the commitment of their subjects may in some senses be worth it, an idea we'll return to later. In Occupy, for example, as contention around what the movement was about and how it should express itself intensified after the initial massive mobilizations, demonstrators were faced with increasingly unsympathetic media coverage. In this crisis of mobilization, radicals asserted the importance of innovation in appeal, while moderates blamed such assertions for the decline in participation.

No figure is cited with such frequency to establish the need for universal humanism in social change as is Martin Luther King Jr. However, King himself was quite open about the exclusions enacted by the messages of his own movement. In a newspaper column on September 1, 1962, he wrote, "No matter what it is we seek, if it has to do with full citizenship, self-respect, human dignity, and borders on changing the 'Southern way of life,' the Negro stands little chance, if any, of securing the approval, consent, or tolerance of the segregationist white South."[8] Elsewhere, he quite starkly laid out his core rhetorical strategy, including a clear specificity of audience:

> The goal of the demonstrations in Selma, as elsewhere, was to dramatize the existence of injustice and to bring about the presence of justice by methods of nonviolence. Long years of experience indicated to us that Negroes could achieve this goal when four things occurred: [1] Nonviolent demonstrators go into the street to exercise their constitutional rights; [2] Racists resist by unleashing violence against them; [3] *Americans of good conscience* in the name of decency demand federal intervention and legislation; [4] The administration, under mass pressure, initiates measures of immediate intervention and supports remedial legislation.[9]

---

8   Clayborne Carson, ed. *Autobiography of Martin Luther King, Jr.*, 166.

9   Ibid., 277. My emphasis.

Given the historical context within which King was working, it is not a stretch by any means to read "the presence of justice" as code for the "federal intervention and legislation" and "Americans of good conscience" as predominantly northern liberal whites, such as those who voted the Kennedys into office. King unambiguously names "the administration" as the ultimate audience of these actions. In King's day, national authorities could be pressured to intervene against regional ones; the awkward coalition of Black liberation with northern industry had worked a century before in the Civil War. In our current context, though, what "higher authority" might be pressured to intervene against endemic homicidal police racism, or a national scapegoating of immigrants, or armed forces with half of the world's military budget, or transnational corporations, or intergovernmental organizations like the WTO or IMF, or indeed the very forces of global capitalism? Unless the United Nations or some benevolent God acquire the power to mobilize the greatest force in history, the same populations governed by these forces are going to have to be the ones to take them on—there is no one to petition.

Topics and Their Publics

Although the Occupy movement is often remembered as a single phenomenon, it should more honestly be considered a problem, constituted more by internal conflicts than any unified collective will. It typified the way leaderless movements employ fights over topics—the "real meaning" of the movement, what it is all about—as a central way different demographics and political tendencies fight out ownership over the movement itself. In the contested claims over "the message" of the Occupy movement, the question of *how* its publics were constituted becomes central to the way it composed its participatory inside while externally appealing to potential participants and allies. And the question hasn't gone away. It has proven just as persistent and thorny in the Black Lives Matter movement: are we talking about police accountability and inclusive representation, or are we talking about overturning an unreformable system built to its core on anti-Black violence? And what kinds of different actions make sense for these very different aims, appealing to which different audiences?

Given the lack of any hard data, as a participant in both the first week of Occupy Wall Street and in nearly every day of Occupy Seattle, one thing seemed clear to me: while the demographic makeup of Occupy Wall Street was noticeably less diverse than most public spaces in Manhattan, Occupy Seattle was noticeably more diverse than most public spaces in Seattle, and Occupy Oakland clearly more diverse than either, racially and otherwise. In the words of one exhaustive study by an independent researcher conducted in tandem with a number of internal Occupy Wall Street research groups, the New York occupation saw "disproportionately high participation rates by professionals and persons with high levels of education. These findings raise specific questions: What do the commitments of our organizing efforts reveal about the kinds of political subjects we enabled?"[10] The study recognizes that "competition over movement purposes sometimes developed along lines of established social privilege/exclusion.... [C]ampaigns for healthcare and financial reform tended to emerge from alliances of wealthier, whiter, professional identified partners."[11] In the study's analysis of 124 political projects within Occupy Wall Street, "only 4 projects in the sample sought to *produce alternative systems* compared to 21 projects producing campaigns to *reform* existing financial, education, legislative, and electoral systems."[12]

A comparison with Occupy Seattle or Occupy Oakland provides a very conditional answer to the study's question about commitments. Neither Occupy Seattle nor Oakland would be so easily typified as disproportionately "professionals and persons with high levels of education," and while concerns about financial regulation, campaign finance reform, abolishing corporate personhood, and raising taxes on "the 1%" were always present, so were statements about police, systemic racism, patriarchy, indigeneity and decolonization, political representation per se, and gender determinism in a way such topics never surfaced in New York before. While I have not done a qualitative study of the political aims expressed, for example, in the general assembly minutes or other conversations in Occupy Seattle and Occupy Oakland, my impression is that they were quite different than those expressed in New York—both in the choice of short-term commitments (as, for example, Seattle's vote to

---

10 James Owens, "Occupy's Precarious Pluralism Report," Occupy Wall Street website, accessed May 24, 2016, http://occupywallstreet.net/sites/default/files /ows_-_occupys_precarious_pluralism_report_final.pdf, 5.

11 Ibid., 3.

12 Ibid., 6. My emphasis.

endorse the October 22, 2011, March Against Police Brutality) and open avowals of "revolutionary" long-term goals. Occupy Seattle's largest cultural event, held at Westlake Plaza in early November, was termed "Rise and Decolonize: Let's Get Free," and featured a number of local MCs, DJs, and B-girls and boys, capped by a raucous dance party. While New York maintained ambiguous attitudes toward police (at least until the military-like raid of the camp on November 15), both Seattle and Oakland passed proposals in general assemblies banning police from the camp. New York declared itself nonviolent before the occupation began, but the general assemblies in Oakland and Seattle voted down such proposals each of the numerous times they were put forward. New York was generally referred to as "Occupy Wall Street," whereas many Seattle participants preferred "Decolonize Seattle," and much of Occupy Oakland identified instead as "The Oakland Commune" to situate itself very explicitly in a revolutionary lineage.

It is certainly possible that New York's larger numbers in the Occupy camps may have correlated with the appeal to less marginalized audiences, although a number of other factors clearly had influence as well, such as the relative size of the cities. The question posed by the movement as a whole, bearing its stunning spectrum of variations in mind, however, stands: what demographic is most appropriate—in what balance of commitment, consciousness, numbers, and influence—to at least *begin* to bring about the sort of social changes desired by movement participants? We should look first at those constituencies most impacted by socio-economic inequality. Sounding almost regretful for opportunities missed, the Occupy Wall Street research study unambiguously states that

> [s]upporting poor peoples' movements against our common opponents seems a better strategy to encourage a powerful social movement that can make our society more democratic. My argument is that communication organizing *can* contribute to such a movement but only when talk is part of action and action is to enable the most excluded to fight their exclusion. The poor cannot always resist, through protest or other means. When activists help the silenced gain the power to speak and be heard, we expand the stage of political

debate and alter the social context in which rulers strive to legitimate their power.

Enacting our equality through common struggle with the least powerful is how we create democratic community and make ourselves democratic subjects. The emergence of that community alters the symbolic and organizational context upon which the ruling order depends and makes another world possible.[13]

Without by any means forgetting the importance of wide-scale mobilizations for social change, and maintaining as an open question the relative importance of numbers versus relevance and commitment in social movement characterization, I will now move on to look at some final characteristics that might typify recent shifts in movements. By looking at the basic set of strategies under contemporary conditions that alter "the symbolic and organizational context upon which the ruling order depends and makes another world possible," we might not only better understand recent movements, but those movements yet to come as well—and why they have shown and will show less interest in approaches and characteristics social movements have taken for granted for decades. These movements may be appealing to essentially different audiences, different people within "The People" under the shifting conditions of neoliberalism, so the sorts of appeals they choose to employ might be expected to change.

AFTER VICTIMHOOD, BEYOND INNOCENCE

Yesterday one of my good friends, an old hippie, was talking about Occupy and—she must've said this five times—the most important thing is that you continue to make sure that everyone knows that you are the *victims*. I mean, I love this woman, I adore her, I have a lot of respect for her as a person.... At the same time there's something so pathological in that. I think there is something very powerful in the whole world seeing that you are not the ones starting shit, but you have to be seen as the *victims*?

I think that in any of the massive disciplined nonviolent movements it must have taken so much courage and so much

---

13   Ibid., 4.

strength to really do what they did. But that wasn't what I heard here: it was in fact that we seem to be weak that we put our weakness at the forefront.... I didn't think about this at the time, but thinking about it now, like, I guess I'm not sure that she had really thought through what that would mean for us to do [that]. I don't really know if I'm willing or able to stand in one place and get my head beaten or watch my friends get their heads beaten so that other people can watch it and feel pity.... Like, fuck that, at the very least, I'm going to run.

—Seattle anarchist[14]

If one characteristic of nonviolence—including its "strategic" variations—is utterly incongruous with the conditions posed by neoliberalism, it is the requirement that one's own victimhood be performed and communicated as a central claim of social movement expression. Sharp's formulation of nonviolence, although prioritizing a fostering of agency, essentially depends on what he calls "political jiu-jitsu" in which counterhegemonic actors assert their victimhood by bringing down repression and suffering publicly before wider audiences. This supposedly removes legitimacy from the regime and assigns it to those suffering repression. Political jiu-jitsu, in Schock's analysis as well, is precisely what is lacking in "violent" approaches. "Martyrdom is a potent catalyst for the political jiu-jitsu dynamic; that is, the murder of unarmed activists highlights the brutality of the regime and encourages previously uncommitted persons to join the cause in a manner that the murder of a violent activist would not."[15] Such approaches are still clearly powerful in some circumstances. In my first week at Occupy Wall Street, it was clearly the diffusion of video images of innocent (white, youthful, female) protesters arbitrarily pepper-sprayed by police that brought out large numbers to join the movement. In the words of the Seattle anarchist whose story about his older hippie friend opened this section, "I mean I don't think she's wrong. There is a lot of power in that, precisely because it puts the person watching on the moral low ground. If you can watch somebody else get really brutally hurt and you're not doing something, you're not there, then you are in

---

14   Personal interview (D).

15   Schock, *Unarmed Insurrections*, 89.

the wrong."[16] Although not as severe as the "murder of unarmed activists" described by Schock, the same "martyrdom" effect can be seen to be working here to "highlight the brutality of the regime and encourage previously uncommitted persons to join the cause." This process of political jiu-jitsu that is so integral to nonviolence, however, presents its own serious problems.

As I noted in the first chapter, the ability of mass publics to watch the suffering of protesters is directly dependent on a mass media sympathetic enough to select and convey those images. Media outlets owned by the very parent companies implicated in protest messages are unlikely to give sympathetic coverage, a factor studied ad nauseam in contemporary media studies literature. Other limitations of such sympathy include novelty, the "narrative arc" of the issue, the legitimacy and legibility of the issue in editorial eyes, as well as the age, gender, social place, and, of course, race of the protesters. The young women in Lower Manhattan and the UC Davis students were all or predominantly white, young, and apparently middle class. Dorli Rainey, whom I stood mere feet from when she was viciously assaulted at an Occupy Seattle protest, is elderly and white—which possibly is why her photo circulated more than any other Occupy image. In Rainey's case, the fortunate presence of medics to hold her up and douse her burning eyes in milk of magnesia presented a photogenic opportunity. The white liquid (mistaken in most accounts for the pepper spray itself) dripped dramatically from her eyes, and her frame hung Christ-like in the medics' supportive arms. Had any of these elements been missing, or had the assault occurred two weeks later when coverage of the still-growing movement was no longer generally deemed newsworthy, Rainey's suffering would have been known only to her friends and those of us present. Only in images where police violence against bodies would be read as *exceptional* can coverage be expected, and only then, in very specific circumstances.

In addition, the very position of spectator presents complexities not always under the control of the insurgents. Gitlin, a staunch advocate of public victimhood and political jiu-jitsu, lets slip occasional acknowledgments that such approaches are as likely to backfire: "When the police shoved demonstrators, clubbed them, and gassed them, the scenes of the action were dubbed 'violent clashes,' as if nonviolent

---

16   Personal interview (D).

demonstrators were responsible for police attacks."[17] Such failed moments are curious exceptions for Gitlin, when in reality they clearly form the rule. When lapdog media representations meet the compassion-fatigue and *ressentiment* of a mass American audience, negative receptions of the protesters' suffering are all too likely. Even sympathetic viewings of "undeserved" suffering risks normalizing persecution of those deemed less reputable. "To be moved by the suffering of some others (the "deserving" poor, the innocent child, the injured hero), is also to be elevated into a place that remains untouched by other others (whose suffering cannot be converted into my sympathy or admiration)."[18] For Brison, victimhood tends to gain a resistant sympathy, at best: "We are not taught to empathize with victims. In crime novels and detective films, it is the villain, or the one who solves the murder mystery, who attracts our attention; the victim, a merely passive pretext for our entertainment, is conveniently disposed of—and forgotten—early on. We identify with the agents' strength and skill, for good or evil, and join the victim, if at all, only in our nightmares."[19]

Political identification through victimhood tends to the third person, never the first. It is an appeal to some protector to live up to their duty on another's behalf and never for the victims themselves to seize power and put an end to the victimizing situation, nor does it offer anything to help potential victims to prevent themselves from becoming an actual one. In short, political pleas of victimhood are inherently representative and mediating, precluding first-person agency for self-defense or to bring about change. It seeks to convince the strong to redirect the application of their strength and never to redistribute strength itself. The victim becomes too suspect a character, their integrity too violated to trust them with their own protection; their victimhood is taken as itself proof of inherent helplessness. What sort of politics, we might ask, does this celebration of victimhood encourage? Brison also warns that it tends to *generate competing narratives of victimization,* not all of which are justified." She agrees with Martha

---

17   Gitlin, *Occupy Nation*, 39.

18   Sara Ahmed, quoted in Rachel Riedner and Kevin Mahoney, *Democracies to Come: Rhetorical Action, Neoliberalism, and Communities of Resistance* (Lanham, MD: Lexington Books, 2008), 51.

19   Brison, *Aftermath*, 10.

Minow "that 'victim talk' tends to provoke counter-'victim talk' (note the recent rhetoric of the 'angry white male victim' of affirmative action) and not all these narratives can be taken at face value, since they are often at odds with one another."[20]

Victim counternarratives are found all too easily these days. Lt. Pike, for example, was awarded $38,000 for the "workplace injury" of "trauma" he suffered after pepper-spraying the UC Davis students. The fact that hundreds of thousands of dollars in crowdfunded support could be raised for homicidal racist Officer Darren Wilson suggests that, for much of the mass-constituted public, these reverse-victimhood claims confuse the issue sufficiently enough to risk defeating the jiu-jitsu effect.

Gandhi himself, although at times executing such jiu-jitsu with masterful timing, at other times may have overplayed it, leading in part to his lessening popularity as the struggle to drive out the British progressed. In one of his less fortunate passages, he wrote, "In a family, when a father slaps his delinquent child, the latter does not think of retaliating. He obeys his father not because of the deterrent effect of the slap, but because of the offended love which he senses behind it. That, in my opinion, is an epitome of the way in which society is or should be governed. What is true of the family must be true of society which is but a larger family."[21] The analogy is objectionable enough in a domestic context—is there ever a point when the "delinquent" (and hence abuse-deserving) child may disagree with the father's judgment? Must the child perpetually suffer to satisfy the father's "offended love," or might they refuse their role in the father's own emotional process? At a societal level, the recommendation is even worse: what institution is analogous to the father, and what sort of "offended love" might institutions "feel"? What level of suffering was required to gratify the "offended love" of British colonialism or today's neoliberal security apparatus? One demonstrator explained the use of homemade shields in an Oakland protest as a response to just this dynamic:

> You don't get to hurt me.... There's a lot of analogies
> that one can make that I'm not going to, but are you

20 Ibid., 34.

21 In Robert L. Holmes and Barry L. Gan, *Nonviolence in Theory and Practice* (Long Grove, IL: Waveland Press, 2012), 80.

really going to ask someone who's constantly brutal-
ized by someone to…materially be injured to prove a
point? That's ridiculous, and it's a privileged fucking
position.… I think they're easy analogies outside of a
political context. It would be like asking the battered
wife to get battered one last time to prove the inhu-
manity of her husband. To me, that makes no sense.
But following the logic of nonviolence you should
steadfastly stand there and get the shit kicked out you.
Because it's proving a point. To who? To some higher authority, to this wife-beater, who actually doesn't
give a shit? Are you proving a point to some higher
authority, the state, who actually doesn't give a shit?
No, of course not. Why would you volunteer yourself
to be hurt?[22]

While this person doesn't acknowledge that other aggrieved parties, rather than the state itself, might form the audience for such
actions, the problem of performative victimhood remains: how can
we guarantee that our audience reacts with compassion rather than
disgust or annoyance?

The public performance of victimhood generally only empowers
those privileged parties whose suffering is not *assumed* as a normal
occurrence, and even then, only under the most generous of circumstances. Mass-mediated publics, should they be made aware of the
suffering, are as likely to be hostile as sympathetic. In response, social
movement participants have begun to favor a tactic different and, in
some ways, opposed to political jiu-jitsu. We might call this tactic
"getting away with it." Schock notes its efficacy in Nepal and Thailand:

The occupation of a single indefensible public place by
the Chinese students [in Tiananmen Square] contributed to the movement's demise, as it was an easy target
for repression. By contrast, the "lightening protests" in
Nepal and Thailand—whereby protestors gathered at
a location, then dispersed upon the approach of authorities, only to reappear at another predetermined

---

22 Personal interview (O).

place—enabled the challengers to outflank the authorities, avoid the direct brunt of violent repression, remain resilient, and give the impression of being more widespread than they actually were.[23]

For communities suffering persecution for centuries, whose presence in prison is more common than in higher education, and for whom "undeserving" has never been an available adjective, voluntary victimhood achieves little for either their own demographic or for mass publics at large. Apparent exceptions prove the rule: King's campaigns self-consciously presented middle-class Black college students, particularly female, as its preferred visage. This, King attested, was effective only for arousing national sentiment against a regional situation. Rodney King was not so much an exceptional target, as a target whose victimhood was captured so vividly on home video, a novel medium at the time. Oscar Grant's death shared some features with Rodney King's beating, as one of the first viral YouTube videos of police murder taken on spectator phones. Neither, however, were intentionally performing their victimhood. In fact, the media actively worked to foreclose any semantic route to victimhood for them. Although Oscar Grant, Michael Brown, Freddie Gray, Aiyana Stanley-Jones, Tamir Rice, Jamar Clark, Laquan McDonald, and Sandra Bland were very obviously innocent of any charge related to the sadism and murder they faced at the hands of police, media sources immediately attempted to legitimize police violence by implicating their character and the character of their parents.

Hill, in her powerful analysis of rhetoric labor and antilynching defense campaigns in US history, provides an illuminating warning on the consequences of embracing the "melodrama" of victimhood claims for contemporary movements:

> After the Civil War, the crime story replaced the story of the heroic rebel at the center of American popular-fiction heroism.... Increasingly, what Nietzsche called *ressentiment* became an ideology against revolutionary legitimacy, rejecting action in the name of liberation and embracing instead action in the name of law

---

23   Schock, *Unarmed Insurrections*, 168.

enforcement. As the nation's soldiers went to war, they acted less in the name of their own personal freedom and more in the name of outraged others in the triangular action that defines the genre of melodrama. In melodrama, three characters create the story line, and only two of the characters are actors in the true sense of the word. There is a chivalric hero who acts to preserve "good," and there is a base villain who threatens the "good." The good itself is an object, not an actor, and is usually represented by a white woman or an idealized female child.[24]

Notably, the third point of the pyramid, the "object" of the good itself, possesses no agency; this already presents radical inconsistencies with the goals of contemporary movements to publicly perform the potential for expanded agency. The idealization of this human object without agency, Hill explains, communicates a scorn for democratic values. "She is defined as 'good' because of her separation from both economic and political struggles for power.... Her elevation as a symbol of the citizenry, dependent on heroic leadership in a time of crisis, is a sign of the erosion of republican beliefs in American culture."[25] As a figure, such a victim acts as a stand-in for the status quo tout court, a "fetish" for all that is threatened by the rage of the Other, embodying in herself the naturalization of familial and class relations:

> The symbol of this "white woman" is the ultimate embodiment of *ressentiment*. Stories about her wronged innocence serve to supplant the role of property in the heart of most actions of law-enforcement and military adventure. In her, the private sphere becomes the fetish for private property itself; at the center of the home, the innocent woman stands in for property and becomes an object whose relationship to labor and conflict is utterly erased and naturalized as outside the realms of human action. Instead of property, Nancy Armstrong argues, the "woman" at the center of domestic fiction

---

24 Hill, *Men, Mobs, and Law*, 12.
25 Ibid.

defines bourgeois subjectivity (and property itself) as outside power.[26]

Perhaps less obviously, the "chivalric hero" also represents a dangerous figure of *ressentiment*. Hill argues that this figure is inherently authoritarian, an appeal to an unquestioned third party who embodies justice in a direct manner, precisely the concentration of legitimacy and power that collective, nonhierarchical deliberation structures seek to avoid. Their judgments are, by necessity, always to remain unquestioned, and their powers always in need of increase. The shift to a plea for the necessity of police, whose development historically paralleled the popularity of the narratives Hill describes, is not far from hand. "[T]he expansion of the state's policing powers has been justified by appeals to the need to protect the same innocent and powerless group from the savage criminal classes.... In this pattern, the public is not allowed to question the chivalric hero. It can only be the grateful recipient of care."[27]

For those already marked with the socially coded traits of alleged villainy, attempts at political jiu-jitsu based on innocence are doomed from the start. In the US context, public tropes of melodramatic victimhood—precisely those that nonviolence advocates such as Hedges insist are of monumental importance in any effective social movement—are so marked by race and class as to always risk reproducing the very legitimizations they set out to undo. Hill shows how this has been true of antiracist liberation struggles in the US:

> Blacks' struggles for social equality in the South were described as a quest to dominate helpless white women. It was against this portrayal of themselves as the powerful demons threatening "the good" that anti-lynching activists had to fight. As a result, they did not offer a simple counter-melodrama of Black innocence, because to do so would have undermined their own citizenship claims. Instead, Ida B. Wells and others who followed her unpacked the mythology of rape that surrounded lynching and found that most

---

26 Ibid.
27 Ibid., 12–13.

people killed by lynch mobs had not even been accused of rape.[28]

Innocence and victimhood go hand in hand. While the figure of
the innocent victim was foundational for movements of the past,
we must ask ourselves if we have reached a point when it must be
overcome.

Beyond Innocence

By most accounts, the majority of the 2.4 million people in prison,
or the nearly seven million under "correctional supervision" of proba-
tion and parole, are not necessarily "innocent." Although only a very
small minority of crimes result in conviction, scholars have not so
far disputed that most convictions are for crimes actually committed.
However, given the massive racial and class disparities in arrest, conviction, and sentencing rates, these convictions can hardly be termed
"justice." When "social justice" rhetoric makes *innocence* a prerequisite
of those people deserving attention, those suffering arguably the greatest injustices under the current order are excluded from the frame. As
Alexander argues, "The time-tested strategy of using those who epit-
omize moral virtue as symbols in racial justice campaigns is far more
difficult to employ in efforts to reform the criminal justice system."[29]

Alexander notes that only months before Rosa Parks's 1955 arrest
on a Montgomery city bus, two other women, Claudette Colvin and
Mary Louise Smith, had also been arrested for similar direct actions
violating Montgomery bus segregation. Yet Colvin, 15, became preg-
nant soon after the arrest, and "[a]dvocates worried that her 'immoral'
conduct would detract from or undermine their efforts to show what
blacks were entitled to (and worthy of) equal treatment."[30] The father of Mary Louise Smith, in turn, was an alcoholic. In Alexander's
words, "It was understood that, in any effort to challenge racial discrimination, the litigant—and even the litigant's family—had to be
above reproach and free from every negative trait that could be used as
a justification for unequal treatment." The NAACP chose to wait for
a figure such as Parks, whose reputation could not be used to defame

---

28 Ibid., 14.

29 Alexander, *New Jim Crow*, 228.

30 Ibid., 227.

her act by the conservative social mores of the day. In our day, conditions have changed (and in many senses actually worsened) since the days of Colvin, Smith, and Parks, but the parameters that determine the preferred character, constituency, and admissible issues of activism reflect the same cultural prejudices. "Challenging mass incarceration," Alexander notes, "requires something civil rights advocates have long been reluctant to do: advocacy on behalf of criminals.... The 'politics of respectability' has influenced civil rights litigation and advocacy, leading even the most powerful civil rights organizations to distance themselves from the most stigmatized elements of the community, especially lawbreakers."[31] As Ta-Nehisi Coates has argued in a number of articles, "respectability politics" are essentially a ploy of changing the subject, derailing critique of undeniable injustices by shifting the topic to talk about the conduct, image, and culpability of those suffering these injustices. Much the same could be said about discussions of nonviolence when they allow conversations about tactics to overshadow the reasons for those actions in the first place.[32]

Alexander does not see this reluctance to engage the disrespectable as a marginal oversight in contemporary antiracism movements; as policing, incarceration, probation/parole, and especially strictures on employment and housing are central to the material reproduction of racism in our day, those suffering their injuries must be the voice of the movement against them. As we've discussed in the first chapter, personal prejudices and social policies in housing, welfare, education, and health access certainly continue to perpetuate racism, but mass incarceration both informs and surpasses each of these factors in influence. After Jim Crow–era legal regimes of segregation North and South were destabilized, they became materially reentrenched through the law-and-order policies like the War on Drugs. What this has meant is that the non-innocent character of the targeted demographic was part and parcel of the logic of the new regime of dispossession. "The new caste system labels black and brown men as criminals early, often in their teens, making them 'damaged goods' from the perspective of traditional civil rights advocates."[33] The genius of

---

31 Ibid., 226.

32 For example, Ta-Nehisi Coates, "Black People Are Not Ignoring 'Black on Black' Crime," *Atlantic*, August 15, 2014.

33 Alexander, *New Jim Crow*, 228.

neoliberal practices of regulated dispossession lies precisely in that they do not need to legally acknowledge their own de facto categories; by off-loading selection to police discretion and enacting potentially objectionable policies disproportionately in communities with fewer resources of political defense, categorical sorting may occur in political contexts with even the most politically "liberal" constituencies. That traditional civil rights advocates have refused to engage the issue is worse than omission; it is utter failure by its own measure. The choice of the citizens of Ferguson to put their lives on the line for Michael Brown, who, as much of American media was quick to point out, was "no angel," was a brilliant and courageous rejection of this white-glove habit of many traditional movements.

Wang points out that traditional civil rights activists are not alone in such complicity; by continually framing contemporary racism exclusively in terms of the murder of Trayvon Martin or the near-legal lynching of the Jena Six, much of today's antiracist discourse only acknowledges the Rosa Parkses of our era—who, under current conditions, often only qualify for such sympathy once they are already corpses. "When we build politics around standards of legitimate victimhood that require passive sacrifice, we will build a politics that requires a dead Black boy to make its point."[34] By making such moments exemplary, nearly the entire spectrum of antiracism winds up addressing only the remnants of Jim Crow–era dispossession practices, while mystifying current ones that are much more widely damaging. As such, many antiracists unwittingly work to reproduce white supremacy in its most potent forms:

> Using "innocence" as the foundation to address anti-Black violence is an *appeal to the white imaginary*, though these arguments are certainly made by people of color as well. Relying on this framework re-entrenches a logic that criminalizes race and constructs subjects as docile. A liberal politics of recognition can only reproduce a guilt-innocence schematization that fails to grapple with the fact that there is an *a priori* association of Blackness with guilt (criminality). Perhaps *association* is too generous—there is a flat-out

---

34 Wang, "Beyond Innocence," 170.

conflation of the terms. As Frank Wilderson noted in "Gramsci's Black Marx," the cop's answer to the Black subject's question—*why did you shoot me?*—follows a tautology: "I shot you because you are Black; you are Black because I shot you." In the words of Fanon, the cause is the consequence. Not only are Black men assumed guilty until proven innocent, Blackness itself is considered synonymous with guilt. Authentic victimhood, passivity, moral purity, and the adoption of a whitewashed position are necessary for recognition in the eyes of the State.[35]

Wang, whose brother received a life sentence without parole at the age of seventeen, is clear about the consequences of such discourse within social movements: those most severely impacted by contemporary regimes of dispossession are effectively barred from participation in the very movements that claim to address these regimes. "When we rely on appeals to innocence, we foreclose a form of resistance that is outside the limits of law, and instead ally ourselves with the State."[36]

Alexander's book became popular just as the Occupy camps were being brutally evicted; writing shortly before Occupy's appearance, she ends her work with strikingly prophetic words of both hope and caution: just as people have always stood up to past regimes of dispossession, so can we anticipate that human dignity will reassert itself against present-day oppressions. Nevertheless, to this hope is joined an unambiguous admonition—such movements must consist of those most familiar with contemporary indignity and dispossession, who have much to say to ears that have so far been unwilling to listen. Such voices may not present themselves as "innocent," and they will not likely be eager to continue their victimhood, publicly or otherwise:

> If Martin Luther King Jr is right that the arc of history is long, but it bends toward justice, a new movement will arise; and if civil rights organizations fail to keep up with the times, they will be pushed to the side as another generation of advocates comes to the fore.

---

35   Ibid., 148.

36   Ibid.

Hopefully the new generation will be led by those who know best the brutality of the new caste system—a group with greater vision, courage, and determination than the old guard can muster, trapped as they may be in an outdated paradigm....

Those of us who hope to be their allies should not be surprised, if and when this day comes, that when those who have been locked up and locked out finally have the chance to speak and truly be heard, what we hear is rage. The rage may frighten us; it may remind us of riots, uprisings, and buildings aflame. We may be tempted to control it, or douse it with buckets of doubt, dismay, and disbelief. But we should do no such thing.[37]

The prophetic quality of Alexander's words is striking in light of Ferguson and the Black Lives Matter movement; even these movements, however, have opened up the questions of an insurgent politics after innocence and without victimhood rather than answering them. While Occupy and Black Lives Matter have finally succeeded after decades of relative quietude in bringing to light essential dynamics of inequality, injustice, and dispossession at the basis of the "American way of life," future movements still face the task of going beyond registering concern and actually constituting alternative ways to live. We will now end with a look at how these movements have opened ways of thinking about this possibility and where movements to come will have to pick up.

AGENCY AND POSSIBILITY IN DEFIGURATIVE POLITICS

I think it redefines what is possible and I think most of what we're doing now. We, in Occupy, we being sort of like the larger milieu of radical politics...[we are] actually pushing forward what is possible.... If you remember, a little over a year ago there were student occupations at Berkeley and all over California, and for the first time, to be fair I guess the first occupations were actually months before in New York,

---

37 Alexander, *New Jim Crow*, 260–61.

you know, the idea of occupying space, of occupation, aside from Iraq and Palestine, but of actually like, taking space in a domestic setting was unheard of. 'Cause it didn't happen, and when people talked about it people would talk about it as an impossibility as not something that we could actually pull off.... Being a college activist radical type, we would discuss whether or not occupying something would make sense, and oftentimes we were just like, no we can't pull it off.... The fact that within the course of a month there were literally like a thousand occupations worldwide, pushed the political horizon of what was.... Occupy has pushed that spectrum in a lot of different ways. And so besides occupation becoming something that by damn if it's actually ok to do, granted the state forces are oppressing, but like, hundreds of thousands, or maybe millions of people were down for it. It's crazy.

—Occupy Oakland participant[38]

Disruption alone does not a social movement make. The rich totality of relations and trajectories; of ephemeral nodes of relationships; of the jagged edges and shifting centers of subjects, publics, and performances; of new futures for the past and unfulfilled histories newly discovered, posit and produce possibilities to the same degree that they erase and disarticulate the past. Indeed, the two processes are one. The "magic" of Occupy, or of the global wave of "unruly politics" in 2011 of which it was part, or of the plenitude of dispersed disruptions that yelled out "Black Lives Matter!" were not confined to any prescription of nonviolence, nor did they bother defining themselves in opposition to it. For any of us who participated, as well as for attentive scholars, their power lay in an impossible dialect of *conversation* with *confrontation*. There was the astounding novelty of a participation finally speaking aloud—publicly!—our secret thoughts, sometimes in the charged dissensus of deliberation, other times in quiet listening, but always through what felt like a rather ungainly practice of trust and love. Finally, things that had forever been whispered were spoken—and screamed—for all to hear. But there was always also what felt like another participation in fear and rage, in collective assertion and rule-breaking, of screaming "No!"

---

38   Personal interview (G).

and "Why?" and, in some sense at least, violence, in exchanges with our constitutive Other of police, officials, indignant citizens, and our former friends: frictions and fractures with the myriad manifestations of the values against which we stood. The splicing of deliberation and panic felt unprecedented, as it may have been; certainly, it is beyond the telling of this project. The movements themselves, first as tragedy and then as farce, seemed to articulate this attachment in their very demise: months after Occupy, after the tents, media committees, "get money out of politics!" working groups, kitchens, medic booths, and libraries had been lost, many Occupies persisted in attempting to hold general assemblies and confrontational public actions; the talking heads who claimed to speak on behalf of Black Lives Matter only surfaced after the disruptions had settled, city by city. Without the accompanying chaotic challenges of the disruptions, however, the words possessed less and less power.

While some scholars have attempted to disavow the necessity of the deliberative,[39] conversational aspect of these movements, others remind us how essential participation and shared deliberation are to the passions by which movements live. Francesca Polletta details how participatory democracies possess a number of the advantages which contributed to these movements' undeniable success in shifting public discourse and constituting new counterpublics of substantial reach.[40] In parallel to some of the claims I have made about performances of unruly politics, Polletta denies that direct deliberation primarily bears *personal* benefits to participants; as her book-length study of the civil rights, New Left, women's liberation, and alter-globalization movements demonstrates, movements where decision-making is devolved are more robust, resilient, and innovative than centralized organizations. These traits, which prove decisive in outmaneuvering foes superior in material resources but potentially lagging in flexibility, are the typical institutional targets of social movements. Social movement theorist Lesley Wood affirms the value of diffuse deliberation, as "when diverse activists with different perspectives can discuss innovations in a reflective, egalitarian manner, they are more likely to be able to incorporate locally new

---

39 See, for instance, Jodi Dean, *Crowds and Party* (New York: Verso, 2016).

40 Francesca Polletta, *Freedom Is an Endless Meeting: Democracy in American Social Movements* (Chicago: University of Chicago Press, 2002).

tactics."[41] In one passage suggesting that these movements' dialectics might not have been as novel as they seemed, Arendt asserted that such deliberative figures have been characteristic of *all* large-scale revolutionary movements of modernity, however often they are repressed by opponents or in the name of the revolution itself:

> The councils, as distinguished from parties, have always emerged during the revolution itself, they sprang from the people as spontaneous organs of action and of order. The last point is worth emphasizing; nothing indeed contradicts more sharply the old adage of the anarchistic and lawless "natural" inclinations of a people left without the constraint of its government than the emergence of the councils that, wherever they appeared, and most pronouncedly during the Hungarian Revolution, were concerned with the reorganization of the political and economic life of the country and the establishment of a new order.[42]

As for the confrontational aspect, upon which this study has focused, social movement scholars have long acknowledged the centrality of material *disruption* in the power of the disenfranchised. As cited in the first chapter, Piven and Cloward conducted a thorough analysis of social movement history in the US and concluded that, in all cases under study, it was the demonstrated potential to leverage disruption in the status quo, to interrupt what Althusser termed the "reproduction of the means of production," which forced concessions and adaptations from elites; consolidations of these concessions by social movement organizations and leaders, both in policy and institution, occurred only afterwards, as effect, not cause, of the changes brought about. If potential to disrupt forms the *material* power of the disenfranchised, performances of *transgression*, acts that *defigure* the symbolic forms of the status quo, make up its rhetorical counterpart; if long-term *influence* is the sociological phenomenon brought about by this power, *agency* is its subjective aspect. This study concludes with

---

41 Lesley J. Wood, *Direct Action, Deliberation, and Diffusion Collective Action after the WTO Protests in Seattle* (Cambridge: Cambridge University Press, 2012), i.

42 Arendt, *On Revolution*, 275.

a look at defiguration practices, those actions so central to opening up the future as they "alter the symbolic…context upon which the ruling order depends and make another world possible."

Semiotic Transgression

I have a hard time understanding what their goals are and how they intend to use these tactics to achieve these goals.… Remember, we're fighting not only to build a movement but to build a consciousness, and that consciousness will only come when we bring people into the streets.… If we do not bring the mainstream over to our side, I don't think we can win.
—Chris Hedges[43]

I have discussed earlier in this chapter how inclusion and exclusion of certain topics, as well as certain "tropes," are marked by specific audiences not always understood as specific. In Hedges's passage above, from a debate with the anarchist group Crimethinc, he commits a similar error in specificity regarding the means of mobilization. Hedges agrees with the radical goals of his conversant, that a change of consciousness is required and that "our side" is something apart from "the mainstream," but he quickly glosses over *how* exactly "we" are to go about "bring[ing] the mainstream over." In this articulation, a conversion in consciousness, what I am terming *defiguration* of status quo symbolic figures through transgression, is indeed required but depends on a *prior* mass mobilization of an already constituted "People," who, importantly, are somehow mobilized on terms already familiar to them. Although the Occupy movement was unprecedented in its nearly instantaneous mobilization of tens of thousands of participants and a large majority of public opinion in polls, such mobilization had, in all locations, stalled by late October 2011 and steadily declined until the camps were raided. The debate in which Hedges admonished the Occupy movement took place in September 2012, many months after its demise. How Hedges expected to mobilize "the mainstream" out of nowhere, relying on appeals familiar to "it" *before* attempting to enact a change in "consciousness," remains mysteriously unstated.

---

43 "Occupy Tactics: Violence and Legitimacy in the Occupy Movement," public debate, September 15, 2012. Video available at https://vimeo.com/49523702.

In one quotation opening this chapter, an interviewee clarified that it was precisely *not* by appealing to "the mainstream" on their own terms—in other words, by not attempting to constitute a new public using worn-out appeals that showed drastically diminishing returns in mobilization—but by revealing what had previously seemed impossible to be possible and by uncovering space for insurgent agency that new means of constituting publics were opened up. As discussed in the first chapter, by negating *hopelessness* rather than *naivety*, this demonstration of possibility and space for agency is particularly suited to neoliberal exigencies. One of the very Occupy Oakland participants of whom Hedges spoke with such disgust as a "cancer" referred to the consciousness/mobilization process as utilizing *transgression* as a mobilization appeal rather than forestalling it until "only...when we bring people into the streets":

> Gramsci—along with Marx, Fanon, and CLR James, in different ways—all point to the importance of radical consciousness emerging from direct participation in social struggle, not the inverse. Just as many of the 30,000 people who shut down the Port of Oakland on November 2nd, 2011 came to see their collective power that day, the broader war of position is contingent upon people not only coming out to a rally, but engaging in a movement with revolutionary goals in a way that they see themselves as part of it, and it as part of them. *The movement doesn't need to manufacture these sentiments among the broader population,* nor should it sit back and wait for changes in popular consciousness to spontaneously happen. A key part of a successful war of position is *helping to draw out the desires that people have been taught are impossible* and create space within our organizing and actions for people to connect with radical organizing and make it their own.[44]

In this formulation, rather than first bringing out the numbers *before* attempting to publicly enact transformational performances,

---

44 Personal correspondence (D).

publics are constituted *through* them. For those attempting semiotic transgression, actions that easily translate into the semiotic system of the status quo are *failure* by definition. For Hedges, on the contrary, it is the *goal*. As mentioned earlier, the right to define the situation is the primary and exclusive "demand" of radical antiauthoritarian actions. While Hedges's reading of the audience wishes to bring out the masses *as is*, transgressive contention aims not only to bring out those bored with "activism" but also to transform the participants in the moment the appeal is received. The radical imaginary revolves around a constitution of a direct *demos* large enough to terminally challenge the status quo, transformed through the very act of its emergence. Though apparently delusional, recent movements seem to reaffirm the potential for exactly this process, as the prairie-fire diffusion of Occupy and Black Lives Matter actions attest; nobody saw them coming exactly because the "public" that came out *didn't exist until the moment of its emergence.*

That participation in these movements was experienced as transformational defiguration was a theme that appeared again and again in conversations with people I interviewed for this book. One trans woman demonstrator in San Francisco compared the process she watched others undergo to coming out as queer and trans; other participants, disoriented by the rapid transformation that they felt part of, in fact sought her out as a guide through their process of what Nietzsche termed "revaluation." She compared participants new to social movements to someone experimenting with cross-dressing—"it takes a long time to reacclimate before he can wear panties under his work clothes"—and further developed this parallel:

> The weirdoes, the outsiders, the queers, the people who already live outside these norms somewhat constantly—we have a leg up, we have something to teach people, because we know how that works, and we understand the process of any transgressive catharsis. And that makes it easier to process. It's like when you're an experienced drug user, and you try a new drug, you're able to be, like, this was this, this was that, here I am now. You know the arc of it. And so knowing the arc of those transgressions is something that a lot of people have, and a lot of other people don't have, and that's

one of those things I'm, like, "how do we share that?" so we can all get on the same page and move forward fast while we still have momentum.[45]

In her investigation, Christina Foust posits a similar transgression as central to contemporary social movement participants, although she typifies it as more marginal than movements since her book have revealed it to be.[46] More egregiously, she bases her analysis on an understanding of transgression as exclusive of and opposed to hegemony, that is, to any new arrangement of meaning. Richard Day makes the same mistake in proclaiming, in his analysis of "the newest social movements" of the alter-globalization era, that "Gramsci is dead."[47] Though both authors correctly assess that participants increasingly do not presume to exert a "new hegemony" in their articulations, or try to put forward what some "new world" that comes after the one they attack might look like, it is too much to claim that they somehow thus negate, escape, or prevent this meaning-making process. Rather, the opening of possibilities through fostering agency "makes space" for new values, without imposing them. This approach also proposes transcendence of a dilemma haunting radical philosophy at least since the 1971 debate between Foucault and Chomsky.[48] Foucault ridicules Chomsky for his imaginary of the future, which risked continuing current nonstate institutions and a reified "human nature" consistent with contemporary subject positions—a continuity which Foucault fears will simply reproduce the current order. While acknowledging Foucault's concern, Chomsky alleges that, without a willingness to venture in imagination beyond the current state of affairs, subjects lack the grounds and motivation to fight *for* a future at all. The notion of semiotic transgression suggests a way out: the now-versus-after-the-revolution temporality shared by both Chomsky and Foucault

---

45   Personal interview (A).

46   Christina R. Foust, *Transgression as a Mode of Resistance: Rethinking Social Movement in an Era of Corporate Globalization* (Lanham, MD: Lexington Books, 2010).

47   Richard Day, *Gramsci Is Dead: Anarchist Currents in the Newest Social Movements* (London: Pluto Press, 2005).

48   Noam Chomsky and Michel Foucault, *The Chomsky-Foucault Debate: On Human Nature* (New York: New Press, 2006).

is irrelevant to today's militant insurgents, who "prefigured" their futures through the lived agency of enacting them, experiencing "future" as a fully present, immediate defiguration of the limitations of the "past." That this "past" was not strictly temporal is tragically revealed as the shared transgressive experience subsides and the "past" reasserts itself as present. For those who partake in such public transgression, however, this return does not make the "past" any more real, nor the fleeting "future" any less so.

Only perhaps in Lacan's sense—in which any creation or destruction of meaning is necessarily violent, and violence but another name for meaning-making—do such moments need to be "violent." In fact, some of them may be the most peaceful of all. What seemed necessary abruptly shatters, the helplessness imposed by a world of no alternatives is suddenly unveiled as a cruel but fragile illusion, and what remains in the new moment of overwhelming agency is the oceanic peace of seemingly infinite possibility. The words of one Oakland Occupier, telling of the moment the port came into view in the massive port shutdown march, attest to the transformative material eloquence of such moments:

> To get to the Oakland port, it's a nice long walk. There were tens of thousands of us, a big mass. I was on the front line. Veterans were first, then the shield bearers were right behind us. As we were marching, you go under this overpass, then you go on this sort of loop around a little bridge, and it peaks, so you can't see what's on the other side. You can't see the opening, so you're literally marching forward, upwards. None of us knew what we were going to see as soon as we crested and looked down. And people were nervous, excited, anxious, exhilarated, all these sorts of things. They were ready, though. They were ready for what was going to happen. At times people would look behind them and see this literally never-ending sea of people, right behind you, following, waiting to back you up, and then we crested, and there were zero police.... And at that point did this expand what was possible because not knowing what was on the other side of the bridge, but still moving. I mean, you could call it the

Gandhian march on the salt factory. People were ready to face whatever was there. It expanded a whole host of possibilities, and then I think that resonated not just in terms of what people thought of as possible experientially, but people who didn't experience it saw that it was doable.[49]

As I finish this book, it appears that the illusion that friendly performances of civility are likely to convince powerful opponents to lay down their arms may finally be abating. Donald Trump has been forced to cancel a number of public appearances because of courageous physical interventions by Black, Latino, Muslim, and other protesters. Only yesterday, a video has gone viral of former city commissioner and anarchist Cara Jennings confronting Florida governor Rick Scott in a coffee shop over his defunding of Planned Parenthood, telling him "You're an asshole!" to his face, until the governor runs for the door. These actions have been met with widespread sympathy and comparatively little condemnation. As protest has more and more directly targeted the contradictions at the very core of American society, broad audiences—if not necessarily "mass" ones—seem to show less concern with liberal niceties and more with who is enacting them, and with what they are actually up to when they do so. Whether the inevitable violence of these conflicts remains primarily semiotic and communicative or spills over into materiality as the Right sharply increases its own injurious and lethal violence, they have already succeeded in beginning to bring to light the immense and very real violence that has been there all along, and which, maybe, we might just be fighting to find our way out of.

---

49 Personal interview (G).

WORKS CITED

Agamben, Giorgio. *What Is an Apparatus? and Other Essays*. Palo Alto: Stanford University Press, 2009.

Ahmed, Sara. *The Cultural Politics of Emotion*. New York: Routledge, 2013.

Alexander, Michelle. *The New Jim Crow: Mass Incarceration in the Age of Colorblindness*. New York: New Press, 2010.

Althusser, Louis. "Ideology and ideological state apparatuses (notes towards an investigation)." In Aradhana Sharma and Akhil Gupta. *The Anthropology of the State: A Reader*. Oxford: Blackwell, 2006.

Amster, Randall. *Anarchism Today*. Santa Barbara: Praeger, 2012.

Anderson, Tim. "Occupy Seattle and Tim Anderson." *Walk the Talk with Kim*. 1150 AM KKNW, November 16, 2011.

Arendt, Hannah. *On Revolution*. New York: Viking Press, 1965.

Balko, Radley. *Rise of the Warrior Cop: The Militarization of America's Police Forces*. New York: PublicAffairs, 2013.

Barry-Shaw, Nikolas, and Dru Oja Jay. *Paved with Good Intentions: Canada's Development NGOs from Idealism to Imperialism*. Halifax, N.S.: Fernwood, 2012.

The Battle of Oakland. Video. Jourdan, Brandon and David Martinez. Global Uprisings website, 2012. Available at http:

//www.globaluprisings.org/the-battle-of-oakland.

"Bay Area News Group Poll Finds 94% Support Occupy Oakland," Occupy Oakland website. February 18, 2012. Accessed May 23, 2016. https://occupyoakland.org/2012/02 /bay-area-news-group-poll-finds-94-support-occupy.

Berger, Dan. *Outlaws of America: The Weather Underground and the Politics of Solidarity*. Oakland: AK Press, 2006.

The Black Power Mixtape 1967–1975. Film. Directed by Göran Olsson. Stockholm: Sveriges Television, 2011.

Boal, Iain A., et al. *Afflicted Powers: Capital and Spectacle in a New Age of War*. New York: Verso, 2005.

Bourdieu, Pierre. *Language and Symbolic Power*. Cambridge: Harvard University Press, 1991.

Brison, Susan J. *Aftermath: Violence and the Remaking of a Self*. Princeton: Princeton University Press, 2002.

Brissette, Emily. "For the Fracture of Good Order." *Counterpunch*, November 4, 2011. Accessed May 24. 2016, http://www.counterpunch.org/2011/11/04/for-the-fracture-of-good-order.

Brown, Wendy. *Regulating Aversion: Tolerance in the Age of Identity and Empire*. Princeton: Princeton University Press, 2006.

Bruner, M. Lane. "Carnivalesque Protest and the Humorless State." *Text and Performance Quarterly* 25, no. 2 (2005).

Buford, Bill. *Among the Thugs*. New York: Vintage Books, 1993.

Burke, Kenneth. *A Rhetoric of Motives*. New York: Prentice-Hall, 1950.

Butler, Smedley D. *War Is a Racket: The Antiwar Classic by America's Most Decorated Soldier*. Los Angeles: Feral House, 2003.

Carson, Clayborne, ed. *The Autobiography of Martin Luther King, Jr.* New York: Warner Books, 1998.

Carter, David. *Stonewall: The Riots That Sparked the Gay Revolution*. New York: St. Martin's Press, 2010.

Chenoweth, Erica, and Maria J. Stephan. *Why Civil Resistance Works: The Strategic Logic of Nonviolent Conflict*. New York: Columbia University Press, 2011.

Chomsky, Noam, and Michel Foucault. *The Chomsky-Foucault Debate: On Human Nature*. New York: New Press, 2006.

Choudry, Aziz. *NGOization: Complicity, Contradictions and Prospects*. London: Zed Books, 2013.

Coates, Ta-Nehisi. "Black People Are Not Ignoring 'Black on Black'

Crime." *Atlantic,* August 15, 2014.

Cobb, Charles E., Jr. *This Nonviolent Stuff'll Get You Killed: How Guns Made the Civil Rights Movement Possible.* New York: Basic Books, 2014.

Comrades from Cairo. "Solidarity Statement from Cairo." Occupy Wall Street website. October 25, 2011. Accessed June 30, 2016. http://occupywallst.org/article/solidarity-statement-cairo.

Cornell, Andrew. *Oppose and Propose! Lessons from Movement for a New Society.* Oakland: AK Press & Institute for Anarchist Studies, 2011.

CROATOAN, "Who Is Oakland: Anti-Oppression Activism, the Politics of Safety, and State Co-optation." Escalating Identity website. April 30, 2012. Accessed May 25, 2016. https://escalatingidentity.wordpress.com/2012/04/30/who-is-oakland-anti-oppression-politics-decolonization-and-the-state.

Cruikshank, Barbara. *The Will to Empower: Democratic Citizens and Other Subjects.* Ithaca: Cornell University Press, 1999.

Cunha, Darlena. "Ferguson: In Defense of Rioting." *Time,* November 25, 2014.

Cunneen, Kerry. "Interview with Kerry Cunneen." *Finn's Revolution* radio program. WUSB. January 22, 2013. Transcript available at https://nopoliticalrepression.wordpress.com/2013/01/24/radio-interview-with-kerry-cunneen.

Darsey, James Francis. *The Prophetic Tradition and Radical Rhetoric in America.* New York: New York University Press, 1997.

Day, Richard. *Gramsci Is Dead: Anarchist Currents in the Newest Social Movements.* London: Pluto Press, 2005.

De Angelis, Massimo. *The Beginning of History: Value Struggles and Global Capital.* London: Pluto Press, 2007.

Dean, Jodi. *Crowds and Party.* New York: Verso, 2016.

Debray, Régis. *Revolution in the Revolution? Armed Struggle and Political Struggle in Latin America.* New York: Monthly Review Press, 1967.

Deleuze, Gilles. "Postscript on the Societies of Control." *October* 59 (1992): 3–7.

Dellinger, David T. *Revolutionary Nonviolence.* Indianapolis: Bobbs-Merrill, 1970.

DeLuca, Kevin M., Sean Lawson, and Ye Sun. "Occupy Wall Street on the Public Screens of Social Media: The Many Framings of the Birth of a Protest Movement." *Communication, Culture & Critique* 5, no. 4 (2012).

Du Bois, William E. B. *Black Reconstruction in America, 1860–1880.* New York: Simon and Schuster, 1999.

Fairclough, Adam. *Better Day Coming: Blacks and Equality, 1890–2000.* New York: Viking, 2001.

Fanon, Frantz. *The Wretched of the Earth.* New York: Penguin Books, 1969.

A Force More Powerful: A Century of Nonviolent Conflict. Film. Produced and written by Steve York. Princeton: Films for the Humanities & Sciences, 2002.

Foucault, Michel. *The Archaeology of Knowledge.* New York: Pantheon Books, 1972.

Foust, Christina R. *Transgression as a Mode of Resistance: Rethinking Social Movement in an Era of Corporate Globalization.* Lanham, MD: Lexington Books, 2010.

Free Association. "Antagonism, Neoliberalism and Movements: Six Impossible Things Before Breakfast." *Antipode* 42, no. 4 (2010): 1019–1033.

Gilje, Paul A. *Rioting in America.* Bloomington: Indiana University Press, 1996.

Gillham, Patrick F., and John A. Noakes, "'More Than A March in a Circle': Transgressive Protests and the Limits of Negotiated Management." *Mobilization: An International Quarterly* 12, no. 4 (2007): 341–57.

Gilligan, James. *Preventing Violence.* London: Thames & Hudson, 2001.

Gines, Kathryn T. *Hannah Arendt and the Negro Question.* Bloomington: Indiana University Press, 2014.

Gitlin, Todd. *Occupy Nation: The Roots, the Spirit, and the Promise of Occupy Wall Street.* New York: It Books, 2012.

Goldman, Emma, *Anarchism and Other Essays.* New York: Dover Publications, 1969.

Gooding-Williams, Robert, ed. *Reading Rodney King/Reading Urban Uprising.* New York: Routledge, 1993.

Gorsevski, Ellen W. *Peaceful Persuasion: The Geopolitics of Nonviolent Rhetoric.* Albany: State University of New York Press, 2004.

Graeber, David. *Possibilities: Essays on Hierarchy, Rebellion, and Desire.* Oakland: AK Press, 2007.

Greenwald, Glenn. *No Place to Hide: Edward Snowden, the NSA, and the U.S. Surveillance State*. New York: Metropolitan Books/ Henry Holt, 2014.

Gregg, Richard B. "The Ego-Function of the Rhetoric of Protest." In *Readings on the Rhetoric of Social Protest, Second Edition*, edited by Charles E. Morris III and Stephen H. Browne, 45–58. State College, PA: Strata Publishing, 2006.

Harries-Clichy Peterson. *Che Guevara on Guerrilla Warfare*. New York: Praeger, 1961.

Hedges, Chris. "The Cancer in Occupy," *Truthdig*, February 6, 2012. Accessed May 24, 2016. http://www.truthdig.com/report /item/the_cancer_of_occupy_20120206.

_____. "Interview with Chris Hedges about Black Bloc." Interview by J.A. Myerson. *Truthout*, February 9, 2012. Accessed May 24, 2016. http://www.truth-out.org/opinion /item/6587:interview-with-chris-hedges-about-black-bloc.

_____. "Thank You for Standing Up," *Truthdig*, January 23, 2012. Accessed May 24, 2016. http://www.truthdig.com/report/item /thank_you_for_standing_up_20120123.

Hill, Lance. *The Deacons for Defense: Armed Resistance and the Civil Rights Movement*. Chapel Hill: University of North Carolina Press, 2004.

Hill, Rebecca. *Men, Mobs, and Law: Anti-lynching and Labor Defense in U.S. Radical History*. Durham: Duke University Press, 2008.

Holmes, Robert L., and Barry L. Gan. *Nonviolence in Theory and Practice*. Long Grove, IL: Waveland Press, 2012.

How to Survive a Plague. DVD. Directed by David France. New York: Sundance Selects, MPI Media Group, 2013.

Incite! Women of Color Against Violence. *The Revolution Will Not Be Funded: Beyond the Non-Profit Industrial Complex*. Cambridge, Mass.: South End Press, 2007.

Indigenous Action. *Accomplices Not Allies: Abolishing the Ally Industrial Complex*. Indigenous Action Media, 2014.

Jacobs, Harriet A. *Incidents in the Life of a Slave Girl*. New York: Dover, 2001.

Katz, Michael. "Why Don't American Cities Burn Very Often?" *Journal of Urban History* 34, no. 2 (2008): 185–208.

"Kazu Haga in Seattle on Kingian Nonviolence in the Context of Occupy." YouTube.com. 02:02. February 7, 2012. Accessed May

24, 2016. https://www.youtube.com/watch?v=PtPLYUe-occ

King, Martin Luther, Jr.. *Stride toward Freedom: The Montgomery Story*. New York: Beacon Press, 2010.

Koestenbaum, Wayne. *Humiliation*. New York: Picador, 2011.

Labrousse, Alain. *The Tupamaros*. New York: Penguin Books, 1973.

Laclau, Ernesto, and Chantal Mouffe. *Hegemony and Socialist Strategy: Towards a Radical Democratic Politics*. London: Verso, 1985.

Lakey, George. *Strategy for a Living Revolution*. New York: Grossman Publishers, 1973.

Lipsitz, George. *The Possessive Investment in Whiteness: How White People Profit from Identity Politics*. Philadelphia: Temple University Press, 2006.

Locke, John. *Second Treatise of Government*. Indianapolis: Hackett Publishing, 1962.

Malcolm X Grassroots Project. "We Charge Genocide Again!" mxgm.org, May 13, 2103. Accessed May 23, 2016. https://mxgm.org/we-charge-genocide-again-new-curriculum-on-every-28-hours-report.

May, Todd. *The Political Thought of Jacques Rancière: Creating Equality*. University Park: Pennsylvania State University Press, 2008.

Milstein, Cindy, ed. *Taking Sides: Revolutionary Solidarity and the Poverty of Liberalism*. Oakland: AK Press, 2015.

Morris, Charles E., and Stephen H. Browne. *Readings on the Rhetoric of Social Protest*. State College, PA: Strata Publishing, 2006.

Mouffe, Chantal. *The Democratic Paradox*. New York: Verso, 2000.

Murakawa, Naomi. *The First Civil Right: How Liberals Built Prison America*. New York: Oxford University Press, 2014.

National Advisory Commission on Civil Disorders. *Report of the National Advisory Commission on Civil Disorders*. Washington, D.C.: U.S. Government Printing Office, 1968.

Neumann, Osha. "Occupy Oakland: Are We Being Childish?" *Counterpunch* website, February 3, 2012. Accessed May 24, 2016. http://www.counterpunch.org/2012/02/03/occupy-oakland-are-we-being-childish.

Nieburg, Harold L. *Political Violence: The Behavioral Process*. New York: St. Martin's Press, 1969.

"Occupy Tactics: Violence and Legitimacy in the Occupy Movement." Vimeo.com. 01:54:47. September 15, 2012. Filmed by Brandon Jourdan. Accessed June 16, 2016. https://

vimeo.com/49523702.

Oliver, Melvin L., James H. Johnson, Jr., and Walter C. Farrell, Jr. "Anatomy of a Rebellion: A Political-Economic Analysis." In *Reading Rodney King/Reading Urban Uprising*, edited by Robert Gooding-Williams, 117–141. New York: Routledge, 1993.

Owens, James, and Occupy Research. "Occupy's Precarious Pluralism Report." Occupy Wall Street website, n.d. Accessed May 24, 2016, http://occupywallstreet.net/sites/default/files/ows_-_occupys_precarious_pluralism_report_final.pdf, 5.

Parenti, Christian. *Lockdown America*. New York: Verso, 2008.

———. *The Soft Cage: Surveillance in America from Slavery to the War on Terror*. New York: Basic Books, 2003.

Pinker, Steven. *The Better Angels of Our Nature: Why Violence Has Declined*. New York: Viking, 2011.

Piven, Frances Fox. "Protest Movements and Violence." In *Violent Protest, Contentious Politics, and the Neoliberal State,* edited by Seraphim Seferiades and Hank Johnston, 19–28. Farnham/Burlington: Ashgate Publishing, 2012.

Piven, Frances Fox, and Richard A. Cloward. *Poor People's Movements: Why They Succeed, How They Fail*. New York: Vintage Books, 1979.

Polletta, Francesca. *Freedom Is an Endless Meeting: Democracy in American Social Movements*. Chicago: University of Chicago Press, 2002.

Positive Peace Warrior Network. "How Will the Walls Come Tumbling Down?"

Rand, Ayn. *Atlas Shrugged*. New York: Random House, 1957.

Riedner, Rachel, and Kevin Mahoney. *Democracies to Come: Rhetorical Action, Neoliberalism, and Communities of Resistance*. Lanham, MD: Lexington Books, 2008.

Schmidt, Jeff. *Disciplined Minds: A Critical Look at Salaried Professionals and the Soul-battering System That Shapes Their Lives*. Lanham, MD: Rowman & Littlefield, 2000.

Schock, Kurt, *Unarmed Insurrections: People Power Movements in Nondemocracies*. Minneapolis: University of Minnesota Press, 2005.

Seferiades, Seraphim, and Hank Johnston. "The Dynamics of Violent Protest: Emotions, Repression, and Disruptive Deficit." In *Violent Protest, Contentious Politics, and the Neoliberal State,*

edited by Seraphim Seferiades and Hank Johnston, 3–18.
Farnham/Burlington: Ashgate Publishing, 2012.

Shami, Leila al-. "Challenging the Nation State in Syria." *Fifth Estate* 396 (2016). Available online at https://www.fifthestate.org /archive/396-summer-2016/challenging-the-nation-state-in-syria.

Sharp, Gene. *Power and Struggle: The Politics of Nonviolent Action Part 1.* Boston: Porter Sargent, 1973.

_____. *The Methods of Nonviolent Action: The Politics of Nonviolent Action Part 2.* Boston: Porter Sargent, 1973.

Shirley, Neal, and Saralee Stafford. *Dixie Be Damned: 300 Years of Insurrection in the American South.* Oakland: AK Press, 2015.

Simons, Herbert W. "Requirements, Problems, and Strategies: A Theory of Persuasion for Social Movements." In *Readings on the Rhetoric of Social Protest*, edited by Charles E. Morris and Stephen H. Browne, 35–45. State College, PA: Strata Publishing, 2006.

Students for a Democratic Society. *The Port Huron Statement.* New York: SDS, 1964.

Taber, Robert. *The War of the Flea: A Study of Guerrilla Warfare Theory and Practice.* New York: L. Stuart, 1965.

Thistlethwaite, Susan Brooks. "UC Davis Pepper Spray and the Power of Nonviolent Witness." *Washington Post,* November 22, 2011.

Thompson, A. K. *Black Bloc, White Riot: Anti-globalization and the Genealogy of Dissent.* Oakland: AK Press, 2010.

Thompson, E. P. "The Moral Economy of the English Crowd in the Eighteenth Century." *Past & Present,* no. 50 (1971): 76–136.

Tolstoy, Leo. *The Kingdom of God Is Within You: Christianity Not as a Mystic Religion but as a New Theory of Life.* New York: Dover, 2006. Reprint of 1894 edition.

Umoja, Akinyele Omowale. *We Will Shoot Back: Armed Resistance in the Mississippi Freedom Movement.* New York: NYU Press, 2013.

Van Deusen, David, and Xavier Massot. *The Black Bloc Papers: An Anthology of Primary Texts From The North American Anarchist Black Bloc 1999–2001, The Battle of Seattle Through Quebec City.* Shawnee Mission, KS: Breaking Glass Press 2007. Available online at http://www.infoshop.org/amp/bgp/BlackBlockPapers2.pdf.

Varon, Jeremy. *Bringing the War Home: The Weather Underground, the Red Army Faction, and Revolutionary Violence in the Sixties and Seventies.* Berkeley: University of California Press, 2004.

Wacquant, Loïc. *Punishing the Poor: The Neoliberal Government of Social Insecurity.* Durham: Duke University Press, 2009.

Wang, Jackie. "Beyond Innocence." *LIES: A Journal of Materialist Feminism* 1 (2012): 145–71.

Williams, Kristian, William Munger, and Lara Messersmith. *Life during Wartime: Resisting Counterinsurgency.* Oakland: AK Press, 2013.

Wolfson, Todd. *Digital Rebellion: The Birth of the Cyber Left.* Urbana: University of Illinois Press, 2014.

Wood, Lesley J. *Direct Action, Deliberation, and Diffusion Collective Action after the WTO Protests in Seattle.* Cambridge: Cambridge University Press, 2012.

Yassin-Kassab, Robin, and Leila al-Shami. *Burning Country: Syrians in Revolution and War.* London: Pluto Press, 2016.

Zunes, Stephen. "Unarmed Insurrections against Authoritarian Governments in the Third World: A New Kind of Revolution." *Third World Quarterly* 15, no. 3 (1994): 403–26.

INDEX

AK Press is small, in terms of staff and resources, but we also manage to be one of the world's most productive anarchist publishing houses. We publish close to twenty books every year, and distribute thousands of other titles published by like-minded independent presses and projects from around the globe. We're entirely worker-run and democratically managed. We operate without a corporate structure—no boss, no managers, no bullshit.

The Friends of AK program is a way you can directly contribute to the continued existence of AK Press, and ensure that we're able to keep publishing books like this one! Friends pay $25 a month directly into our publishing account ($30 for Canada, $35 for international), and receive a copy of every book AK Press publishes for the duration of their membership! Friends also receive a discount on anything they order from our website or buy at a table: 50% on AK titles, and 20% on everything else. We have a Friends of AK ebook program as well: $15 a month gets you an electronic copy of every book we publish for the duration of your membership. You can even sponsor a very discounted membership for someone in prison.

Email friendsofak@akpress.org for more info, or visit the Friends of AK Press website: https://www.akpress.org/friends.html

There are always great book projects in the works—so sign up now to become a Friend of AK Press, and let the presses roll!